READING COLUMBUS

LATIN AMERICAN LITERATURE AND CULTURE

General Editor
Roberto González Echevarría
Bass Professor of Hispanic and Comparative Literatures
Yale University

READING COLUMBUS

Margarita Zamora

University of California Press
Berkeley · Los Angeles · London

E
112
.Z35
1993

The publisher gratefully acknowledges a grant
from the Program for Cultural Cooperation
between Spain's Ministry of Culture and United
States Universities.

University of California Press
Berkeley and Los Angeles, California

University of California Press, Ltd.
London, England

Library of Congress Cataloging-in-Publication Data

Zamora, Margarita.
    Reading Columbus / Margarita Zamora.
        p.   cm. — (Latin American literature and
    culture ; 9)
    Includes bibliographical references and index.
    ISBN 0-520-08052-1 (alk. paper). — ISBN 0-520-08297-4
    (pbk. : alk. paper)
    1. Columbus, Christopher—Literary art.
    2. America—Early accounts to 1600—History and
    criticism.   I. Title.   II. Series: Latin American
    literature and culture (Berkeley, Calif.) ; 9.
    E112.Z35   1993
    970.01'5—dc20   92-39234
                                                                CIP

Printed in the United States of America
1   2   3   4   5   6   7   8   9

26 932940

In memory of
Juan Clemente Zamora y López-Silvero and
Rosario Munné y García de Andina

Et convertat faciem suam ad insulas, et capiet multas.

And he shall turn his face to the islands and take many.

(Daniel 11:18a, as cited by Columbus,
Libro de las profecías)

Contents

Appendix

Illustrations

Illustrations

Acknowledgments

This book began to take shape in the classroom, stimulated by questions my students at the University of Wisconsin raised regarding the validity and usefulness of reading Columbus in courses devoted to the study of Spanish-American literature and culture. Their probing of issues too often taken for granted in the traditional academic disciplines, chief among them the interface of literature and history, prompted me to write an early version of the essay "'All these are the Admiral's exact words.'" For that initial stimulus I owe them a debt of gratitude.

Institutions that provided research support include the University of Wisconsin Graduate School, the Program for Cultural Cooperation Between Spain's Ministry of Culture and United States Universities, the Institute for Research in the Humanities of the University of Wisconsin, and the Cyril B. Nave Bequest.

This work would not have been possible without the resources and assistance offered in the United States by the Memorial Library of the University of Wisconsin, Madison; the John Carter Brown Library of Brown University; the Newberry Library; the William L. Clements Library at the University of Michigan, Ann Arbor; the James Ford Bell Library of the University of Minnesota; and the American Geographical Society Collection at the University of Wisconsin, Milwaukee. For generously sharing their time and expertise, I would like to express thanks to John Parker of the James Ford Bell Library, Daniel J. Slive of the John Carter Brown Library, and Mark Warhus of the Office for Map History, American Geographical Society Collection, University of Wisconsin, Milwaukee. I am very grateful to have been able to consult materials in the archives and libraries of Portugal at the Biblioteca Central da Marinha, the Biblioteca Municipal de Evora, and the Biblioteca Nacional. The staff at the Biblioteca Colombina in Seville, Spain, was especially helpful in facilitating my access to the Columbian postils, even as a major reorganization of the collection was in progress and the library was essentially closed to the public.

For their support of this project in its formative stages I am grateful to Biruté Ciplijauskaité, Roberto González Echevarría, Nellie McKay, Elaine Marks, Stephanie Merrim, and Enrique Pupo-Walker. For sharing work-in-progress with me I am indebted to Tom Conley, Stephen Greenblatt, David Henige, Dennis Martin, and Steven Hutchinson. To Claudia Card, E. Michael Gerli, Roberto González Echevarría, Stephen Greenblatt, and Juan Clemente Zamora, each of whom made valuable comments and suggestions on the manuscript, I reserve a special thank you. My most heartfelt thanks go to Judith Green, for her support through every stage of this project.

Three editors at the University of California Press have left their mark on this volume. I appreciate the efforts of Eileen McWilliam, who guided the project through a rigorous review process, Amy Einsohn, who attentively copyedited the text, and Dore Brown, who carefully helped shape the manuscript into a book. The work's most constant reader has been David Henige, from whose knowledge of Columbian history I and the manuscript have greatly benefited.

Finally, I wish to thank the editors of various journals for granting permissions to reprint revised versions of my earlier publications. The following pieces have been incorporated into the essays in this volume: "Todas son palabras formales del Almirante: Las Casas y el *Diario* de Colón," *Hispanic Review* 57 (1989): 25–41; "Text, Context, Intertext: Columbus's *diario de a bordo* as Palimpsest" [coauthored with David Henige], *The Americas* 46, no. 1 (1989): 17–40; "Abreast of Columbus: Gender and Discovery," *Cultural Critique* 17 (Winter 1991): 127–49; "Reading in the Margins of Columbus," *Amerindian Images* [reprint of *Hispanic Issues* 9], ed. René Jara and Nicholas Spadaccini (Minneapolis: University of Minnesota Press, 1992): 183–97; "Christopher Columbus's 'Letter to the Sovereigns': Announcing the Discovery," *New World Encounters*, ed. Stephen Greenblatt (Berkeley: University of California Press, 1993): 1–11.

Note on Editions and Translations

Editions and translations are identified in the text and notes by the following abbreviations. All translations not otherwise credited are the author's.

Alvar	*Diario del descubrimiento*. Ed. Manuel Alvar. 2 vols. Gran Canaria: Cabildo Insular de Gran Canaria, 1976.
Cioranescu	*Oeuvres de Christophe Colomb*. Trans. Alexandre Cioranescu. Paris: Gallimard, 1961.
Colección	*Colección de obras completas de Bartolomé de Las Casas*. Ed. Consuelo Varela. Madrid: Alianza, 1989.
Dunn & Kelley	*The Diario of Christopher Columbus's First Voyage to America, 1492–1493*. Ed. and trans. Oliver Dunn and James E. Kelley, Jr. Norman: University of Oklahoma Press, 1989.
Fernández de Navarrete	*Colección de viajes y descubrimientos que hicieron por mar los españoles desde fines del siglo XV* [1825]. Martín Fernández de Navarrete. 5 vols. Buenos Aires: Editorial Guaranía, 1945.
Ferro	*Diario di bordo: Libro della prima navigazione e scoperta delle Indie*. Ed. and trans. Gaetano Ferro. Milan: Mursia, 1985.
Jane	*Select Documents Illustrating the Four Voyages of Columbus*. Trans. and ed.

Cecil Jane. 2 vols. London: Hakluyt
Society, 1930.

de Lollis

Scritti di Cristoforo Colombo. Ed. Cesare
de Lollis. Vol. 1, pt. 1. Rome: Minis-
terio della pubblica istruzione, 1892–
94. (Part of the collection entitled *Raccolta de documenti e studi pubblicati della
R. Commissione Colombiana.*)

Major

*Four Voyages to the New World: Letters
and Selected Documents.* Ed. and trans.
R. H. Major. Gloucester, Mass.: Peter
Smith, 1978.

Morison

*Journals and Other Documents on the Life
and Voyages of Christopher Columbus.*
Ed. and trans. Samuel Eliot Morison.
New York: Heritage Press, 1963.

Rumeu

*Libro Copiador de Cristóbal Colón: Corres-
pondencia inédita con los Reyes Católicos sobre los viajes a América. Estudio
histórico-crítico y edición.* 2 vols. Ed.
Antonio Rumeu de Armas. Madrid:
Testimonio, 1989.

Sanz

*Diario de Colón: Edición facsímil del "Li-
bro de la primera navegación y descubrimiento de las Indias."* Ed. Carlos Sanz.
Madrid: Bibliotheca Americana Vetustissima, 1962.

Varela

*Cristóbal Colón: Textos y documentos
completos.* Ed. Consuelo Varela. Madrid: Alianza, 1984.

West & Kling

*The "Libro de las profecías" of Christopher
Columbus: An en face Translation.* Trans.
and comm. Delno C. West and August Kling. Gainesville: University of
Florida Press, 1991.

Introduction

Los niños con los juegos, los mozos con las letras, los mancebos con los deleites, los viejos con mil especies de enfermedades pelean, y estos papeles con todas las edades. La primera los borra y rompe, la segunda no los sabe bien leer, la tercera, que es la alegre juventud y mancebía, discorda. Unos les roen los huesos que no tienen virtud, que es la historia toda junta, no aprovechándose de las particularidades, haciéndola cuento de camino, otros pican los donaires y refranes comunes, loándolos con toda atención, dejando pasar por alto lo que hace más al caso y utilidad suya. Pero aquellos para cuyo verdadero placer es todo, desechan el cuento de la historia para contar, coligen la suma para su provecho, ríen lo donoso, las sentencias y dichos de filósofos guardan en su memoria, para trasponer en lugares convenibles a sus actos y propósitos. Así que cuando diez personas se juntaren a oír esta comedia, en quien quepa esta diferencia de condiciones, como suele acaecer, ¿quién negará que haya contienda en cosa que de tantas maneras se entienda?

(Rojas, *Celestina*)

Children with their sports, boys with their books, young men with their pleasures, old men with a thousand sorts of infirmities, skirmish and war continually; and these papers with all ages. The first blots and tears them; the second knows not well how to read them; the third (which is the cheerful livelihood of youth, and set all upon jollity) doth utterly dislike them. Some gnaw only the bones, but do not pick out the marrow, saying there is no goodness in it— that it is a history, huddled, I know not how, together, a kind of hodgepodge or gallimaufrey; not profiting themselves out of the particularities, accounting it a fable or old wife's tale, fitting for nothing save only for to pass away the time upon the way. Others call out the witty conceits and common proverbs, highly commending them, but slighting and neglecting that which makes more to the purpose and their profit. But they for whose true pleasure it is wholly framed reject the story itself, as a vain and idle subject, and

gather out the pith and marrow of the matter for their own good
and benefit, and laugh at those things that savour only of wit and
pleasant conceit, storing up in their memory the sentences and say-
ings of philosophers, that they may transpose them into such fit
places as may make, upon occasion, for their own use and purpose. So that when ten men shall meet together to hear this com-
edy, in whom perhaps shall happen this difference of dispositions,
as it usually falleth out, who will deny but that there is a contention in that thing which is so diversely understood?[1]

Reading is a contentious practice, Fernando de Rojas affirmed in the
prologue to *Celestina*, a work published during Columbus's third
voyage to the Indies. For the act of reading is never perfectly
smooth; it is usually carried out in tension with the text as well as
with other readings. As Rojas could have predicted, the ink from
Columbus's pen was hardly dry when Isabella and Ferdinand expressed their dismay, in September 1493, over the report on the voyage he submitted to them upon his return from the first navigation.[2]
Clearly, what they had anticipated reading was different from the
text they received.

Since then, scholars have made careers and reputations out of
arguing about what exactly Columbus meant by what he wrote. No
aspect of his writings has been more controversial than the question
of the Discovery itself. In one corner are those who insist that Columbus died believing he had found a new route to Asia and had
in fact landed on the Asiatic mainland. But other scholars, using the
selfsame texts for evidence, claim with equal vigor that Columbus
knew all along, or very early on, that he had found a new continent.
Only slightly less controversial are such topics as the route Columbus followed, where he made landfall, the authenticity of the texts
attributed to him, the nature of the enterprise, and Columbus's
views of the Indians. The Columbian texts have something to say
about all of these issues, but they say different things to different
people and, apparently, in different ways.

The essays in this volume approach Columbian writing precisely
at its historical stress points; that is, they revisit those aspects of the
texts that have caused readers the greatest anxiety or have resulted
in significant disagreements among scholars of the Discovery.
Doubtless, my arguments and interpretations will provoke further
disagreement and dissent. But I trust that my interrogations of both

the Columbian texts and the assumptions made by previous readers will provide new vantage points from which to reconsider persistent questions about Columbian writing.

Typically, the Columbian texts have been under the purview of scholars working in disciplines devoted to determining the nature of the past. They treat the texts as evidence, and their readings are based on particular assumptions about the texts' authenticity, reliability, and accuracy. To date, there is no consensus: the Columbian texts have been deemed both very reliable and largely untrustworthy testimonies on the Discovery. All the essays here consider this problem, either implicitly or explicitly. But rather than focus on the relation between the texts and the events they refer to, I approach the texts as texts and emphasize the mediated nature of reading and writing.

For just as every text arises in a particular context and a specific set of circumstances, so do readings of that text. And although we cannot reconstruct those contexts in all their complexity and specificity nor approach writing and reading as if they were only responses to circumstances, to disregard the contexts within which texts become meaningful is to ignore an important aspect of how writing and reading help make history. The results of an interpretation that treats the mediated character of a text's mode of existence as a central focus of the analysis can be unsettling to those who feel most comfortable with the positivist assumption that the past can be essentially reconstituted in the present through the study of documentary sources. Yet if mediation is not taken into account, one runs the risk of producing a flat, static picture of historical writing.

In putting these differences between two critical perspectives on Columbian writing in such stark terms, I am overstating the problem somewhat in order to draw a clear distinction between two ways of reading that differ in purpose and emphasis. One can read to understand the past or to understand how stories about the past are told. Both these manners of reading require an awareness of the nuances and ambiguities of language, of the plural condition of meaning, of the importance of exegesis and interpretation in understanding the written word. But a historical reading seeks ultimately to recreate what really happened, through an archaeology of the word. Instead, the essays in this volume seek to understand the ways in which writing about the past makes it meaningful.

Several of the essays, for example, concern the pragmatics of Columbian writing; that is, they consider how a text may have been used by its author and readers, under what circumstances, and with what consequences. They focus, in other words, on the rhetorical rather than the referential qualities of writing. The readers to whom a text is explicitly or implicitly addressed, the circumstances surrounding the act of writing, the author's intentions, and the reader's expectations are only a few of the kinds of mediations that affect how information is selected and conveyed and, of course, the meaningfulness or usefulness of that information to those who receive it.

Such rhetorical inflections are most evident in the case of so-called creative writing. But in fact every text, even the most ostensibly objective of legal documents, can be shown to respond inventively to its circumstances, if only in the determinations the writer makes regarding exactly what information would be relevant to readers and most appropriate to the situation, and the form in which that information should therefore be presented. The creative dimension of historical writing and its relevance to the study of the past has been a recent focus of studies exploring the relation between historiography and literary criticism, history and the language arts.[3] These essays, however, strive to move the discussion beyond the specific fields of history and literature in order to consider the effects of other modalities of expression, including nonwritten forms, on Columbian writing's representation of the Discovery.[4] Such an approach necessarily transcends traditional disciplinary boundaries, touching as it does on a variety of fields in order to explore the cognitive bridges between them. Its object of study, however, is the text. It is, therefore, literary in the larger (and today archaic) sense conveyed by the Latin *litterarius*—of reading and writing. It does not distinguish between "literary" and "historical" texts. Indeed, as I will argue, in the analysis of Columbian writing the notion of disciplinary boundaries is highly questionable, if not obsolete.

In this regard these essays pose an alternative to the two traditions in the study of Columbian writing, history and literary criticism, by raising the types of questions that cannot be explored with a single methodology alone. The essay "'This present year of 1492,'" for example, considers the influence of the medieval notarial arts on the articulation of the enterprise of the Indies, as well as the circumstances that dictated the norms of the exchange between the writer and his addressees. "Voyage to Paradise" takes up the vexing question of Columbus's destination by looking at the relations between the Columbian texts' representation of the journey of discovery, its geography, and the cartographic paradigms to which they respond. "Gender and Discovery" approaches Columbian writing as a response to the contractual documents of commission issued by the Crown on the eve of the first voyage, and then evaluates gendered imagery in the Columbian texts in relation to the commercial and political goals of the enterprise as expressed in the royal contract.

Another important stress point in the interpretation of the Columbian texts concerns their transmission to later readers. The part reading plays in perpetuating writing is perhaps too obvious for comment. A text that is not read at least once stands little chance of survival. But the role of reading in transforming writing is generally not recognized as a significant problem in the study of texts. As Rojas had already pointed out in the fifteenth century, the relations between readers and texts are usually more complicated than simple, more combative than congenial. The three stages he identified in the life of the text as an object of reading suggest that it is an invasive activity. The "Carta a Luis de Santángel" (15 February 1493), announcing the Discovery, illustrates this point. Within a few months of Columbus's return, the letter (the only Columbian text to be published in his lifetime) appeared in Spanish, Italian, Latin, and in Italian verse. A manuscript copy in Santángel's hand is preserved in the Archivo General de Simancas. None of these versions are identical. The Latin editions, for instance, are addressed not to Santángel, the keeper of the royal privy purse, but to Gabriel Sánchez, the general treasurer of the kingdom of Aragon, whom the texts misidentify as Rafaél Sánchez. The versions differ from each other in other small ways, in part because all but the Spanish text are translations, and they differ quite significantly from the text that was probably their common matrix, the "Carta a los Reyes" of 4 March 1493, also announcing the Discovery.[5]

Moreover, a comparison of the letter to Santángel and the letter addressed to the Crown the following month suggests that the "earlier" version was probably derived from the later one and that the

February letter was at least substantially revised, if not completely composed, by someone other than Columbus. As it turned out, the derivative February letter not only modified but actually took the place of—or, more precisely, masqueraded as—the original announcement of the Discovery for almost five hundred years. Samuel Eliot Morison's assessment of the letter's authority and privilege is representative of the esteem in which most scholars have held it: "This letter is the first and rarest of all printed americana. It tells not only what the Admiral himself thought, but the most important things he wished the sovereigns to know. . . . Columbus composed this letter on board the caravel Niña, on his homeward passage" (Morison, 180). The 4 March letter, lost or suppressed for half a millennium, was known to have existed at all only because it was mentioned in a postscript to the 15 February version.[6] The consequences of this censorial reading and rewriting are taken up in more detail in the opening essay, "Reading Columbus."

Two other essays focus on the decisive mediation of Bartolomé de Las Casas, who copied, edited, paraphrased, and commented on a significant number of Columbus's writings, some of which survive only in Las Casas's versions. Conversely, the Columbian texts that remain lost today, including the *diarios* of the second, third, and fourth navigations, are, in part, unavailable because Las Casas did not transcribe them.[7] Thus, much of our understanding of the Discovery, much of what we know of what Columbus thought or said, as well as what we do not, is the result of Las Casas's intervention in the transmission of the Columbian texts. Although neglect, scribal error, official suppression, and foul play may also have contributed to the deformation and attrition that Columbus's words have suffered since their original inscription, nothing has had as comprehensive and profound an effect on them as Las Casas's hand. The scope and character of Las Casas's editorial interventions in the reconstitution of his source, the since lost *diario* of the first voyage, is the subject of the essay "'All these are the Admiral's exact words'"—a phrase that appears frequently in Las Casas's edition of Columbus's journal. "In the Margins of Columbus" considers the effects of Las Casas's mediation in the transmission of Columbian writing by examining the annotations and commentary he inscribed in the margins of the Columbian texts.

I use the phrase "Columbian writing" throughout these essays in recognition of the problems inherent in the notion of authorship and, especially, in acknowledgment of the mediated condition of the texts under consideration. From this perspective, *Reading Columbus* is an ironic title, since not only is it impossible to determine with absolute certainty which portions of these texts are Columbus's "very words," but the very signature "Columbus" must be seen as an aggregate, a corporate author as it were.

Discourse appears frequently and prominently in the pages that follow. The term has a long history: In Latin *discurrere* means "to run back and forth," a purely physical action. In its evolution through medieval Latin and into the modern European languages, however, the word retained of the original sense only the connotation of movement to and fro, and it came to designate intellectual activity, specifically, the process of reasoning or argumentation. More recent usage has branched into seemingly antithetical directions, with the twin senses of formal presentation or discussion (in Spanish *discurso* means "speech") and dialogue or exchange.

Upon further consideration, however, the one meaning implies the other. A lecture or speech may be performed as a monologue, but it is inherently dialogical insofar as it is a reaction to the current state of knowledge or opinion on the topic. Moreover, every lecture or speech addresses someone (even if only implicitly) and, perhaps most importantly, seeks to elicit a response (even if only to squelch dissent). Knowledge is not created by an individual genius working alone; it is the product of intellectual give and take, of the movement of ideas back and forth, of conversations comprising many voices.

To speak of the "discourse of the Discovery" then, suggests an exchange. Using the analogy of conversation or dialogue helps to underscore that the Discovery was a dynamic process constituted not by persons acting and speaking autonomously, but in formal official exchanges in the public sphere, situations that were inherently contractual—that is, dialogical in a figurative sense.

These essays consider the Discovery, then, not as a single and unique event, but as a process defining how Europeans were to relate to the newly found peoples and the territories they inhabited. In these terms, the Discovery and its discourse continued for decades, even centuries, after Columbus, as Las Casas's treatment of the Columbian texts illustrates. The exchange in question, however, was not between Europeans and Indians, but rather almost exclusively among Europeans themselves. The indigenous peoples of the New World suffered the Discovery, resisted or collaborated in various ways, but they were not participants in defining the terms of the Europeans' discourse. Neither Guacanagarí, the Haitian *cacique* who helped Columbus recover from the Santa María disaster on Christmas Day 1492, nor Cahonaboa, who subsequently destroyed the Spanish settlement established with the aid and protection of Guacanagarí and named La Navidad in commemoration of that first collaboration, were able to affect the essential European character of that process. The most significant contribution of the indigenous peoples—their resistance—constituted a rejection of the Europeans' definition of the Discovery and its implementation—but they were not allowed a voice in the discourse. Cahonaboa was eventually duped, captured, and sent to Spain in shackles. Guacanagarí remained a faithful ally of Columbus even in the face of the ever-increasing devastation inflicted by the discoverers on the other tribes of the island. Yet neither indigenous collaboration nor resistance have a say in this encounter. When the indigenous peoples speak through the Columbian texts at all, it is only because others do the talking for them.

One final clarification. Each of the essays in this book probes the tensions and contradictions in the discourse of the Discovery from a different perspective. But each new vantage point, by definition, also limits the angle of vision, by restricting the types of questions raised and, thereby, the character of the responses. Thus while each essay affirms a position with respect to the object of study and the issues raised, the volume as a whole does not resolve the complexities, incongruities, and tensions that inhabit the Columbian texts into a totalizing theory that would be compelling in its homogeneity. Such a perspectivistic strategy is heterogeneous not out of a relativistic reluctance to "take a stand" but, rather, out of a conviction that a critical stance is itself, like the texts it addresses, the contingent product of interactions at a particular time and place.[8]

Reading Columbus

Christopher Columbus's act of writing to the Crown to announce the Discovery was an event almost as momentous as the act of discovering itself. Not only did his letter make the fact of the historical event known to others, but the very future of the enterprise depended on how it was represented to those who were in the position to decide its fate.

Like writing, reading has consequences, and our thoughts today about Columbus's first voyage are at least as much the result of how the Columbian texts were read as of the manner in which they were written. This essay considers the earliest readings of Columbian writing through a comparative lens, focusing on two versions of the announcement of the Discovery. Both were presumably written by Columbus, although, as I note below, that is a matter of some debate. The dispute over the actual authorship of these versions aside, however, the significant variations between the two texts suggest that one constitutes a reading of the other, an emendation of the original scriptural act that created a new and different image of the Discovery.

Of course, not every act of reading literally constitutes a new text. But reading is always, if only in a metaphorical sense, a rewriting. As readers, we privilege certain aspects of the text, repress others, misunderstand some, and perhaps on occasion even understand only too well the story before us. Readings are, in any case, always in creative tension with the text. In underscoring the generative quality of the act of reading, my purpose is to explore the role reading has played in the writing of the history of the Discovery.

As the *Diario* of the first navigation tells it, on 14 February 1493, in the midst of a life-threatening storm, Columbus wrote to Ferdinand and Isabella, announcing the Discovery. He sealed the letter inside a barrel, along with a note asking whoever found it to deliver it to the sovereigns unopened, with the promise of a substantial reward if the instructions were followed; he then tossed the barrel overboard to the fate of the wind and the waves.[1] Given the raging storm and the fact that Columbus had not yet sighted any land, although he calculated that he was sailing in the vicinity of the Azores, the composition of this letter seems more an act of desperation than of premature optimism. On 4 March he wrote to the king of Portugal and to the Spanish sovereigns again. According to the *Diario*, Columbus had managed to find his way to tranquil waters in the mouth of the Tagus River on that day, and both letters were apparently posted overland.

Two other letters, both dated 15 February 1493, also announcing the Discovery, have been ascribed to Columbus. One was addressed to Luis de Santángel, the other to Rafaél (Gabriel) Sánchez. Both these men were officials of the Crown of Aragon who had been instrumental in facilitating the Columbian enterprise. Neither of these letters, however, are mentioned in the *Diario*, and the place of composition stated in the letters contradicts Columbus's itinerary.[2]

Until quite recently the only versions of the announcement known to have survived were the almost identical texts of the letters addressed to Santángel and Sánchez. Within a few months of Columbus's return, these had been published in various editions and in three different languages throughout Europe. The letter of 14 February apparently was lost at sea. The only remaining traces of it are the references in the *Diario* and in subsequent histories derived from that account of the first navigation.[3] The letters of 4 March, to João II of Portugal and to Isabella and Ferdinand, also disappeared without a trace, but probably for the opposite reason—not because they were lost en route to the addressees, but because they indeed were received and read. As official documents of considerable import, they undoubtedly would have been copied and the originals handled with utmost care. Nonetheless, until 1989 we had only references to their existence: the *Diario* mentions the letter to the Portuguese king; the postscript of the published letters to Santángel and Sánchez mentions the letter to the Spanish sovereigns; and correspondence from the Crown to Columbus acknowledges receipt of a letter that most scholars believe was probably the text of 4 March. But the letters themselves fell victim to accident or, more likely, to deliberate suppression by officials treating them as state secrets at the Portuguese and Castilian courts. They were wholly lost to us until 1989, when Antonio Rumeu de Armas published an undated and unsigned copy of the 4 March letter, based on a manuscript of uncertain origin, probably from the mid-sixteenth century.[4]

The letters dated 15 February to Santángel and Sánchez, on the contrary, were so vigorously and widely circulated that they appear to have been part of a concerted propaganda campaign. After thorough study of the enigmas surrounding the composition and publication of the letters to Santángel and Sánchez, Demetrio Ramos Pérez concluded that the evidence overwhelmingly suggests they are a sanitized version of another text (probably the letter of 4 March to Ferdinand and Isabella), composed by officials at court (perhaps by Santángel himself) to broadcast the official version of the Discovery.[5] Moving beyond the letters' inconsistencies concerning dates and place of composition, Ramos shows how the letters of 15 February responded to the political climate in Europe during the months immediately following the conclusion of the first voyage.

Some of Ramos's assumptions about the lost letter to Ferdinand and Isabella of 4 March have proved inaccurate in light of Rumeu's edition. Yet the thrust of Ramos's argument that the version of 15 February was composed as propaganda, appears to be strengthened by the 4 March text. Though similar, the February and March versions offer fundamentally distinct representations of the Discovery.

If one accepts the hypothesis that Columbus himself authored the originals of each of these announcements of the Discovery, then all three letters can be considered distillations of the *diario* of the first voyage; that is, products of Columbus reading himself. Both Ramos and Rumeu have tested a similar hypothesis and found that the correlation of specific passages is often very close, although the letters also present significant divergences from the *Diario*. The fundamental problem with this approach, however, is that all of the surviving versions of the itinerary of the first voyage are secondhand. Ferdinand Columbus and Las Casas both quoted or paraphrased extensively from the *diario* of the navigation in their accounts of that voyage, but their texts can only be considered reconstitutions of whatever Columbus may have written. Even Las Casas's edition of the *Diario*, the closest version we have to Columbus's own account, is a highly edited summary of a copy of the text, composed by Las Casas in the sixteenth century.[6] Two other factors also tend to undermine any conclusions drawn from such a comparative analysis. First, no holographs of these texts are available. The closest extant versions of the original letter of 15 February are an archival copy of the text addressed to Santángel and the surviving first editions of the published texts. The copy of the letter of 4 March to Ferdinand and Isabella published by Rumeu is some 150 years removed from the original. Such lacunae make it essentially impossible to draw any solid conclusions about the sources of the variations or even the significance of the similarities.

With Rumeu's publication of the 4 March letter, however, two different versions of the announcement of the Discovery are now available. Indisputably, one of them is a reading of the other. And while it may be impossible to verify with absolute certainty which of these texts was the original and which the revision, or to determine who did the rewriting, a comparison of the two versions provides an opportunity to consider the consequences that the earliest readings of Columbian writing have had on our understanding of the Discovery.

Rumeu (1:27–41) contends that Columbus must have penned two different versions of the announcement, one addressed to the Crown and the other to Santángel and to Sánchez, all of which he then sent to court together on 4 March 1493. Ramos, on the other hand, proposes that someone, probably Santángel himself, composed the version of 15 February specifically for publication, working from either a letter Columbus sent him or, more likely, the letter of 4 March to the sovereigns.[7] In any case, it is difficult to dispute that a pen other than Columbus's intervened in the 15 February version, especially if one is persuaded by Ramos and Rumeu that its publication must have been carried out with the Crown's blessing and under official supervision.

A comparison of the letter to Santángel with the letter of 4 March strongly suggests that the former underwent stylistic revision on its way to publication. Generally more concise and better organized than the royal version, the Santángel text systematically summarizes various passages that are more elaborate in the letter to Isabella and Ferdinand. Many of these concern the technical aspects of the exploration, such as the recording of distances, directions, geographical information received from the Indians, and so on. The descriptions of people and landscape in the letter to Santángel tend to be of a more general character, often collapsing details given in the 4 March letter about particular islands into sweeping characterizations of all the islands as a group. Some revisions seem to have been undertaken for the purpose of resolving ambiguities or contradictions in the 4 March text. In the letter to Santángel, for example, a passage describing Columbus's predicament and actions on the north coast of Cuba and explaining his critical decision to cut short the exploration of what he thought was the mainland differs from its 4 March counterpart not only in its specific wording but also in the greater degree of detail it provides with respect to Columbus's thoughts and actions (see Appendix, note 4).

Other changes, however, cannot be attributed to the reviser's desire for economy or clarity, simply to facilitate reading. By far the more interesting differences are those which suggest that the royal text was systematically censored on its way to becoming the public version of the announcement. It is in this redactive process, whose traces emerge between the lines of text when the two versions are compared, that a particular way of reading the Discovery unfolds.

The *Santa María* disaster is a case in point. The letter to the sovereigns tells of leaving behind the flagship to serve in building a fortification for the Spaniards who were to remain at La Navidad. It does not mention, however, what the *Diario* entry for 25 December amply explains: that it became necessary to abandon the vessel and leave the men on the island after the *Santa María* had run aground on a reef, due to the negligence and cowardice of some of the crew, and was unfit for the return trip. Despite Columbus's reticence, the implications of Spanish misconduct must have been clear. Deliberately, it would seem, no reference whatsoever to the fate of the *Santa María* appears in the Santángel version.

Ships are in fact a prominent topic in the letter of 4 March. Columbus proffers elaborate observations on the advantages of using smaller vessels for exploration and apologetically explains that he had taken larger ones against his better judgment, bowing to pressure from a fearful crew that was reluctant to trust the smaller ships in oceanic navigation. None of these comments appear in the 15 February version, perhaps because they were considered potentially useful to rival expeditions, or perhaps to delete the implication of cowardice among the crew. Whatever the reason, these passages were purged from the public announcement.

Also absent from the 15 February version is any mention of the treachery of Martín Alonso Pinzón, captain of the *Pinta*, who vexed Columbus throughout the voyage, according to the *Diario* and an allusion to "one from Palos" in the letter of 4 March. The full extent of Columbus's complaint about Pinzón is difficult to ascertain because the manuscript of the 4 March copy is severely damaged in this section, but it is evident that Columbus wanted to alert the Crown to Pinzón's insubordination and self-interest in straying from the rest of the fleet to explore on his own. The Santángel letter, however, is completely silent on this issue. Nor does it mention another source of friction—the generalized resistance to the project Columbus encountered at court prior to his departure. The 4 March letter, on the other hand, lingers on the ridicule and ill treatment Columbus had to endure from his detractors, seeming to relish the implicit "I told you so."

Other differences between the royal and public versions of the announcement may seem insignificant at first but, on closer examination, reveal important semantic alterations. Consider, for example, the following almost identical passages:

Quanto tienen y tenían davan por qualquiera cosa que por ella se le diese, hasta tomar un pedazo de vidrio o de escudilla rrota o cosa semejante, quiera fuese oro quier fuese otra cosa de qualquier valor; los cavos de las agujetas de cuero ovo un marinero más de dos castellanos y medio; y destas cosas ay diez mill de contar.	*Yo defendí* que no se les diesen cosas tan siviles como pedazos de escudillas rotas y pedazos de vidrio roto y cabos de agugetas; *haunque cuando* ellos esto podían llegar, les parescía haver la mejor ioya del mundo; que se acertó haver un marinero por una agugeta, de oro de peso de dos castellanos y medio, y otros de otras cosas que muy menos valían, mucho más.
("Carta a los Reyes"; Rumeu, 2:437)	("Carta a Luis de Santángel"; Varela, 142; emphasis added)
Everything they have or had they gave for whatever one gave them in exchange, even taking a piece of glass or broken crockery or some such thing, for gold	*I forbade* that they should be given things so worthless as pieces of broken crockery and broken glass, and lace points, *although when* they were able to

<table>
<tr><td>

or some other thing of whatever value. One sailor got more than two and a half castellanos [in gold] for the ends of leather latchets. There are ten thousand like occurrences to tell.

</td><td>

get them, they thought they had the best jewel in the world; thus it was learned that a sailor for a lace point received gold to the weight of two and a half castellanos, and others much more for other things which were worth much less.

</td></tr>
</table>

(Morison, 183)

Both passages deal with the highly favorable rate of exchange the Europeans obtained from the Taínos owing to their portrayed generosity or naiveté (or, more likely, to their different value system). In each text the same anecdote of the sailor who managed to negotiate a nice chunk of gold for a leather latchet is presented as a sort of paradigm of present and future transactions. But in the Santángel version the added words "Yo defendí" and "haunque cuando" affect not just the tone, but the entire import of the passage. For what in the letter to Isabella and Ferdinand was simply an example of the potential for exploiting future trading partners is transformed in the letter to Santángel into a situation created and welcomed by the Indians themselves, despite Columbus's explicit sanctions against such crass abuse. The two short phrases added to the Santángel text turn the Indians into the instigators who invite and perpetuate the uneven negotiations Columbus gallantly tried to prevent—a consummate example of blaming the victim.

Simple differences in the organization of the two texts also produce important semantic variations. For example, consider the passages that describe the Indians' reception of the Spaniards:

<table>
<tr><td>

generalmente en quantas tierras yo aya andado, creieron y creen que yo, con estos navíos y gente, venía del çielo, y con este acatamiento me rreçibían, y oy, en el día, están en el mesmo propósito ni se an quitado dello, por mucha conversaçión que ayan tenido con ellos; y luego en llegando a qualquiera poblazón, los hombres y mugeres y niños andan dando bozes por

</td><td>

y creían muy firme que yo con estos navíos y gente venía del cielo . . . Oy en día los traigo que siempre están de propósito que vengo del cielo, por mucha conversación que ayan havido conmigo. Y estos eran los primeros a pronunciarlo adonde yo llegava, y los otros andavan corriendo de casa en casa y a las villas cercanas con bozes altas "Venit, venit a ver la gente del

</td></tr>
</table>

las casas: "Benid, benid a ver la
gente del çielo."
("Carta a los Reyes";
Rumeu, 2:437)

cielo." Así todos, hombres
como mugeres, después de
haver el corazón seguro de nos,
venían que non quedavan
grande ni pequeño, y todos
traían algo de comer y de bever,
que davan con un amor maravi-
lloso.
("Carta a Luis de Santángel";
Varela, 142–43)

generally, in whatever lands I
traveled, they believed and believe that I, together with these
ships and people, came from
heaven, and they greeted me
with such veneration. And today, this very day, they are of
the same mind, nor have they
strayed from it, despite all the
contact they [the Spaniards at
La Navidad] may have had with
them. And then upon arriving
at whatever settlement, the
men, women, and children go
from house to house calling out,
"Come, come and see the
people from heaven!"

and they are still of the opinion
that I come from the sky,[8] in
spite of all the intercourse
which they have had with me,
and they were the first to announce this wherever I went,
and the others went running
from house to house and to the
neighboring towns with loud
cries of, "Come! Come! See the
people from the sky!" They all
came, men and women alike, as
soon as they had confidence in
us, so that not one, big or little,
remained behind, and all
brought something to eat and
drink which they gave us with
marvelous love.
(Morison, 184)

In isolation, the passage in the letter to Santángel appears to be primarily an expansive paraphrase, a rhetorical intensification that
employs repetition, additional modifiers, and detail to recreate
more vibrantly the scene of arrival. But, more importantly, the passage has also been relocated and recontextualized. In the letter of 4
March these observations appeared immediately preceding the passage describing the opportunities for exploitative barter, a juxtaposition that highlighted the patently unheavenly conduct of the
Christians in response to their hosts' generous and reverent reception. In the letter to Santángel, the welcoming of the Europeans as
divine beings follows the mention of the sanctions Columbus
placed on unfair trading. Thus the scene of arrival now effectively

confirms and even underscores the Admiral's laudable ethical comportment, and the reverential reception given to the Europeans by the Indians appears well-deserved.

Moreover, in the letter to Santángel, the passage immediately preceding that of the arrival describes the evangelical dimension of the expedition and Columbus's generosity toward the Indians. In repositioning and recontextualizing the scene of arrival, the letter in effect redefines the terms of exchange: The crass exploitation of the natives related in the royal missive is refashioned into a reciprocal interaction that bespeaks the noble Christian character of the Spaniards. The letter that announces the Discovery to Christian European readers presents the image of a paternal Columbus who brings the word of God to the heathens and seeks to protect them not so much from Spanish greed as from their own naiveté, a man worthy of the Indians' adoration and the Crown's favor.

Perhaps the most striking difference between the letter to the sovereigns and the published letter to Santángel is the deletion of several concluding paragraphs in the latter. Three of these paragraphs contain direct petitions to the Crown for favors and the fulfillment of the honors and rewards promised Columbus in the "Capitulaciones de Santa Fe" (17 April 1492). Specifically, these include a request for the concession of favors for services rendered, together with a letter of petition to the Pope asking for a cardinalate for Columbus's legitimate son Diego, and a request for the appointment of Pedro de Villacorta, a Columbus favorite, to the post of paymaster of the Indies. The nature of the petitions themselves is probably not as significant as is the fact that the royal letter contains them while the Santángel version does not. Such petitions, of course, would have been inappropriate, indeed irrelevant, in a letter addressed to anyone but the Crown, and they may have been omitted by Columbus himself if he in fact wrote the original version of the letter to Santángel (even before the idea of publication came into play).

Nonetheless, the petitions in the royal letter significantly color the reader's conceptualization of the Discovery in underscoring the contractual character of the enterprise. As the petitions remind us, Columbus's fate rested in the Crown's perception of the success or failure of his endeavor. The purpose of the letter announcing the Discovery to the royal sponsors of the expedition was not simply to transmit an objective account of what Columbus witnessed and experienced. Rather, it was a fairly transparent attempt to advocate for the protagonist's interests before Isabella and Ferdinand. From this perspective, every observation on the lands and peoples is marked by the contractual pragmatics that determine and define the acts of writing and of reading. Nowhere is this more evident than in Columbus's supplication that "la honrra me sea dada según el serviçio" (441; honor be bestowed upon me according to [the quality of] my service). In the final analysis, the announcement of the Discovery in the letter of 4 March is the account of the quality of the service rendered by the protagonist and a petition for commensurate compensation.

Ferdinand and Isabella seemed to have recognized Columbus's announcement as such a request, as their response of 30 March indicates:

> Don Cristóbal Colón, nuestro almirante del Mar Océano e visorrey y gobernador de las islas que se han descubierto en las Indias: vimos vuestras letras, y hobimos mucho placer en saber lo que por ellas nos escribistes, y de haberos dado Dios tan buen fin en vuestro trabajo, y encaminado bien en lo que comenzaste, en que él será mucho servido, y nosotros asimismo y nuestros reinos recibir tanto provecho. . . . Placerá a Dios que demás de lo que en esto le servides, por ello recibiréis de Nos muchas mercedes, *las cuales creed que se vos harán con* (sic) *vuestros servicios e trabajos lo merescen.*
> (Rumeu, 1:35; emphasis added)

> Don Cristóbal Colón, our admiral of the Ocean Sea and viceroy and governor of the islands that have been discovered in the Indies: we read your letters, and derived great pleasure from learning what you wrote to us in them, and that God has given such success to your labor, and set what you began on such a good path, in which He, and we also, will be well served, and our kingdoms will receive so much profit. . . . It will please God that besides the service you have rendered to Him, you will receive from Us many favors for it, *which favors you can trust will be granted unto you according to the merit of your services and labors.* (emphasis added)

In the salutation the Crown explicitly acknowledges and confirms the titles of admiral, viceroy, and governor promised to Columbus in the "Capitulaciones." Moreover, echoing his letter of 4 March, this letter directly links the bestowal of royal favors to his labors and the quality of his service. In deleting the contractual pragmatics of

Columbus's announcement, the Santángel version redefined the Discovery—from an enterprise marked by significant national and private interests to a heroic, selfless mission on behalf of Christendom.

Yet another paragraph from the letter to the sovereigns, but absent from the Santángel version, contains arguably the most important contribution the recent publication of the 4 March letter has made to our understanding of the Columbian enterprise. Columbus asserts that the project was undertaken for the expressed purpose of helping to finance a Spanish military campaign to reconquer the Holy Land:

> Concluio aquí: que mediante la graçia divinal, de aquél ques comienço de todas cosas virtuosas y buenas y que da favor y victoria a todos aquéllos que van en su camino, que de oy en siete años yo podré pagar a Vuestras Altezas çinco mill de cavallo y çinquenta mill de pie en la guerra e conquista de Iherusalem, *sobre el qual propósito se tomó esta empresa.*
>
> (Rumeu, 2:440; emphasis added)

> I conclude here: that through the divine grace of He who is the origin of all good and virtuous things, who favors and gives victory to all those who walk in His path, that in seven years from today I will be able to pay Your Highnesses for five thousand cavalry and fifty thousand foot soldiers for the war and conquest of Jerusalem, *for which purpose this enterprise was undertaken.* (emphasis added)

The topic of the reconquest of Jerusalem becomes very prominent in Columbian discourse from the third voyage on. The passage cited above is repeated almost verbatim in a letter Columbus addressed to Pope Alexander VI in 1502 (Varela, 312). The recovery of Jerusalem is also a principal theme of the *Libro de las profecías* and of two letters, one addressed to Queen Isabella; the other to the sovereigns together, both written in 1501. The royal missive of 4 March strongly suggests that the project had already been discussed with the Crown prior to the inception of the first voyage. And yet such a remarkable statement of purpose, which would undoubtedly have impressed any Christian reader, does not appear in the version of the letter published precisely to broadcast the news of the voyage's success throughout Christendom.[9] This deletion is even more perplexing if one is persuaded by Ramos's contention that the letter's publication was intended not only for general propaganda but specifically to thwart Portuguese pretensions at the Vatican and to pave the way for Castilian negotiations for a bull of concession of the newly found lands from the Pope.[10] In any case, the Crown may have felt the commitment to evangelization proclaimed in the letter was sufficient to ensure that the Church would be well-disposed toward the enterprise without the additional, and much more costly, commitment to a campaign for the Holy Land. Whatever the reasons, the link between the Discovery and the reconquest of Jerusalem was dropped from the published version, rendering the enterprise of Discovery less religiously committed and certainly less messianic than Columbus seems to have intended.[11]

Thus the active promotion of the Santángel version of Columbus's announcement of the Discovery, together with the suppression of the royal version, created a revised image of the event that was the product of reading at least as much as of the original scriptural act, whatever that may have been. For almost five hundred years our sense of the Discovery has been the product of a reading that appears to have been little concerned with the objective representation of the geographical and anthropological aspects of the lands in question, or with historical accuracy. The Santángel version was much more interested in its own reception; that is, it was fashioned for the readers it sought to engage and the reactions it hoped to elicit. So, undoubtedly, was the letter of 4 March to the sovereigns that the Santángel text supplanted in the public arena, although it did so in significantly different ways, as we have seen.

The first mediation in the transmission of Columbian writing to future readers was an erasure, as Rojas suggested in the prologue to *Celestina*, a reading that eradicated one text and created another. The 15 February Santángel/Sánchez texts replaced the royal missive as the "original" announcements of the Discovery, and the surrogate versions were invested with all the privilege and authority of primogeniture. The unprecedented blanketing of Europe with copies and translations of the 15 February version of the announcement all but ensured that it would be the one transmitted to posterity. A sobering reminder that acts of reading, like storms at sea and other acts of God or Fate, have the power to erase—and to rewrite—the text of history.

"This present year of 1492"

Despite its brevity, the so-called prologue to the *Diario* of the first voyage should be of fundamental interest to readers of Columbian writing. As preface to the most complete account of the navigation to have survived, it has served as the definitive introduction to the Discovery for almost two hundred years. Moreover, it is the discursive bridge between the official prediscovery documents issued by the Crown commissioning Columbus to undertake the enterprise and Columbus's testimony on his compliance with their conditions and the fulfillment of his charge. Bartolomé de Las Casas, in the introductory rubric to his edition of the *Diario*, recognized the text's importance, explaining that he had largely summarized much of Columbus's account of the voyage proper but had rendered verbatim the Admiral's prologue.[1]

Las Casas's privileging of the prologue apparently has not impressed modern scholars of the *Diario*, who rarely take note of the text except in passing or to chastise Columbus (or Las Casas) for fabrication, historical inaccuracy, or worse.[2] Yet Las Casas, who was one of the first and undoubtedly the most comprehensive of the early historians of the Columbian enterprise and must have been aware of the misrepresentations the text contained, nevertheless was struck by the prologue, apparently for reasons other than historical accuracy. In chapter 35 of the *Historia de las Indias* he explains it this way:

> salió [Colón] del puerto y barra que se dice de Saltes, porque así se llama aquel río de Palos; y porque comenzó desde allí sus navegaciones para estas Indias, y el prólogo dél, así por contar algo de la toma de Granada y hacer minción de la echada de los judíos, como porque se conciba la intinción de los Reyes y suya, y también por la antigüedad y simplicidad de sus palabras, parecióme no ir fuera de la historia referillo aquí, en el cual comienza Cristóbal Colón decir a los Reyes así . . .
>
> ([Madrid: Biblioteca de Autores Españoles, 1958], 1:126–27)

[Columbus] departed from the port and bar called Saltes, because that is the name of that river of Palos; and because he began a book about his navigations to these Indies there and its prologue, in order to tell something about the seizure of Granada and to mention the expulsion of the Jews from these kingdoms, and so that the intention of the sovereigns and his own may be understood, and also because of the antiquity and simplicity of his words, it seemed to me it would not be inappropriate to the history of the matter to relate it here, in which [prologue] Columbus begins to address the sovereigns thus . . .

A transcription of the prologue in its entirety follows. Immediately after the transcription Las Casas turns to the particulars of the first voyage. Unlike his practice elsewhere in the *Historia*, where he usually comments lavishly on the significance of the Admiral's actions and words, here Las Casas offers no commentary on the prologue, nor any interpretation of how it might illuminate the account of the discovery or Columbus's thinking.

The two aspects of the prologue that seem to have attracted Las Casas's attention are the "intention" the text presumably expresses, which Las Casas attributes to both Columbus and the Crown, and the manner in which that intention is expressed ("la antigüedad y simplicidad de sus palabras"). My working hypothesis here is that, despite what Las Casas would like us to believe, the so-called prologue is not to be read as a repository of information regarding an extrinsic referent—the historical event of the Discovery—but as an essentially rhetorical composition, which is therefore referentially unreliable. Rather than serving an informative function (that is, communicating accurate information about extrinsic events), the prologue has as its primary purpose a hortatory, or performative, function. It seeks to engender an attitude in the recipients of the message, conducing its readers to action of a particular kind.[3]

To speak about the prologue's performative force is an essentially pragmatic consideration. It situates the act of reading in the interface between writer and addressee, words and their effects. In the case of the prologue, such a position is especially problematic because the original text has been lost since the sixteenth century. The version we have was copied and manipulated by scribes and later edited by Las Casas. It is possible, however, to speculate about alternatives to the text's condition and status before Las Casas intervened in its transmission, thereby imbuing it with his own intentions. Perhaps the most momentous consequence of his intervention was the explicit labeling of the text in question as a prologue—a simple, seemingly neutral operation that altered the way the account of the first voyage is read.

Despite Las Casas's attempt to underscore the prologue's informative function ("in order to tell something about the seizure of Granada and to mention the expulsion of the Jews from these kingdoms, and so that the intention of the sovereigns and his own may be understood"), his description of the text connotes his admiration of its rhetorical qualities—"la antigüedad y simplicidad de sus palabras," as he puts it. By *antigüedad*, Las Casas does not mean the literal "ancientness" of the text (it was only a few decades old when he first consulted it), but rather the text's privilege and authority as the oldest, indeed the original, word on the Discovery. As the earliest Spanish dictionary—Covarrubias's, published in 1611—notes, the adjective *antiguo* implies "priority" (from *ante*, "before") and also "authority." Of the various connotations of *simplicidad* mentioned by Covarrubias, the one that seems most appropriate in this context is the biblical one: "Hombre simple, en la Escritura, vale hombre sencillo sin ningún doblez, justo y bueno" (A simple man, in the Scriptures, means a candid man without deceitfulness, just and good).[4] This definition is the moral complement of the notion of authoritativeness expressed in the word *antigüedad*. In praising Columbus's words for their "antigüedad y simplicidad," Las Casas is preparing his readers to be persuaded of the truthfulness of the Columbian message and of Las Casas's belief, repeated throughout the *Historia*, that Columbus had been destined by God to undertake the Discovery.

The existence of this prologue, however, is not mentioned by Ferdinand Columbus, the other early biographer of Columbus to have consulted the primary sources directly. Nor does he even implicitly paraphrase its contents when he recounts the first voyage in his *Vida del Almirante Don Cristóbal Colón*. If the text Las Casas labels the prologue to the *Diario* was not a prologue until he made it so, then it may well have been what it most patently appears to be in form and pragmatics—the first letter about the voyage-in-progress from Columbus to the Crown.[5]

Let us suppose that the so-called prologue in fact began its life as the first official missive of the voyage from Columbus to Isabella and Ferdinand. Like most of what Columbus is known to have written, this text probably was conceived and executed as a letter. Perhaps it prefaced the account of the first voyage in the (now lost) manuscript Columbus presented to the Crown, but, more likely, it simply accompanied that manuscript as a covering letter. Nothing intrinsic to this Letter of 1492 (as I will refer to the "prologue" from here on) indicates that it was composed specifically to serve a prefatory role in the account of the first voyage, although the only extant copy is the one that prefaces the *Diario*. Conceivably, the piece could have been written for mailing directly to Isabella and Ferdinand from the Canaries during the fleet's hiatus there for repairs on the first leg of the voyage. Consistent use of the present tense, however, indicates that this text was not written in chronological sequence with the voyage itinerary. The *diario* proper begins with the entry for 3 August 1492, with the departure from Palos narrated in first person plural of the preterite tense: "Partimos viernes 3 días de agosto de 1492 años . . ." (Varela, 17; We departed Friday, 3 August 1492).

Nor, apparently, was the Letter of 1492 composed after the account of the journey was completed, in typical prologue fashion, for the verb tenses imply that it was written in 1492, some time after the fleet arrived in the Canaries. For Columbus to have placed the letter at the very beginning of his account, as Las Casas did in the *Diario*, would have involved at the very least some revision and rearrangement of the account of the journey. More importantly, however, it would have constituted a violation of Columbus's promise to the Crown, made in the letter itself, that his account would be a strict, chronological, "day-by-day" record of the navigation.

The solemnity with which Columbus must have approached the composition of the Letter of 1492 is not difficult to imagine. Given the royal addressee and the circumstances in which the text was prepared, it must have been one of the most deliberate and carefully crafted pieces Columbus ever wrote. Far from any casual intimacy or spontaneity, understandable in the day-by-day account, the letter had to achieve the highest degree of epistolary eloquence. It would be expected to conform to the standards and guidelines of the *ars dictaminis* (the art of letter writing), which prescribed the conventions of medieval correspondence, from the loftiest epistles to distinguished authorities to the most pedestrian of missives.[6] On this letter, Columbus knew, hinged the Crown's recognition of the success of his expedition, the confirmation of the rights and privileges promised him, and royal favor for future voyages.[7] To fail to live up to the standards required of such a momentous communication in a society so governed by ritual and convention would not only put Columbus (and his achievements) in a bad light, but could also jeopardize the future of the enterprise itself.

Following the guidelines recommended in dictaminal manuals, the Letter of 1492 opens with a lavish *salutatio*, or greeting, exalting Isabella and Ferdinand. There follows an elaborate *exordium*, often referred to as the *captatio benevolentiae* and considered the most important part of an epistle because in it the writer had to capture the addressee's attention, invoke his or her benevolence, and lead into the matter at hand by relating it to an attractive general principle or theme. The *exordium* was the most rhetorically intense and demanding section of a letter since the reader's favor and receptiveness to the writer's purpose depended on its effective "priming" of the addressee. The historical errors for which the Letter of 1492 is famous are found precisely in this section. The *exordium* was typically followed by the *narratio* (i.e., explanation by narrative of fact), a section that dictaminal manuals recommended should be brief, simple, and to the point. The *narratio* portion of Columbus's letter relates his taking leave of the sovereigns at Granada, his arrival at Palos and the equipping of the three caravels, his departure for the Indies by way of the Canaries, and the purpose of his mission: to undertake the embassy from Ferdinand and Isabella to the Grand Khan. It presents a succinct, precise account of the enterprise to that point, correctly dated and in some cases detailed down to the day of the week and time of day when the events in question took place.

The closing section of the letter introduces the account of the voyage proper, stating Columbus's intentions to write a timely day-by-day account ("todo este viaje muy puntualmente de día en día"), to make a new navigation chart of the lands and waters of the Ocean Sea and, moreover, to compose "un libro y poner todo por el semejante por pintura" (a book and similarly record all of the same in a drawing; Dunn & Kelley, 21). Presumably this was to be an illustrated account of the voyage.[8] This section, which should correspond to the dictaminal *conclusio*, reads more like a continuation of the *narratio*, since it informs the reader of what Columbus proposes

to do. As a closing, it seems clumsy, for it leaves the letter uncomfortably open-ended. As an introduction to the subsequent day-by-
day account of the voyage, it is equally clumsy, however, since it
introduces not one but three different textual entities—the day-by-
day record of the voyage, the cartographic "text," and the illustrated
"libro"—only the first of which follows in the *Diario*. The final three
lines of the letter allude to Columbus's zeal in carrying out his mission and are reminiscent of the popular rhetorical topic "idleness is
to be shunned."[9] Columbus's purpose seems to be to ingratiate his
royal readers by reminding them of the great labors and deprivations that await him:

> y sobre todo cumple mucho que yo olvide el sueño y tiente mucho
> el navegar porque así cumple las quales serán gran trabajo.
>
> (Varela, 17)
>
> and above all it is very important that I forget sleep and pay much
> attention to navigation in order thus to carry out these purposes,
> which will be a great labor.
>
> (Dunn & Kelley, 21)

To rename as the Letter of 1492 the text Las Casas labeled the prologue to the *Diario* is to bring into relief important differences in the
way the text functions if read as a letter to the Crown instead of as
a prologue to the *Diario*.[10] The two genres are kindred spirits; indeed, prologues often mimic epistolary rhetoric in order to establish
the immediate and direct rapport with the reader that both genres
typically strive for. Though similar in their rhetorical effects, however, prologues and letters are not equivalent genres in their discursive pragmatics—a crucial distinction in understanding the significance of this Columbian text with respect to the larger context of
writing in which it was produced. The (hypothetical) recontextualization of the text from a prologue to the *Diario* to Columbus's first
direct in-progress communication with the Crown draws to the fore
the text's most distinctive characteristics—its performative qualities
and, more specifically, its predominantly hortatory thrust.

The majority of the documents generated by the Discovery are
implicitly, if not explicitly, dialogic; that is, they are rejoinders in an
ongoing colloquy in which information was requested, supplied,
questioned, and interpreted, back and forth, by both the Crown
and Columbus. This dialogue of texts was initiated by Ferdinand

and Isabella in the documents of commission. The Letter of 1492, as Columbus's first response, establishes not only the terms, but the tone and tenor of his voice in the exchange. It was in fact the first opportunity for Columbus to "speak" directly to the sovereigns in his official capacity as their envoy in the enterprise of the Indies. He must have also been acutely aware that it was his first opportunity to speak to posterity since the letter, as part of the official record of the first voyage, would ultimately be preserved in the royal archives. (Like many other Columbian texts, including the *diarios* of the three later voyages, however, neither the original nor any registered copy is known to have survived.)

Pragmatically speaking, the Letter of 1492 belongs to the group of prediscovery documents that defined the parameters of the enterprise and the nature of the relationship between the Crown and Columbus. The most important of these were the "Capitulaciones de Santa Fe" (17 April 1492) and the "Carta de Merced" (30 April 1492).[11] All subsequent communications perforce would conform to, and certainly could not violate, the terms of this foundational dialogue of 1492. That the letter was conceived with an eye to the contractual prediscovery documents issued by the Crown is suggested by the insistent manner in which the year 1492 is repeated as the date of composition. The letter may not have reached the sovereigns until 1493, with the account of the now-completed first voyage, but Columbus took great pains to establish this text as a document of the same vintage as the prediscovery texts that defined the scope of the enterprise and the soon-to-be admiral's privileges. Despite Columbus's concerted effort to situate the text in the same historical moment as the prediscovery "Capitulaciones" and the "Carta de Merced," the letter's significance resides in the ways in which it deviates from those documents with which it sought to be identified.[12]

The "Capitulaciones" is an overtly imperialistic document, calling for the subjugation of all territories and peoples encountered by the expedition, as Rumeu de Armas has noted.[13] It is an imperialism, however, in which hegemony is conceived primarily in economic terms. For example, the verbs referring to Columbus's duties and privileges—*ganar, descubrir, regir* (acquire, discover, govern)—describe actions that are accessories to the stated commercial goals of the voyage—*comprar, trocar, hallar, haber* (buy, barter, locate, possess). Political domination is articulated, not as the primary goal of the enterprise, but as a means to facilitate the exploitation of whatever markets might be found. The fundamental issue the "Capitulaciones" addressed was acquisition, not so much of territories or subjects, but of markets. The type of expansion it prescribed was quite distinct from the reconquest of Muslim territories that had just culminated on the Iberian peninsula with the defeat of Granada. Surprisingly, there is no mention of any evangelical purpose whatsoever in the documents commissioning the expedition, and no religious were listed among the men who sailed with Columbus. There were probably some ex-convicts, however, pardoned by the Crown by special decree (30 April 1492) to fill out the crew for the dangerous voyage—hardly what one would expect of a mission with evangelical intentions.[14]

The "Carta de Merced" describes and confirms, in highly technical terms, the political concessions and privileges promised Columbus in the "Capitulaciones," to be conferred upon the successful completion of the voyage. Although this document does not delve into the economic aspects of the remuneration, neither does it mention evangelization as part of Columbus's obligations to the Crown or as grounds for the conferring of any of the royal favors.[15] Such silence is quite perplexing given that these were the official documents by which the Reyes Católicos (Catholic Monarchs) authorized an embassy to foreign lands.[16] For according to medieval kingship theory, Christian kings were expected to be missionaries and crusaders on behalf of the Church, and this was precisely how Ferdinand and Isabella conceived and justified their actions in the reconquest of the Iberian peninsula from the Moors. Yet it was the Columbian Letter of 1492, and not the royal documents of commission and confirmation, that introduced the evangelical element into the contractual terms of the enterprise of discovery.[17]

The prediscovery documents generated by the Crown are also curiously enigmatic about Columbus's destination. Not once is it explicitly stated as Asia, which most historians believe to have been the goal of the voyage.[18] The characteristic phrasing in the texts—"certain islands and mainlands in the Ocean Sea"—is tantalizingly vague. Although Rumeu makes a strong case that such ambiguity was intended to confound Portuguese spies, it is equally conceivable that the blanket terminology was intended to serve whatever eventuality might result, reflecting the degree of uncertainty at court regarding what Columbus was likely to find. In any case, Ferdinand Columbus concedes that his father expected to run into some large island in the western Ocean Sea before reaching Asia.[19] The source of the popular conviction that the goal of the first voyage was none other than to reach the Asian mainland by sailing west is Columbus himself. As he writes in the Letter of 1492:

> Vuestras Altezas, como cathólicos cristianos y príncipes amadores de la sancta fe cristiana y acreçentadores d'ella y enemigos de la secta de Mahoma y de todas idolatrías y heregías, pensaron de enbiarme a mí, Cristóval Colón, a las dichas partidas de India para ver los dichos príncipes y los pueblos y las tierras y la disposición d'ellas y de todo, y la manera que se pudiera tener para la conversión d'ellas a nuestra sancta fe, y ordenaron que yo no fuese por tierra al Oriente, por donde se costumbra de andar, salvo por el camino de Occidente, por donde hasta oy no sabemos por cierta fe que aya passado nadie."
>
> (Varela, 15–16)

> Your Highnesses, as Catholic Christians and Princes, lovers and promoters of the Holy Christian Faith, and enemies of the false doctrine of Mahomet and of all idolatries and heresies, you thought of sending me, Christóbal Colón, to the said regions of India to see the said princes and the peoples and the lands, and the characteristics of the lands and of everything, and to see how their conversion to our Holy Faith might be undertaken. And you commanded that I should not go to the East by land, by which way it is customary to go, but by the route to the West, by which route we do not know for certain that anyone has previously passed.
>
> (Dunn & Kelley, 19)

The passage could hardly be less ambiguous on the destination and the purpose of the voyage: to reach certain regions of "India" by sailing the uncharted western route in order to see the Grand Khan, his peoples and lands, and how they might be converted to Christianity.[20]

Just as the Letter of 1492 rewrites the "Capitulaciones" by adding the religious dimension, it also revises the earlier document by deleting any mention of the economic goals that defined the enterprise in the Crown's contract. Under the circumstances, one would expect Columbus to have at least acknowledged the commercial transactions he had been commissioned to undertake. He did take the time in the Letter of 1492 to recapitulate almost verbatim the political and juridical rights and privileges promised to him in the "Carta de Merced," but wholly ignores the generous financial remuneration promised him in the "Capitulaciones."

Taken together, the supplying of the evangelical element so conspicuously absent in retrospect from the Crown's definition of the enterprise and the simultaneous suppression of the mercantile character of the voyage of discovery appear to share the same strategy. The Letter of 1492 responds to the documents of commission and confirmation daringly—by emendation. Columbus's detractors have argued that the omission of economic matters must be understood as an attempt to shift attention away from the meager yields of the first voyage, a resounding failure in commercial terms, by substituting souls for the gold that is so elusive in the *Diario*. For this explanation to be plausible, however, the letter would have to have been written after the navigation was completed (despite internal evidence to the contrary) for the purpose of blunting or masking the disappointing economic returns of the voyage. Perhaps. But the pragmatics of the letter clearly situate it in the context of an ongoing process of communication with the Crown, a dialogue that exceeds the historical and textual limits of the first navigation. The economics of the first voyage and its immediate contractual conditions are of secondary importance when compared to the larger ideological economy of the enterprise. Columbus was tied to Ferdinand and Isabella in a relationship of vassalage, with duties and obligations for all the parties concerned, a bond that transcended the specific circumstances of the first navigation. The Letter of 1492 refers to this greater economy and, in that context, the corrective tenor of Columbus's inaugural reply in his exchange with the Crown acquires its full significance.

The ideological terms of the relationship of vassalage as set forth by Columbus in this letter place his immediate obligations to the Crown on the plane of a higher, divine authority. The letter opens with a phrase Las Casas claimed was customary in Columbus's writing and demonstrated his extreme piety: "In Nomine Domini Nostri Jesu Christi." Its formulaic nature notwithstanding, this rubric is in fact emblematic of both the epistle and the enterprise it describes. For if the letter was written "in the name of Christ" so, the text tells, was the navigation itself carried out in his name:

por la información que yo avía dado a Vuestras Altezas de las tierras de India y de un Prínçipe que es llamado Gran Can (que quiere dezir en nuestro romançe Rey de los Reyes), como muchas vezes él y sus anteçessores avían enbiado a Roma a pedir doctores en nuestra sancta fe porque le enseñasen en ella, y que nunca el Sancto Padre le avía proveydo y se perdían tantos pueblos, cayendo en idolatrías e resçibiendo en sí sectas de perdiçión; y Vuestras Altezas, como cathólicos cristianos y prínçipes amadores de la sancta fe cristiana y acresçentadores d'ella y enemigos de la secta de Mahoma y de todas idolatrías y heregías, *pensaron de enbiarme a mí, Cristóval Colón, a las dichas partidas de India.*

(Varela, 15; emphasis added)

because of the report that I had given to Your Highnesses about the lands of India and about a prince who is called "Grand Khan," which means in our Spanish language "King of Kings"; how, many times, he and his predecessors had sent to Rome to ask for men learned in our Holy Faith in order that they might instruct him in it and how the Holy Father had never provided them; and thus so many peoples were lost, falling into idolatry and accepting false and harmful religions; and Your Highnesses, as Catholic Christians and Princes, lovers and promoters of the Holy Christian Faith, and enemies of the false doctrine of Mahomet and of all idolatries and heresies, *you thought of sending me, Christóbal Colón, to the said regions of India.*

(Dunn & Kelley, 17–19; emphasis added)

The sentence is long and complicated by many clauses, but the syntax unambiguously (albeit tortuously) links Ferdinand and Isabella's decision to send Columbus sailing with the report he had given them earlier regarding the Grand Khan's ignored petition to be instructed in the Christian faith. Explained in this way, the voyage becomes the long-awaited and repeatedly requested Christian mission to the Tatar emperor's realm. Here, the expedition's sole purpose is to minister the Faith to "so many peoples . . . falling into idolatry and accepting false and harmful religions."

It would be difficult to exaggerate the self-consciousness and premeditation that must have accompanied the act of writing such a statement of purpose, especially one that was so obviously different from the Crown's. The initial draft must have been subject to various careful revisions before achieving a form worthy of its royal ad-

dressees and appropriate for reposing in the archives of the kingdom. In style, the letter is far more polished than the typical
Columbian text, and there were almost certainly other readers involved in helping Columbus prepare the final version, among them
perhaps his friends at the monastery of La Rábida near Palos, where
he spent almost two weeks before proceeding to Seville and on to
Barcelona for his audience with Isabella and Ferdinand. And yet the
letter contains blatant "errors" concerning the time and place of key
historical events mentioned in the text. It affirms that in the year
1492, *in the same month of January,* Ferdinand and Isabella took Granada and there made the decision to send Columbus on his embassy to the Grand Khan. Moreover, it states that *in the same month*
and *in the same place* they decided to expel the Jews from Spain. The
historical record, however, shows that the facts were as follows:
Granada surrendered in early January, the "Capitulaciones" commissioning Columbus were not signed until mid-April in Santa Fe,
not Granada (the last breakdown in the negotiations between the
Crown and Columbus occurred precisely in January), and the decree of expulsion of the Jews was signed at the end of March, before
Ferdinand and Isabella entered Granada. These chronological and
geographical inaccuracies are especially surprising in a text presumably written by Columbus during the Palos-to-Canaries portion of
the voyage, in early August 1492, that is, just a few months after the
events had taken place.

Alain Milhou, in *Colón y su mentalidad mesiánica,* has attributed
Columbus's lack of factual accuracy to the predominance in the text
of a grander ideological theme. In linking disparate events chro-
nologically and geographically, Milhou argues, Columbus was establishing an important conceptual connection among the Reconquest, the expulsion of the Jews, and his own mission to the Indies
and the Grand Khan. Milhou also points out that this apparent attempt at ideological coherence conformed to the official political
messianism that had dominated the royal policies of Aragon and
Castile since the thirteenth and fourteenth centuries. This is arguably the most penetrating and cogent explanation offered to date for
these so-called errors. Moreover, it has the additional elegance of
not relying on the presumption of someone's bad faith to make its
case.[21] However, it is important to add to these observations another
deduction essential to understanding the rhetoric and ideology of

the *Diario*: The Columbian enterprise had no expressed evangelical purpose until it was represented as such in the Letter of 1492. Perhaps this explains why the evangelical dimension of the colonization developed so slowly that the first native of the Indies was not baptized until late 1496.

Yet the letter's considerable ideological novelty with respect to the other prediscovery documents must be situated in a rhetorical context if its point is not to be missed. The sense of the enterprise this text expresses is ultimately not the product of abstract values suspended in some kind of historico-ideological soup, but is a specific articulation of those values in light of the pragmatics dictated by the circumstances. Above all, the letter's rhetorical profile indicates that it was fashioned in the dictaminal tradition as an instrument of persuasion; strict historiographical exigencies of accurate and disinterested recording were subsumed by the intent to influence royal favor and policies regarding territorial and commercial expansion.

A reading that looks to the Letter of 1492 only for its informative qualities (i.e., the accurate documentation of historical events) would deem it defective for its inaccuracies, all the while missing the larger significance of the so-called errors. Viewed rhetorically as well as ideologically, the misrepresentations become central elements in a discourse whose modality is predominantly figurative and whose communicative pragmatics are essentially persuasive. From this perspective, Columbus comes into focus as a man of letters, an adept practitioner of the medieval art of letter-writing, a genre that straddled the boundaries of poetics, oratory, and the notarial arts. The blending of literary, political, and juridical modes of discourse was quite typical of medieval epistolography; indeed, it was not unusual to find poets moonlighting as secretaries and notaries.[22] Surely, then, an ambitious soon-to-be viceroy and governor of the Indies might brush up on the *ars dictaminis* in preparation to address the Crown.

The most interesting part of the Letter of 1492, considered rhetorically, is the *exordium*, where the famous "errors" appear. It is in this section that the figurative dimension of the letter's discourse predominates. Columbus's purpose appears to be simple enough at first glance—to give the background of historical events that immediately preceded, and therefore helped explain, the sovereigns'

decision to commission the voyage described in the subsequent *narratio*. But the repetition (*repetitio*) of the year 1492 ("este presente
año de 1492," "del mesmo año de 1492," "a tres días del mes de
agosto del dicho año"), the month ("a dos días del mes de enero,"
"en aquel presente mes," "en el mismo mes de enero"), and the
place ("en la muy grande çiudad de Granada," "en las torres de la
Alfambra, que es la fortaleza de la dicha çiudad," "y partí yo de la
çiudad de Granada") suggests that the literary illusion of coincidence (i.e., at the same time and in the same place), and not historical precision, was what the author sought to create. Such a con-
currence could only be achieved at the expense of historical
accuracy. While ideological coherence may have been one of the desired results of this operation, both the process by which it was
achieved and its effect on the reader have their source in epistolary
rhetoric. The letter manipulates the facts in order to predispose the
reader to grant the writer the ends he seeks. We can speculate that
the sought-after results included one or more of the following: the
privileges promised Columbus upon the successful completion of
the voyage, royal disposition for future voyages, fame for the protagonist of the event, and spiritual rewards in the afterlife.

If the Letter of 1492 constitutes a radical departure from the terms
that defined the enterprise in the "Capitulaciones de Santa Fe" and
the "Carta de Merced," it does so not by explicit statement and direct polemic, but through a figurative rewriting of the historical record. The letter purposefully violates historiographical norms in favor of greater rhetorical efficacy. Moreover, it rejects the objective
juridical mode characteristic of the royal diction in the prediscovery
documents to embrace an essentially tropological and hortatory
mode of representation and argumentation.

The significance of the "errors," the import that makes them
meaningful rather than simply mistaken, consists in the figurative
relations the letter establishes among the historical events in order
to render them parts of a greater whole—that is, the evangelical
mission considered a fundamental duty of all Christians under the
militant ecumenical Catholicism that inspired the Crusades, the Reconquest, and the expulsions of heterodox elements from the Christian community. In the fifteenth century the united kingdoms of
Castile and Aragon were the vanguard of this mission.

The specific rhetorical mechanism used to achieve this figurative coherence is metonymy: a figure that alludes, through connotation, to a greater or smaller entity which itself is not explicitly mentioned (i.e., the part for the whole).[23] Through metonymy the capture of Granada from the Muslims, the expulsion of the Jews, and the voyage to the Indies are reconstituted as parts of a larger spatio-temporal event—the Christian mission—that in turn renders the individual events coherent and meaningful. The figurative coincidence of these events in the same month, year, and place transforms the time, January 1492, and the place, Christian Spain (represented through synecdoche by the conquered city of Granada, the last stronghold of the infidel on the Iberian peninsula), into a historical paradigm of Christian evangelism and a metaphor for expressing the meaning and purpose of Christian history.[24] In this figurative context, the Columbian enterprise becomes a transaction in a nobler economy—the acquisition of souls for the Faith. Originally a commercial endeavor, a trading expedition, it is reconceptualized as a Christian mission. From this perspective, it makes perfect sense that the Letter of 1492 suppresses the original commercial rationale for the enterprise expressed in the documents of commission and confirmation.

There is yet another important consequence of this inscription of the voyage into a Christian economy. The prediscovery documents established not only a verbal exchange between the Crown and Columbus, but a reciprocity of action, of duties, responsibilities, and rewards pertaining to the very specific set of circumstances of the first voyage. Had this voyage been deemed insufficiently successful in economic terms, the commission undoubtedly would have been terminated. Under the new terms of the Letter of 1492, the duty to perform and the obligation to fulfill falls to both Columbus and the Crown. From this angle, the "Capitulaciones" between the Catholic Monarchs and Columbus becomes a subcontract, as it were, under the greater Christian "contract" in which all the parties concerned were ultimately obliged to perform before God.

Once the commercial enterprise has been transformed into an evangelical mission to the Grand Khan, the apostolic duty as prescribed under the terms of Christian kingship resides with the Crown first of all. Columbus's obligations, in turn, transcend the strictly commercial and political limits prescribed in the "Capitulaciones." He must sail to the Indies, inquire into all aspects that might affect the evangelical effort, and report back on all he has learned:

> y para esto pensé de escrevir todo este viaje muy puntualmente.
> . . . y sobre todo *cumple* mucho que yo olvide el sueño y tiente mucho el navegar, porque así *cumple*; las cuales serán gran trabajo.
>
> (Varela, 16–17; emphasis added)

> and for this purpose I thought of writing this whole voyage, very diligently. . . . and above all *it is imperative* that I forget sleep and pay much attention to the navigation in order to *fulfill* [these obligations], which will be a great labor.

His compliance in deed and word (i.e., the account of the voyage) is, in the final analysis, only a preliminary to Isabella and Ferdinand's fulfillment of their obligation, as "príncipes amadores de la sancta fe cristiana," to save all those peoples whom Columbus warned in his letter were "falling into idolatry and accepting false and harmful religions." The procuring of gold and spices, mandated in the "Capitulaciones" and fervently sought in the *Diario*, thus becomes secondary to the conversion of souls.

Columbus's duty to perform, as articulated in the Letter of 1492, is ultimately that of any Christian vassal aiding his sovereigns in the fulfillment of their duty as Christian kings to the Pope and through him to God. Additionally, this redefinition of the mission to the Indies makes Columbus and the Crown all protagonists of the same historical action. The letter thus includes Isabella and Ferdinand, not just as addressees in the *salutatio*, but as actors in the *exordium*. This adds an attractive twist to the *captatio benevolentiae*, allowing the recipients to admire themselves as copartners with the author in the saintly and heroic mission the letter so eloquently describes.

Earlier I noted that the Letter of 1492 may have served as a cover letter to the account of the first voyage Columbus presented to the Crown upon his return, but it was probably not intended as a prologue in the literary sense in which Las Casas conceived of it in the *Historia* and the *Diario*. I develop this argument more fully in the next essay, but here want to touch on the fundamental differences between reading the text as a letter and reading the same text recast by Las Casas as the prologue to the *Diario*. In *ars dictaminis* the epistle is conceived as a fundamentally communicative vehicle, within the context of specific pragmatic circumstances. Although prologues often assume an epistolary form, precisely in order to establish rapport with the reader, and often employ elegant diction and figurative language to enhance the effect on the audience, prologues differ from the epistolary genre in at least one significant way—pragmatically. Prologues are essentially supplemental, accessory texts whose sole reason for being is the main text that follows. Moreover, prologues derive their significance principally in relation to the main text, functioning as a reader's guide to or commentary upon the arguments of the ensuing text. Typically, prologues contain very specific references to the text that follows, especially comments concerning its significance, sense, and the rationale for writing it. They are guides to interpretation, in effect "illustrating" the narrative. The genre's primary function is to constitute a method or model for reading the main text.

The Letter of 1492 performs these prefatory duties with respect to the *Diario* only partially and imperfectly. As noted earlier, the piece explicitly alludes to three distinct textual entities (the voyage itinerary, the illustrated book, and the cartographic text), none of which had been completed at the time of its own composition according to its internal testimony. Its anomalous relation to the *diario* of the first navigation is especially pointed: the letter suppresses mention of the commercial dimension of the voyage even as entry after entry throughout the day-by-day account relates the obsessive search for gold and spices. In constructing a paradigm of the enterprise of discovery as a Christian mission, the letter deliberately transgresses the limits of the first navigation, and the account of it, in order to exhort the Crown to sustain a comprehensive enterprise of conversion of "all the peoples and lands of India." Clearly, such a feat could hardly have been achieved in one expedition (especially the one described in the *Diario*, which had so little to do with evangelization).

Thus the Letter of 1492 becomes fully coherent only in the context of the prediscovery exchange between Columbus and the Crown, which established the duties, obligations, and rewards of all the parties concerned. As a rejoinder in this dialogue, the letter corrects and amends the original mercantile and political terms of the enterprise defined by the Crown, adding the missing religious element. In this way, it renders Isabella, Ferdinand, and Columbus ultimately accountable to a divine authority, and thus seeks the

Crown's favor for future expeditions with more than a little spiritual arm-twisting. From the vantage point of this exchange, the Letter of 1492 comes into focus as an essentially hortatory composition, in the Augustinian sense of rhetoric as language crafted to serve and promote the new world order of Christian imperialism—even as it promoted Columbus's more worldly interests in future voyages.

The factual "errors" render the letter an unreliable historical source but also one of the most influential pieces of writing ever produced. Soon after, Spain's colonization of the Indies began to adjust to the terms and obligations set forth in the figurative discourse of the Letter of 1492. It was this text, and not the royal documents of commission and confirmation, that defined the Discovery as an evangelical enterprise, a *negotium crucis* (business of the cross).[25] The oxymoronic quality of such a phrase, the figurative tension inherent in the trope of opposites, is perhaps the only way adequately to capture the strain of the contradictions inherent in the historical action the letter strives to promote.

"All these are the Admiral's exact words"

Este es el primer viaje y las derrotas y camino que hizo el Almirante don Cristóval Colón cuando descubrió las Indias, puesto sumariamente, sin el prólogo que hizo a los Reyes que va a letra y comien- ça d'esta manera: . . .

(Varela, 15)

This is the first voyage and the courses and the way that the Admiral Don Christóbal Colón took when he discovered the Indies, summarized except for the prologue that he composed for the king and queen, which is given in full and begins this way: . . .

(Dunn & Kelley, 17)

So begins the *Diario* of Columbus's first voyage, a text whose importance to scholars of the Discovery and lay readers alike would be difficult to overstate. Yet there is no convincing evidence to suggest that anyone since the sixteenth century has seen the complete text of the day-by-day account Columbus himself wrote. The original manuscript, the copy of it made at Queen Isabella's request, and any other copies that may have been made have all disappeared.[1] Ferdinand Columbus apparently worked from the original or a copy to compose his father's biography, inserting verbatim passages from Columbus's journal throughout his own account of the first voyage. Bartolomé de Las Casas produced a heavily edited summary of the text and later (just when is in dispute) borrowed extensively from it in composing the first part of his *Historia de las Indias* (1527–c. 1563).[2] Columbus's *diario*, therefore, has reached modern readers in fragments, through Ferdinand's biography, Las Casas's history, and the latter's summary, known as the *Diario*, the most complete version of the original text to have survived to the present day.

For more than four centuries, access to the Discoverer's own impressions of the first voyage has been possible only through the versions of them created by his son and, especially, by Las Casas. Both men were extremely interested readers of Columbus. Ferdinand was involved in lawsuits pertaining to the succession of the Admiralty and ransacked the *diarios* in order to highlight the unique and heroic nature of his father's achievements. While composing his summary, Las Casas was immersed in a lifelong political and literary campaign to defend the rights of the conquered and promote their peaceful evangelization.

At one time a colonizer of Española (Haiti) and Cuba and an *encomendero* who was granted an allotment of Indian laborers for service on his estate, Las Casas experienced a religious conversion in 1514, returned the Indians to the governor of Cuba, and left for the Spanish court to plead for better treatment of the indigenous peoples. Thus began his advocacy of Indian rights, to which he remained committed (some would say obsessed) for the rest of his life. Among his principal political achievements, beginning with his appointment as priest-procurator of the Indies, was his successful lobbying of Charles V's consent to establish "towns of free Indians," where Spanish farmers and natives would work together to create a new Christian society. He promoted sweeping reforms in colonial policy toward the Indians, many of which were enacted under the New Laws of 1542. He even managed to persuade the king to declare a moratorium on new conquests, while their legitimacy was being officially debated by Las Casas himself and others back in Spain.[3]

In 1547 he returned to Spain from the Indies for good. He would never again see the lands and peoples he continued to champion until his death in 1566. Yet many scholars consider this his most fruitful period. It was certainly his most prolific as a writer. During the final two decades of his life, Las Casas wrote most of two major histories of the Indies, the *Apologética historia sumaria* (c. 1559) and the monumental *Historia de las Indias* (1527–c. 1563), the *Brevíssima relación de la destrucción de las Indias* (completed in 1542, published in 1552), and countless other treatises and petitions on behalf of Indian rights. It is also likely that during this time, around 1552, he undertook the editing of Columbus's *Diario* and the "Relación del tercer viaje."

Las Casas was intimately familiar with most of what Columbus wrote. His friendship with the Columbus family, particularly with the eldest son, Diego, who inherited the governorship of Española during Las Casas's residence there, allowed him to consult, copy, and edit materials from the family archive. Many of the texts that passed through Las Casas's hands between the mid-1520s and the early 1550s survive today only in the copies he made. No other readers, with the possible exception of Ferdinand, have had at their disposal the wealth of Columbian sources that Las Casas consulted for the composition of his histories and treatises. Traces of this intimate acquaintance with Columbus's writings are found throughout Las Casas's works, most clearly and profusely in the *Historia de las Indias*, his history of the early decades of Spanish colonization in the New World. Much of Las Casas's history of the first decade, devoted to Columbus's voyages, was composed through the paraphrase or outright quotation of the Admiral's writings. Indeed, his principal "primary" source is the *Diario*, his own version of Columbus's *diario* of the first voyage; almost the entire *Diario* is paraphrased or quoted in the *Historia*.

Las Casas's writings, like his political activities, were single-mindedly and without exception committed to liberating the Indians from the abuse of the colonizers and to promoting their peaceful evangelization. All of his writings, both the overtly polemical and the historiographical texts, have a critical, even denunciatory edge intended to undermine the theory and practice of Spanish conquest. One target of his ire was the terminology in which Spanish relations with the Indians were articulated. He condemned, for example, use of the word *conquista* (conquest) to designate Spanish incursions into new Indian territories because, in his words, it was "un vocablo tiránico, mahometano, impropio e infernal" (a tyrannical, Muhammadan, improper, and infernal vocable) contrary to all Christian teachings.[4] Due to his influence, the New Laws of 1542–43 discarded *conquista* in favor of Las Casas's (and Columbus's) preferred term *descubrimiento* (discovery).[5] The New Laws, which many believe to have been promulgated as a direct result of Las Casas's instigation, constituted not only a reform of the legal parameters of the practice of colonization but also of the very language officially used to express it.[6]

The program of reform to which Las Casas had committed himself so completely and the accompanying ideological position he had carved out in his writings would certainly have influenced his editorial criteria and practice in transcribing Columbus's account of the first navigation. If one situates the edition of Columbus's journal in the context of Las Casas's other works, it becomes clear that the edition was intended, at least in part, to serve as an aide mémoire and citation source for the composition of his histories and treatises. As such, it would not need to have been a complete or even a representative version of the journal. Las Casas would have transcribed passages selectively, with an eye to those that could serve his purposes in future works. The very nature of the *Diario*, with its clarifying interpolations, marginal commentaries, crossouts, and errors, suggests a deliberate yet hasty, utilitarian, and above all selective method of transcription colored by Las Casas's commitment to the indigenes' cause. On closer examination, it becomes evident that Las Casas produced the *Diario* through a systematic and comprehensive editorial manipulation of Columbus's account of the first navigation. Yet owing to the disappearance of the original *diario* and its copies, Las Casas's edition has been allowed to take its place, as if it were a literal transcription of Columbus's exact words.

The textual problems posed by Las Casas's editorial intervention in the transmission of the *diario* of the first voyage have been studied only partially, usually with the purpose of speculating on the integrity of his version with respect to the lost original and on his fidelity as a copyist. The authenticity of the text, on the other hand, has been debated since the manuscript was discovered at the end of the eighteenth century. Among the most vitriolic attacks against Las Casas are those of Henri Vignaud and Rómulo D. Carbia, both of whom considered much, if not all, of the edition a fraudulent fabrication.[7] In a defense of Las Casas published in 1939, Samuel Eliot Morison affirmed that the *Diario* was reliable beyond reasonable doubt, and this view has prevailed in recent studies.[8] Consuelo Varela and Robert H. Fuson, for example, have pointed out probable lexical, orthographical, and grammatical interventions made by Las Casas in order to emend linguistic errors presumably committed by Columbus, whose command of Spanish was far from perfect. These critics have also identified probable errors committed by Las Casas, especially in the miscorrection of Italian and Portuguese interference in Columbus's Spanish, and in the spelling of certain Arawak terms. However, after pointing out numerous instances of editorial manipulation in the text, both Varela and Fuson accept the *Diario* as a faithful and accurate rendering of the original text, although each recognizes that Las Casas's interventions are problematic in isolated cases.[9]

It is not my purpose here to evaluate the criticism on the *Diario* but rather to underscore that the vast majority of studies address the text's integrity at the level of content, its historiographical authenticity as the primary source on the Discovery. Yet by reducing Las Casas's role in the transmission of the text to that of a mere copyist, this type of criticism ignores the fundamental consequences of Las Casas's intervention in the transcription of Columbus's journal.[10] The role of faithful amanuensis is indeed the one professed by the editorial voice in the *Diario*, but a close reading reveals that Las Casas actually played a much more active part in its composition than is generally assumed. His interventions in the *Diario* are frequently ideologically charged with the same interests that motivated his writing practices elsewhere, and they go far beyond simple changes to facilitate the faithful transcription of Columbus's words. Las Casas not only summarizes and paraphrases Columbus; he insinuates himself as a new subject into the text by imposing on it an editorial rhetoric that could not have existed in the original journal. Through a selective process of transcription and omission, these editorial interventions altered the original text's content and, perhaps even more fundamentally, also altered the way in which the text can be read. To put it another way, the mediating presence of the editor's voice in the text intervenes in the process of reading and interpretation as well as in the *Diario*'s representation of the Discovery. Thus we must move beyond a historical-philological assessment of Las Casas's accuracy and fidelity as transcriber if we are to appreciate fully the definitive role Las Casas played in the transmission of Columbus's words.

THE EDITOR SPEAKS

Las Casas insinuates himself as a new third-person subject in the text, and his editorial presence is felt at all levels. Perhaps the most salient intervention is an editorial commentary that assumes two distinct forms—evaluative and nonevaluative—both marked by a grammatical change of person. Among the other operations performed by the new subject are summarizing, expanding (almost always anachronistically), and interweaving the citation or paraphrase of Columbus's words, in the first person, with indirect narrative in the third-person singular. In every instance the intervention consists of a manipulation of the "exact words of the Admiral" through the introduction of a new editorial subject who comments, reorganizes, adds, subtracts, highlights, or subordinates various aspects of the original text.

The editorial commentary introduces a new voice into the narrative, a voice that stands out from what are presented as Columbus's "very words" by assuming a metalinguistic and critical attitude toward them. In the majority of cases this type of intervention is signaled by a change in grammatical person, although sometimes the insertion is marked only by a palpable semantic distance—typically, a detectable anachronism—from the context. In most modernized editions of the *Diario*, direct quotations appear in quotation marks and editorial interpolations are placed in parentheses. There are no such punctuation marks in the manuscript, however; only the editorial commentary itself signals the shift. Undoubtedly, some of Las Casas's interventions remain undiscernible as interventions.

The most common type of detectable metalinguistic intervention in the *Diario* comprises the phrases that introduce direct quotations, setting them apart from the indirect discourse. The variants are many ("Todas son palabras del Almirante," "Todo ésto dize el Almirante," "Dize más el Almirante," etc.), but their function is always the same—to give prominence to certain passages by setting them in relief against the background of the indirect discourse. Moreover, by identifying them as Columbus's *ipsissima verba*, the editorial commentary actually privileges these passages through the increased authority the testimonial mode lends them.

The following passage, taken from the account of the exploration of Cuba, is representative of the numerous instances in which the narrative voice moves from third to first person when relating Columbus's impressions of the Indians:

> Dixo qu'el domingo antes, onze de noviembre, le avía parecido que fuera bien tomar algunas personas de las de aquel río para llevar a los Reyes porque aprendieran nuestra lengua, para saber lo que ay en la tierra y porque bolviendo sean lenguas de los cristianos y tomen nuestras costumbres y las cosas de la fe, "porque yo vi y conozco," dize el Almirante, "qu'esta gente no tiene secta ninguna ni

son idólatras, salvo muy mansos y sin saber qué sea mal ni matar a otros ni prender, y sin armas y tan temerosos que a una persona de los nuestros fuyen ciento d'ellos, aunque burlen con ellos, y crédulos y cognosçedores que ay Dios en el çielo, e firmes que nosotros avemos venido del çielo, y muy presto[s] a cualquiera oraçión que nos les digamos que digan y hazen el señal de la cruz. Así que deben Vuestras Altezas determinarse a los hazer cristianos, que creo que si comiençan, en poco tiempo acabarán de los aver convertido a nuestra sancta fe multidumbre de pueblos."

(12 November; Varela, 54–55)

He said that the Sunday before, the eleventh of November, it had seemed to him that it might be well to capture some people of that river in order to take them to the king and queen so that they might learn our language and in order to know what there is in that land, and so that, returning, they might be interpreters for the Christians, so that they would take on our customs and faith. Because I saw and recognize (says the Admiral) that these people have no religious beliefs, nor are they idolaters. They are very gentle and do not know what evil is; nor do they kill others, nor steal; and they are without weapons and so timid that a hundred of them flee from one of our men even if our men are teasing them. And they are credulous and aware that there is a God in heaven and convinced that we come from the heavens; and they say very quickly any prayer that we tell them to say, and they make the sign of the cross, †. So that Your Highnesses ought to resolve to make them Christians: for I believe that if you begin, in a short time you will end up having converted to our Holy Faith a multitude of peoples.

(Dunn & Kelley, 143–45)

Here, the transition from indirect to direct discourse occurs precisely at the point where the narration of Columbus's intention to take slaves back to Spain ends and the exhortation to the Catholic Monarchs to commit themselves to the evangelization of the Indies begins. The metalinguistic intervention "dize el Almirante" marks the exact start of the testimony on the idealized moral nature of the Indian as a creature living in a moral golden age—a state which, says Columbus, is especially apt for the implantation of the Christian faith. The change signaled here by Las Casas may seem unremarkable at first glance, a parenthetical clarification resulting in little if any interruption in the scanning of the eyes across the page. Yet it constitutes not merely a change of grammatical person but one of voice and tenor, as well. His addition of "dize el Almirante" gives

the utterance that follows new substance and weight, the reso-
nance, as it were, of the "Admiral's" personal authority. The precise
timing and timbre of this editorial intervention seem neither coincidental nor arbitrary but tactical and intentional.

Invariably in the *Diario* the editorial commentary that marks the
transition from indirect discourse to the first-person testimonial
mode concurrently signals an ideological transition in the text. Typically, the first-person narration describes the Eden-like quality of
the new lands and the innocence and gentleness of the Indians. In
other words, Las Casas reserves the testimonial mode for the lyrical
and idealizing themes, as distinct from the more prosaic and often
exploitative aspects of the Discovery. Throughout the *Diario*, Columbus's exhortations to the Crown to commit itself to a politics of
evangelization are rendered by Las Casas as the Admiral's personal
appeals, inscribed in the first person.

The metalinguistic commentary also interrupts the third-person
narration to reinforce the fidelity of the editorial voice, the narrative
posture explicitly assumed by the new writing subject. The third-
person passages are filled with brief interpolated phrases ("Dize el
Almirante," "diz que," "dize él") that periodically interrupt the narrative flow to remind the reader of the testimonial nature of the original Columbian discourse, but even more to underscore the new editorial subject's faithfulness to it.

There are also numerous interpolated comments that appear to
have resulted from Las Casas's having carelessly slipped from Columbus's voice into his own without differentiation: the expression
"conviene a saber," added for emphasis, so characteristic of Las
Casas's writing style; the expressed concern about the integrity of
the copy he was working with (e.g., entry of 30 October); anachronisms such as giving the Arawak name of the island of Guanahaní
before relating the first contact with the natives from whom Columbus would have learned it (11 [sic; 12] October); speaking of Florida
many years before it was discovered (21 November); and the comical exclamation of incredulity regarding the ephemeral islands Columbus earnestly was seeking in the vicinity of what only much
later became known as Florida.[11]

But if there is any carelessness at all, it is in the maintaining of
the illusion of scribal fidelity, not in any negligent breaching of it.
For Las Casas's edition of the *Diario* systematically violates the integrity of Columbus's words. Such breaks, when they are detect-

able, reveal the fictive nature of the editorial voice and the rhetorical character of the editorial practice it represents. Indeed, Las Casas's manipulation of the Columbian discourse is so extensive and complex that it seems more accurate to describe the *Diario* as a rewriting, not a transcription, of Columbus's journal. Unless the original is recovered, it will remain impossible to determine with all certainty where and how Las Casas altered the text. However, only a reading that suppressed the editorial voice could arrive at the conclusion that the *Diario* is essentially equivalent to the original journal of Christopher Columbus. That some readers have done so is both a tribute to Las Casas's dexterity and evidence of these readers' desire (no doubt shared by Las Casas) to suspend disbelief, to read around the cracks in the text, in order to maintain Columbus's authority, the text's integrity, and thus the *Diario*'s privileged status as the primary source on the Discovery.

As noted, we can identify many of the modifications performed by Las Casas relying exclusively on evidence contained in the *Diario*, without recourse to Columbus's original text. Far more interesting than the simple identification of these interventions, however, is the consideration of how they affect the process of signification in the edition, that is, how Las Casas's manipulation of the Columbian discourse may have altered the sense of the original, yielding a new account of the Discovery, different from whatever Columbus's may have been.

Once we approach the *Diario* not as a simple transcription but as an edition, we soon begin to see how Las Casas's editorial presence infuses the discourse with an alien intention, to wit, his own ideological goals. In the process the *diario*, or "libro de su primera navegación y descubrimiento d'estas Indias," as Las Casas called it, becomes Las Casas's *Diario* of Columbus's first voyage. In using the third-person possessive *su* to identify the text he was working on as belonging to Columbus, Las Casas himself suggests a distinction between the *diario* and the text he was in the process of deriving from it. Mikhail Bakhtin explains the decisive role intentionality plays in defining the act of expression this way:

> To study the word as such, ignoring the impulse that reaches out beyond it, is just as senseless as to study psychological experience outside the context of that real life toward which it is directed and by which it is determined. . . . As a living socio-ideological concrete thing . . . language, for the individual consciousness, lies on

the borderline between oneself and the other. The word in language is half someone else's. It becomes "one's own" only when
the speaker populates it with his own intention, his own accent,
when he appropriates the word, adapting it to his own semantic
and expressive intention.[12]

Through his editorial interventions Las Casas not only insinuates
himself into Columbus's *diario*, he takes possession of it, adapting
it to his own semantic and expressive intention, as Bakhtin puts it.

EDITING AS APPROPRIATION

There are at least two layers of writing, two scriptural acts and two
intentions, cohabiting in the *Diario*: Columbus's and Las Casas's. It
is conceivable, even probable, that Columbus himself may have
done several different redactions, so that the *diario* was born of ac-
cretion and revision rather than of a single creative act. Scribes may
also have altered the original by introducing corruptions in the copy
Las Casas worked with. Las Casas actually complained of having
trouble making out certain passages, attributing the difficulty to
scribal sloppiness or error. Royal documents confirm that two
scribes, rather than the usual one, were responsible for producing
the first copy of Columbus's account. Nevertheless, for readers of
the *Diario* the traces of those scribal pens are hardly detectable. The
suspicion or even knowledge that the original text may have been
altered several times along the way does not affect the reading process significantly. The *Diario* acknowledges the presence of only two
writings: "the Admiral's" and Las Casas's. Both appear as produc-
ers of the text, although Las Casas would have one believe they did
so in fundamentally different ways: Columbus was the author, Las
Casas only the passive and faithful conduit of the Admiral's words.
Yet in his brief introduction Las Casas himself alerts the reader to
the contingent nature of the *Diario*, asserting that it is mostly an abbreviation of another text. The *Diario*, then, is both derivative and
creative. It incorporates Columbus's journal and so is dependent on
it for its own existence, but it also modifies it. The relation of the
Diario to the journal implies two separate and different acts of writing, Las Casas's and Columbus's, that have been brought together
to constitute a single discursive whole. The *Diario* is not Columbus's
journal, nor even its equivalent; it is its substitute, a new text, the

product of the assimilation and transformation of Columbus's words by Las Casas's.

Julia Kristeva coined the term "intertextuality" to argue that all texts are constituted through the assimilation and transformation of one text by another.[13] From this perspective, every act of writing becomes the reelaboration of something previously read; every text is a reaction to or the product of another reading. This formulation of the text as an intertextual phenomenon threatened to become tautologous in its amplitude and has been refined subsequently by Kristeva herself and others, but it has usually retained two fundamental characteristics: the transformational aspect of the intertextual process and the intentionality that motivates it.[14] Intertextuality as an essentially creative process transforms the sense of the assimilated utterance in a manner that invariably reflects the intentionality of the new act of writing which incorporates it. Both these ideas, the transformational and intentional aspects of the intertextual process, are essential to understanding the effects of Las Casas's editorial interventions in generating the *Diario* from Columbus's journal.

The intertextual model generally has been used to identify the presence of assimilated utterances and analyze their function in the signifying process of a text; in other words, to scrutinize how text A is assimilated and transformed in the process of creating a new text B, or how new texts come into being precisely by assimilating other texts. This type of analysis implies an original autonomy of the text and its intertexts which, despite the transformation suffered by the intertexts, continues to be discernible and presumably verifiable by the reader. It is through the semantic tension arising from the initial autonomy of the intertext and its subsequent assimilation—its new formal and semantic dependency—that new meanings are produced. Even a faithful paraphrase or summary of a text involves an interpretation and a selection based on the synopsis-writer's own criteria regarding the importance of certain portions of the text relative to others. As Genette has observed, no reduction is transparent, insignificant, or innocent: "dis-moi comment tu résumes, je saurais comment tu interpretes" (tell me how you summarize, I will know how you interpret).[15] The same can be said of any expansion, excision, or commentary.

In the absence of Columbus's journal we cannot analyze the specific character of Las Casas's paraphrase. But a few observations on the nature and purpose of paraphrase as it was understood in rhetorical theory from classical antiquity into the Renaissance will give us a sense of the types of activities Las Casas may have undertaken. In the rhetorical handbooks, paraphrasing is alternately described as the alteration of the form of expression of an idea to achieve the best possible way of conveying it, or as the variation of style with the retention of the sense of the original expression. Three basic modes are identified by classical rhetoricians: elaboration, abbreviation, and transposition. But in actual practice the paraphrased text often differed greatly from the original, retaining only the general sentiment expressed.[16]

Paraphrase was also used as an exegetical tool, whether as a stylistic rephrasing of authors whose vocabulary was no longer understood (as often in the case of Homer) or as a work with creative literary pretensions of its own. The concept of paraphrase as a creative interpretation that transforms the original text through a change in form, not content, was the theoretical context in which Las Casas's reworking of Columbus's words took place. This is not to say that he was striving for a new literary creation to take the place of Columbus's journal. He clearly understood his task as a historiographical one. But his reconstitution of the Columbian text in the *Diario* was informed by a rhetorical tradition that emphasized the creative dimension of linguistic expression no matter what the discipline. As the classical rhetorician Isocrates put it:

> it is in the nature of language that it is possible to set forth the
> same subject in many different ways, to make the lofty humble and
> to lend greatness to what is small, to describe old material in a
> modern way and to give the patina of age to what has recently happened. Therefore we should not avoid what others have spoken on
> before, but try to outdo our predecessors. For past actions are the
> common inheritance of all of us, while their timely use, appropriate
> formulation and proper verbal expression are the private domain of
> the cultivated.[17]

As an editorial practice, paraphrase is inherently evaluative. Even the simplest of selections entails a devaluation of the material chosen for omission and a revaluation of the material that is retained and recontextualized. This process of reconstitution through selection produces a new discourse, one that depends on the original text for its existence and continually signals its presence and privilege, but in so doing also must differentiate itself from its source. In assuming the role of faithful amanuensis, Las Casas attempted to downplay the transformations suffered by the journal, yet the editorial insistence that what we have in the *Diario* are "the very words of the Admiral" does not negate the intertextual character of the relationship. Rather Las Casas has rendered the journal an intertext of itself. Thus it may be more precise to characterize the relationship between the *Diario* and the journal as intratextual, especially since the autonomy of these texts, though evoked and even promoted in Las Casas's edition, is not verifiable in the absence of the original. Historical circumstances have made the point, more poignantly than any theoretical pronouncement could, that the perceived autonomy of the text and its intertexts is fundamentally a rhetorical phenomenon, not an empirical one. Despite the disappearance of the journal as a historical object, it is nonetheless important to readers that the *Diario* presents it as if it were an autonomous text. The implied integrity and autonomy of the original journal is significant in this intertextual context precisely because the *Diario* renders its constituent parts in new rhetorical relations.

The following passage from the *Diario* entry for 6 November is worth quoting at length because it contains the three most striking and most frequently discussed characteristics of the Columbian representation of the Discovery: a mercantilistic discourse typified by observations regarding the possibilities for economic exploitation of the land and people, a poetic discourse idealizing the new human and geographical landscapes, and a hortatory Christian-evangelical discourse etched in a language reminiscent of the Spanish Reconquest.[18] The narration begins in the paraphrastic mode:

> Vieron muchas maneras de árboles, yervas y flores odoríferas. Vieron aves de muchas maneras diversas de las d'España, salvo perdizes y ruiseñores que cantaban y ánsares, que d'estos ay allí hartos; bestias de cuatro pies no vieron, salvo perros que no ladravan. La tierra es muy fértil y muy labrada de aquellos mames y faxoes y habas muy diversas de las nuestras; eso mismo panizo y mucha cantidad de algodón cogido y filado y obrado; y que en una sola casa avían visto más de quinientas arrovas y que se pudiera aver allí cada año cuatro mill quintales. Dize el Almirante que le pareçía

que no lo sembravan y que da fruto todo el año: es muy fino, tiene el capillo grande. Todo lo que aquella gente tenía diz que dava por muy vil preçio, y que una gran espuerta de algodón dava por cabo de agujeta o otra cosa que se le dé. Son gente, dize el Almirante, muy sin mal ni de guerra, desnudos todos, hombres y mugeres, como sus madres los parió. Verdad es que las mugeres traen una cosa de algodón solamente, tan grande que le cobija su natura y no más. Y son ellas de muy buen acatamiento, ni muy negro[s] salvo menos que Canarias. "Tengo por dicho, Sereníssimos Prínçipes," dize aquí el Almirante, "que sabiendo la lengua dispuesta suya personas devotas religiosas, que luego se tornarían cristianos, y así espero en Nuestro Señor que Vuestras Altezas se determinarán a ello con mucha diligençia para tornar a la Iglesia tan grandes pueblos, y los convertirán, así como an destruido aquellos que no quisieron confessar al Padre y el Hijo y el Espíritu Sancto; y después de sus días, que todos somos mortales, dexarán sus reinos en muy tranquilo estado y limpios de heregía y maldad y serán bien resçebidos delante el Eterno Criador, al cual plega de les dar larga vida y acreçentamiento grande de mayores reinos y señoríos, y voluntad y disposición para acreçentar la sancta religión cristiana, así como hasta aquí tienen fecho. Amén. Oy tiré la nao de monte y me despacho para partir el jueves en nombre de Dios e ir al sueste a buscar del oro y esperías y descobrir tierra." Estas todas son palabras del Almirante, el cual pensó partir el jueves, pero porque le hizo el viento contrario no pudo partir hasta doce días de noviembre.

(Varela, 53–54)

They saw many kinds of trees and plants and fragrant flowers; they saw birds of many kinds, different from those of Spain, except partridges and nightingales, which sang, and geese, for of these there are a great many there. Four-footed beasts they did not see, except dogs that did not bark. The earth was very fertile and planted with those mañes and bean varieties very different from ours, and with that same millet. And they saw a large quantity of cotton collected and spun and worked; in a single house they had seen more than five hundred *arrobas*; and that one might get there each year four thousand *quintales* [of it]. The Admiral says that it seemed to him that they did not sow it and that it produces fruit [i.e., cotton] all year. It is very fine and has a large boll. Everything that those people have, he says, they would give for a very paltry price, and that they would give a large basket of cotton for the tip of a lacing or anything else given to them. They are people, says the Admiral, quite lacking in evil and not warlike; [and] all of them, men and women, [are] naked as their mothers bore them. It is true that the women wear a thing of cotton only so big as to cover their genitals and no more. And they are very respectful and not very black, less so than Canarians. I truly believe, most Serene Princes, (the Admiral says here), that, given devout religious persons knowing thoroughly the language that they use, soon all of them would become Christian. And so I hope in Our Lord that Your Highnesses, with much diligence, will decide to send such persons in order to bring to the Church such great nations and to convert them, just as you have destroyed those that did not want to confess the Father and the Son and the Holy Spirit, and that after your days (for all of us are mortal) you will leave your kingdoms in a tranquil state, free of heresy and evil, and will be well received before the Eternal Creator, may it please Whom to give you long life and great increase of your kingdoms and dominions and the will and disposition to increase the Holy Christian Religion, as up to now you have done, amen. Today I pulled the ship off the beach and made ready to leave on Thursday, in the name of God, and to go to the southeast to seek gold and spices and to explore land. All these are the Admiral's words. He intended to leave on Thursday, but because a contrary wind came up he could not leave until the twelfth of November.

(Dunn & Kelley, 168–70)

For the sake of argument, let us accept the touted fidelity of Las Casas's version with respect to the content of Columbus's journal. A more provocative question is whether the *Diario's* sense of the Discovery is, therefore, the same as that conveyed by the journal. Several observations on this topic can be made even in the absence of the original text.

First, one notices that Las Casas's editorial rhetoric in the passage presents the mercantilistic portions of the narrative indirectly, from the third-person point of view. The reader is given a valuation of the land, its flora and fauna and, especially, its fertility in producing marketable commodities. The language in this portion of the passage is characterized by the proliferation of quantifiers (*mucho, harto, cantidad, quinientas arrobas, cuatro mil quintales, vil precio*), underscoring the sheer abundance of goods. The quantifying tendencies of this mercantilistic discourse are abandoned in favor of comparative evaluation when the focus turns to the Indians. The idealizing discourse on the moral qualities of the natives is presented from what seems to be a first-person point of view, although the first-person pronoun that usually signals the testimonial passages in the *Diario* is not in evidence. The editorial comment "dize el Almirante" apparently is intended to highlight the testimonial character of Columbus's utterance, but since Las Casas never used quotation marks—these were imposed only much later by modern editors—the matter is ambiguous. In contrast, the Christian-evangelical discourse addressed to the Catholic Monarchs is thrice marked as being in the first-person testimonial mode: it begins with a verb in first-person singular; the editorial voice interrupts Columbus's eloquent exhortation to Isabella and Ferdinand in order to underscore its testimonial nature ("dize el Almirante"); and the formulaic phrase "Estas todas son palabras del Almirante" signals the end of the quote. The latter formula serves not only to indicate the end of the quoted material but, more pointedly, to remind readers of the accuracy and authority of the statement. The editorial voice accentuates the authority of these testimonial remarks by announcing that they are Columbus's ipsissima verba, a literal and faithful rendering of the original text, and by inserting comments in the first person into the third-person narrative.

Whether Las Casas's paraphrases are reductive or accurate renderings of the words Columbus himself used and the emphasis he placed on them in his *diario*, we cannot say. But the indirect discourse is clearly subordinated, rhetorically speaking, in the discursive hierarchy, to the first-person testimonial utterances. Because the Christian-evangelical passages are usually represented in the first person and the mercantilistic ones in the third, the former are endowed with greater authority even if the latter constitute the bulk of the text. The representation of some passages in the first person and others in the third creates a hierarchy of voices in the text that effectively alters the rhetorical homogeneity of Columbus's original utterance. Such a fragmentation of Columbus's homogeneous first-person narrative voice in the journal into distinct voices that represent not only disparate points of view but different acts of writing has important consequences. For in altering the rhetorical homogeneity of the original text, Las Casas lends the different voices he has created an ideological autonomy that places them in an intertextual relation to one another. Thus the affirmation that the *Diario* communicates essentially the same meanings as the journal is impossible to sustain; when viewed from an intertextual perspective, Las Casas's editorial intervention is undeniably evaluative and interpretive.

I would argue further that not only is it possible to do an intertextual reading of the *Diario*, but that ultimately such a reading is inescapable. The result of Las Casas's editorial intervention is precisely to split or separate Columbus's journal into distinct gradations of writing, as it were—its now discrete parts rendering it effectively an intertext of itself. Las Casas, as the new subject, disrupts the unity and linearity of the original discourse, altering the narrative voice of the journal, which was undoubtedly in the testimonial first-person, through paraphrase, summary, and other editorial interventions. As a result, the commentaries that signal direct citation, as well as the repetition of the first-person pronoun, set in relief against the background of the indirect discourse a new text whose prestige and authority are underscored by its direct link to the original text and the testimonial authority of the Discoverer himself. The passages in which the editor's voice invades Columbus's utterance as an editorial commentary on it constitute a third intertext. Thus the dialogue among the different voices not only breaks the textual unity and linearity but also imposes a hierarchical relationship on the voices or "texts" within the text.

In the new narrative economy of the *Diario* the first-person passages are assigned the role and acquire the value of the Original Text. The third-person paraphrase plays the part of the "faithful" summation. The metatext, or editorial commentary, articulates the points of transition between the two and determines the nature of their relationship by defining the significance of their interaction. The editorial commentary also controls the reading process insofar as it functions as the reader's guide in passing through the various textual layers. It signals both the points of transition and the new attitude the reader is to assume toward the writing as a result of the transition.

To the editorial voice belongs the most privileged position in the intertextual hierarchy, since it functions as the reader's guide. It orients us in interpreting the text, directing us toward those passages marked by the editorial rhetoric as most important or significant.

We come to depend on the editorial voice to guide and orient our reading. In the final analysis, not only do we read *what* the editor wants us to read, but also *how* the editor wants us to read the text.

In second position in the intertextual hierarchy are the passages in the first person. Represented as the ipsissima verba of the Discoverer, this text is imbued with the authority of eyewitness testimony and with the personal prestige of the Admiral of the Ocean Sea. Although Las Casas criticizes Columbus in some of his marginal notes in the *Diario*, the accent the editorial voice places on those passages that show the Admiral in a flattering light creates a protagonist of heroic proportions.[19] In turn, the words designated in the summary as exactly Columbus's participate in the prestige the editor has fashioned for him.

The lowest position in the hierarchy belongs to the passages narrated in third person, which constitute the bulk of the *Diario*. Uttered by the editor, they are not identified as his words. Yet although they are attributed to Columbus, as third-person statements they are divorced from his subjectivity and authority. Not surprisingly, all of the instances of editorial "carelessness," of anachronisms and interpolations that have been detected, occur in the paraphrase. It seems almost as if Las Casas were less respectful of this "text," which was less worthy of Columbus. In effect, the third-person paraphrase functions rhetorically as an anonymous text. Despite the editor's brief interjections assuring the reader of his fidelity to the original words, the paraphrase does not really partake of either Columbus's or Las Casas's authority.

Intertextuality, the generative force that transforms the journal into the *Diario*, alters the meaning of the original utterance, whatever that may have been. The editorial rhetoric in the summary privileges the poetic-idealizing discourse and the Christian-evangelical discourse above all others, creating a new sense of the Discovery, a view that is a product of the hierarchical relationship of the texts within the text. The vision of the Indies that issues from the *Diario* is of a place whose moral and natural attributes affiliate it with the classical Golden Age and the biblical Garden of Eden. It is a predominantly beautiful, pristine, and innocent world—just as Las Casas presented it in the *Brevíssima relación de la destrucción de las Indias*, the *Historia de las Indias*, and his other polemical treatises and histories.[20]

THE "PROLOGUE" AND THE "BOOK"

A public subject will become private property if you do not
idle round the common and open ground nor strive to render word for word like a faithful translator or get yourself in
a fix, a cramped imitator, afraid to put a foot wrong out of
diffidence or respect for the laws of the genre.

Horace, *Ars Poetica*

In an earlier essay, "'This present year of 1492,'" I proposed reading
the so-called prologue to the *Diario*, not as the preface Las Casas
claimed it was, but rather as an autonomous textual entity, the Letter of 1492, that Las Casas chose to append to his edition of Columbus's journal. Here, I want to reconsider the effects of Las Casas's
having designated the letter as the prologue to his edition of Columbus's *diario* of the first voyage.

Las Casas's editing of Columbus's journal at the very least privileged, if not outright invented, its prologue through what we may
call a metaliterary intervention. Such interventions are the result of
an editor making an explicit formal evaluation of a text and assigning to it characteristics that are traditionally literary. There are only
two instances of this in the *Diario*, but they are among the most profoundly consequential of Las Casas's editorial manipulations. The
first is found in the brief rubric that heads the text, where Las Casas
advises the reader that what follows is a summary of Columbus's
account of the first voyage, "sin el prólogo que hizo a los Reyes que
va a la letra" (except for the prologue that he composed for the sovereigns, which is given in full). The second metaliterary intervention appears in the journal entry for 11 October: "Esto que se sigue
son palabras del Almirante en su libro de su primera navegaçión y
descubrimiento d'estas Indias" (Varela, 30; What follows are the formal words of the Admiral from his book on the navigation and discovery of these Indies). Earlier I discussed the type of editorial commentary, evident in these passages, that privileges certain portions
of the text. What interests me here is Las Casas's identification of
two distinct parts of the *Diario*, one which he calls a "prólogo" and
the other a "libro."[21]

In fact Las Casas not only labels the two parts—the "book" and
its "prologue"—but also underscores the importance of the latter
vis-à-vis the rest of the *Diario* by announcing a special editorial

treatment of it—verbatim transcription instead of summation. The editorial restraint expressed here, as elsewhere in the *Diario*, is a powerful device for the enhancement of a particular portion of the text relative to its context. In the case of the prologue, however, Las Casas highlights not simply its content, but especially its introductory function with respect to the "libro." In explicitly designating this portion of the text as the prologue to the "libro," Las Casas has prescribed the role it is to play in the act of reading; he has defined the prologue's communicative pragmatics in the context of the greater textual whole of the *Diario*.

The most immediate effect of this editorial intervention is the creation of one coherent composition out of what had been two autonomous texts, the Letter of 1492 and the day-by-day account of the navigation. To present the *Diario* as a book with a prologue suggests a degree of coherence, elaboration, and formality of composition that undermines the claims of a spontaneous, immediate reportage made by Columbus in the so-called prologue itself.[22] But for what purpose? In order to make sense of Las Casas's metaliterary interventions, we need to take a closer look at the prologue genre.

The written prologue derives from the oratorical *prooemium*, the introductory section of a speech in classical rhetoric. Like its oratorical counterpart, the prologue is typically the site of maximum rhetorical craft harnessed to establish an immediate rapport with the audience. In addition to capturing a reader's good will and attention, a prologue introduces the reader to the text that follows, an orientation that facilitates reading but, more importantly, guides the reader's interpretation of the ensuing text.

Perhaps the most illuminating paradigm for understanding the role of Las Casas's prologue in the *Diario* is the medieval *accessus ad auctores*. Originally, the *accessus* was what A. J. Minnis has called an "academic" prologue: a didactic introduction to an authoritative (canonical) text, composed for the purpose of literary pedagogy—understood in the medieval sense of textual exegesis at the service of demonstrating the link between linguistic expression and the communication of ethical (i.e., Christian) values.[23] This literary pedagogy was designed to facilitate the use of literature as evidence in the discussion of Christian truths, through the uncovering in texts of intrinsic moral lessons. The *auctor* was conceived not only as a writer but also as an authority to be respected and believed. Thus the *accessus ad auctores*, in introducing the text to the student-reader, typically focused on pragmatic and ethically charged questions, such as the author's intention (*intentio auctoris*) and the purpose or usefulness of the text (*utilitas*), as well as considering more formal questions about subject matter and stylistic and rhetorical qualities.

The key to understanding Las Casas's intention in turning the Letter of 1492 into a prologue for the *Diario*, to my mind, is to be found in the ethical didacticism of the *accessus* tradition. In the *Diario* and again in the *Historia de las Indias*—where the Letter of 1492 is reproduced "porque se conciba la intinción de los Reyes y suya" (Varela, 127; so that the intention of the sovereigns and [Columbus's] own may be understood)—Las Casas uses the device of a prologue to emphasize his ideological moralistic concerns.[24] Although the Letter of 1492 does not follow the form of a typical medieval academic prologue, Las Casas seems to have intended it to function pragmatically as an *accessus*. By redefining the enterprise of the Indies as a Christian mission, the prologue guides the reader to a Christian interpretation of the ensuing text.

Alberto Porqueras Mayo, who has written one of the most comprehensive studies of the prologue genre, has shown that by the end of the fifteenth century prologues had assumed their definitive generic form.[25] Among the genre's defining characteristics, Porqueras cites its conventionality, its typographical and stylistic differentiation from the main text, and, especially, its permeability to that text in content as well as form. To his list should be added the prologue's direct communication with the reader on the subject of the main text, that is, the prologue's essentially metatextual character, the reflection it provides on the conditions of its textuality.

The prologue that Las Casas selects for the *Diario*, however, disappoints our generic expectations. It prepares us for a main text whose ideology, ethics, and diction are commensurate with Christian values and ideals. As I have noted, the prologue defines the enterprise of the Indies exclusively as an evangelical mission to spread the faith among the peoples of the Grand Khan, and it exhorts the Crown to carry on its fight against the infidel from the Iberian peninsula to "all the lands of India." But once we leave the prologue, the *Diario*'s articulation of the voyage frequently corresponds to the mercantilism and imperialism of the enterprise as defined by the Crown, echoing the stated goals and language of the royal documents of commission, the "Capitulaciones de Santa Fe" and the "Carta de Merced." Each new island encountered by Columbus is described as extremely fertile, auriferous, and imminently exploitable. The Taíno inhabitants are portrayed as easy marks for establishing a trading relationship much more favorable to the Europeans and as incapable of resisting even minor military force.[26]

Contrary to the prologue's emphasis on evangelization, the conversion of the Indians is rarely mentioned in the *Diario*. The first reference to evangelization in the itinerary of the voyage proper does not appear until the entry for 11 October:

> "Yo," dize él, "porque nos tuviesen mucha amistad, porque cognosçí que era gente que mejor se libraría y convertiría a nuestra sancta fe con amor que no por fuerça, les di a algunos d'ellos bonetes colorados y unas cuentas de vidrio que se ponían al pescueço, y otras cosas muchas de poco valor, con que ovieron mucho plazer y quedaron tanto nuestros que era maravilla.
>
> (Varela, 30)

> I, he says, in order that they would be friendly to us—because I recognized that they were people who would be better freed [from error] and converted to our Holy Faith by love than by force—to some of them I gave red caps, and glass beads which they put on their chests, and many other things of small value, in which they took so much pleasure and became so much our friends that it was a marvel.
>
> (Dunn & Kelley, 65)

Thus begins by far the longest sustained first-person quotation in the text, which Las Casas allows to run uninterrupted by paraphrase until the entry for 25 October. Placed at the very beginning of the earliest testimony on the Indians, it sets the tone and tenor for the rest of the quoted section, in which evangelization is mentioned only twice, and then only in passing.

Moreover, a careful reading of the passage cited above leaves the unsettling impression that the clause about conversion may have been added as an afterthought or perhaps even as an interpolated product of a later revision (by Las Casas?). At the very least, the passage expresses two quite dissonant purposes. The offering of cheap gifts to win the Indians' friendship and whet their appetite for trading is perfectly consistent with the commercial goals of the enterprise; indeed, later in the text Columbus remarks on the ease with which Europeans would be able to exploit the Indians, who accepted the trifles offered them "as if they were the greatest treasure in the world." Yet if, as the passage asserts, the purpose was to encourage the natives to become "friendly" to Christianity, the gifts seem a vulgar, indeed contemptible, offering.

The significant discursive discontinuity in this passage is marked grammatically by a clause that is semantically anomalous in its context. Such incongruities are typical of the *Diario*'s treatment of the evangelical dimension of the enterprise, which is usually introduced somewhat arbitrarily and abruptly, and then only sporadically, into the account of the voyage through the Indies. Nevertheless, it is precisely this aspect of the text that Las Casas's editorial manipulations seek to privilege, as we have seen. By designating the Letter of 1492 as the prologue to the *Diario*, he tried to predispose readers to interpret the entire narrative of the voyage as the prologue defined it—the account of an evangelical Christian mission to the Indies of the Grand Khan—despite the paucity of references to religious conversion in the account.

Las Casas's assessment of the prologue in the *Historia* collapses the roles of addresser and addressee that define the pragmatics of the Letter of 1492. In suggesting that Columbus and the Catholic Monarchs speak as a united voice, with one and the same intention, Las Casas effectively erased the exceptional rhetorical and ideological character of the Letter of 1492 as Columbus's corrective response to the prediscovery documents issued by the Crown. This univocality could only be figurative and retrospective, of course, for at the time Columbus wrote to Isabella and Ferdinand they had not yet made an explicit commitment to proselytizing in the Indies. Nevertheless, as an editorial tactic, Las Casas's comment has the important effect of rendering the prologue part of the postdiscovery rather than the prediscovery family of writings, a piece composed after the fact as an introduction to the specific historical action the *Diario* relates. Such a tactic was essential to establishing the prologue's metatextual role as reader's guide and interpretive paradigm for the *Diario*.

In setting Columbus's and the Crown's presumed Christianizing intention in relief, Las Casas also, through his editorial "voice," imbues that intention with a new purpose of his own: to render the idealizing dimension of Columbus's testimony on the peoples of the

New World as the moral paradigm for the proper way Christian Europeans should behave in the Indies. With the goal of reforming Spanish colonial policy, Las Casas uses the prologue, like an *accessus*, to establish the exemplariness of Columbus as an *auctor*—an authority to be trusted and emulated. In the aftermath of legal battles between the Columbus family and the Crown, during which the Admiral's reputation was tarnished considerably, Las Casas was not only Columbus's first editor but also the rehabilitator of his good name. It is Las Casas who ensured Columbus's canonical stature by rendering him *the* scriptural authority on the Discovery.

I do not mean to suggest that Columbus himself could not have had a similar Christian vision of the Discovery in his unedited *diario*. There is simply no way of knowing. We can with certainty, however, conclude that the sense of the Discovery presented in the *Diario* is to a large degree the result of Las Casas's editorial manipulations. It is undoubtedly not coincidental that the *Diario* complements and supports the evangelical revolution of Spanish colonial policy that Las Casas advocated in his other works.[27]

Las Casas's voice is omnipresent in the *Diario*. Not a line in the text is unaffected by his editorial intent, including the first-person passages in which he decides to let Columbus speak for himself and quotes "the Admiral's very words." Even quotation, recontextualized, is a form of rewriting, as Borges's character Pierre Menard reminds us in his remarkable verbatim rendition of *Don Quijote*. Interrupting and interrupted by the editorial commentary, the paraphrases, the metaliterary evaluations, and other editorial manipulations, Columbus's voice is not exclusively his own. He speaks through, and for, Las Casas.

And yet traces of the long-missing *diario* of the first voyage can be glimpsed in the palimpsest Las Casas published as the *Diario*. That lost original version appears to have constituted a disjunctive discourse on the Discovery that was idealistic and poetic and, at the same time, mercantilistic and imperialistic. The *Diario*'s editorial rhetoric subordinates the latter and enhances the former, in an attempt to resolve the tensions and contradictions residing in the Columbian text into a coherent Christian discourse. Whether or not this was also Columbus's intention in the original, as Las Casas claimed, will remain an open question as long as the missing *diario* of the first navigation remains lost to us.

In the Margins of Columbus

The decisive mediation of Bartolomé de Las Casas in the transmission of the Columbian texts to future generations of readers has been largely ignored, as I have argued earlier in this volume. Yet today we would not have any version of the *diarios* of the first or third voyages were it not for his edition of the former and his transcription and paraphrase of the latter in the biography of Columbus that comprises the first book of the *Historia de las Indias*. Las Casas was not only a transcriber, editor, and biographer of Columbus, however. He was also his first Reader, with a capital R to distinguish his activities from the type of reading that leaves few if any traces of itself. Few of the texts Las Casas worked with are free of marginal or interpolated notes registering his reactions to Columbus's words. Much of this annotation was then incorporated into the *Historia*, a work that can be described as a collection of citations and paraphrases of the Columbian texts tied together by Las Casas's running commentary. The notes even made their way into the marginalia of the *Historia*, recording to the point of practical if not rhetorical redundancy Las Casas's reflections and responses to Columbus.[1]

Unlike a typical reader's occasional underscorings, Las Casas's notations reflect a consistent and coherent philosophy of reading that, in turn, as the commentary is assimilated into the *Historia*, becomes a way of writing the history of the Discovery. Compared to the works of Ferdinand Columbus and Gonzalo Fernández de Oviedo y Valdés, the other early biographers of Columbus and historians of the Discovery, Las Casas's *Historia* has a pronounced exegetical character, which not only incorporates but also proclaims the primacy of the texts it contains.[2] Las Casas was alone among the early Columbianists in interpreting the historical event through an explicit commentary on and exegesis of his sources; in rendering the figure of Columbus not only as the protagonist of the events but as the narrator of the story he himself had written; and in holding Columbus accountable not just for his actions but for the way he told the story of what occurred. Words, Las Casas believed, contain the germs of deeds within them, and so his critical history of Spain in the Indies begins with a criticism of what Columbus wrote about his experiences there. The results of this historiographical strategy have been to both enrich and irrevocably alter the Columbian texts. Las Casas's marginal commentary on the Columbian texts—his creative reading practice—constitutes a way of interpreting, revising, and ultimately yet another way of rewriting the history and story of the Discovery.

Common usage dictates that the adjective "marginal" be reserved for the inessential, peripheral, or supplemental, that which lies outside the boundaries defining the central. Paradoxically, however, it is precisely in its relation to the margins that the center takes shape. As something added, even if only as an afterthought, the supplemental element implies the incomplete or insufficient character of the entity to which it is appended. Deconstructive analysis uses this "logic of the supplement" to subvert the distinction between essential and inessential, inside and outside, in order to question the hierarchies that designate certain things as central and others as unessential.[3] But what is a "center" if it relies on the margins to define its centeredness? The reversal implicit in this question, the attribution of importance to that which has been characterized as supplementary or marginal, is the way deconstructionists typically relativize the activity of interpretation or evaluation of cultural products. In undermining the very decidability of what is important or meaningful and what is less so or not at all, deconstruction ultimately seeks to prevent any particular evaluation from establishing itself as authoritative or, at least, from doing so for very long.

By invoking the notion of marginality, I want to call attention to how Las Casas's marginal comments, which have long been considered an unessential part of the Columbian texts, in fact exert a significant effect on our reading of Columbus. But beyond this initial "decentering" of Columbian writing, I also employ the notion of marginality in a way quite different from that typically used by deconstructionists. "The margins" therefore will also serve as a position from which to identify and trace the moves of a strategy for writing the Discovery that is explicitly supplemental and self-consciously revisionist. Las Casas's discourse is characterized precisely by its accessory nature, indeed derives its strength and authority from its secondary condition. From this perspective, I will also examine the countermoves of a reading tradition that has consistently suppressed the marginal text and the consequences of this tacit censorship for our understanding of Columbian writing.

Implicit in this approach is an awareness that even if hierarchies bear their own deconstruction within them, if the center can be uncentered by attributing importance to an element previously thought to be marginal, the very act of decentering carries with it tangible consequences because it is always, even if only momentarily, itself also a centering. In calling attention to the marginalia, in situating my own reading in the margins, I am advocating a reorientation in the discussion of Columbian writing that takes into full account Las Casas's mediation in its transmission. For his mediation was in no way neutral. On the contrary, in the interplay between margin and center in his work on Columbus, Las Casas made literary choices with profound political, ethical (he would have said "moral"), and ultimately historical consequences. In the process he profoundly altered some of these texts, inscribing in them his voice and his vision. In refocusing the discussion of Columbian writing on the marginalia, I seek to demonstrate that rather than constituting an incidental or extraneous appendage to the main texts as we have them, Las Casas's commentary has become their necessary supplement. Implicit in my argument acknowledging the integrality of the central and the marginal writings is a protest of established editing practices that suppress or subordinate one in favor of the other.

Las Casas's interest in Columbus was not purely, or even primarily, historiographical. Ethnographical, literary, juridical, moral and, perhaps above all, political concerns attracted him to "the Admiral's" writings. His reading of Columbus was done with an eye to provoking the Spanish authorities to a moral awakening: that the many unchristian, unjust, and unlawful aspects of the conquest required the reform of colonial laws and practices damaging to the Indians. Only occasionally does this case assume the form of historical argumentation in the *Historia*; more often than not, it is articulated through a blending of sermonlike moralization, ethnological description, and theological commentary packaged in the litigator's rhetoric or the literary forms of biography or the interpolated story.[4] Anthony Pagden has observed that the *Historia* "reads less like a 'history' than a series of overlapping depositions" in which Columbus is presented as, among other things, Las Casas's opening and preferred witness.[5]

The mode of discourse in the *Historia* alternates between quotation or paraphrase of Columbus's writings and an exegesis or commentary on that text based on Las Casas's experiences in the Indies, eyewitness testimony whose authority is vouched for by his erudition and his commitment to Christian precepts. His narrative of events often reads more like a chorus of textual "voices" to which the historian's writing responds in confirmation, correction, or outright condemnation. In book 1 of the *Historia*, for example, the biography of Columbus and the history of the enterprise of the Indies are related through paraphrase, direct quotation, and verbatim transcription of long passages or even (apparently) entire documents. The various texts are formed into a cohesive narrative structure and coherent historical argument through Las Casas's exegesis and commentary, through his interpretation of the texts' significance. The historian's task, as he explains in the prologue to the *Historia*, is the "discovery" of a past not so much forgotten as "hidden":

> muchos otros sabemos haver sido a quien la grandeza y dignidad y numerosidad de las obras y hechos en sus tiempos acaecidos, viéndolos *ocultados y cubiertos* con niebla del olvido, habiendo respecto a la utilidad común, que *descubiertas*, dellas esperan seguirse, porque se *manifiesten*, convida y solicita o induce a querer escribirlas.
>
> ([Madrid: Biblioteca de
Autores Españoles, 1957], 3;
emphasis added)

> Many others, because we know ourselves to be among those to whom the greatness, dignity, and multitude of works and deeds that have occurred in their time, seeing these things *concealed and covered* by the fog of oblivion, out of respect for the common good that one hopes will derive from them once they are *discovered*— which invites and solicits or induces [us] to want to write them— [are moved to compose histories] in order to *make them manifest*.

The phrasing recalls Columbus's own—"cometí viaje de nuevo al cielo y tierra que fasta entonces estaba oculto . . . salió a pareçer de mi industria" (Varela, 264; I undertook a new voyage to the sky and land that up to that point had been hidden . . . [which] appeared because of my labor)—suggesting an intriguing parallel between the original discovery of the Indies as divinely inspired revelation and their historiographical "rediscovery" by Las Casas in the *Historia*.[6] But Las Casas's wording is also reminiscent of biblical hermeneutics, the most common purpose of which was to discover, through the exegesis of biblical texts, the spiritual meanings latent in sacred history and the truths and moral values it could teach. Of the four types of interpretation recognized by the Church—literal, moral, allegorical, and anagogical—Las Casas favors the second in his interpretation of the texts that tell the story of the Discovery. His exegesis typically culminates in a critique of conduct in light of Christian precepts. In his prologue he clearly states the reforming intent of his history even as he reiterates its moralizing didactic purpose:

> Quise tomar este cuidado y acometer entre otras muchas ocupaciones este trabajo, no poco grande, . . . por la utilidad común, espiritual y temporal, que podrá resultar para todas estas infinitas gentes, . . . [y] por librar mi nación española del error y engaño pernicioso en que vive.
>
> (*Historia*, 15)

> I wanted to take on this charge and undertake this no small labor on top of all the others . . . because of the spiritual and temporal benefits that may result for all these infinite peoples, . . . [and] in order to deliver my Spanish nation from the pernicious error and self-deception in which it lives.

The exegesis of the Columbian texts is the opening blast in the *Historia*'s battle to change the course of events in the Indies by awakening Spain's moral conscience to the horrors of the conquest and its consequences. Following the Columbian model of discovery expressed in the text Las Casas selected as the prologue to the *Diario* (a text also transcribed into the *Historia*), he advocates in place of conquest an exclusively evangelical mission under the direction of religious and supported by peaceful persuasion rather than force.

For this mission he prefers the term *descubrimiento* (in the sense of the term as employed in the Columbian text) to *conquista*, which is a "vocablo tiránico, mahometano, impropio e infernal" (a tyrannical, Muhammadan word, improper and infernal).[7]

To speak about the Columbian texts' role in Las Casas's historical discourse it is helpful, however, to consider first the formative stages of a reading method and writing practice that culminated in the *Historia*'s critique of Spanish colonization. Many of the same Columbian passages invoked in the *Historia* are also the subject of Las Casas's marginalia in his edition of the *Diario* and "Relación" of the third voyage. (Although that edition is undated, most scholars have concluded, as we will see, that Las Casas's commentary in the *Historia* is derived from it, and not vice versa.) The most strongly worded of these passages concern the Indians, specifically Columbus's perceptions and treatment of them, which is also a primary focus of the *Historia*, and so I have chosen to concentrate on this aspect of the marginal commentary.

II

The original manuscript of Las Casas's edition of the *Diario* and "Relación," preserved at the Biblioteca Nacional in Madrid, presents the two documents in sequence on seventy-six continuously numbered folios. The main text attributed to Columbus, the marginal comments, and the numerous corrections are all in Las Casas's handwriting. The text's appearance is striking in that the margins are very generous, in contrast to Las Casas's other holographs, where each page is typically covered with text, notes, and corrections.[8] The marginal commentary assumes various forms. There is a sketch (unique in the *Diario*) of a quill pen in the left margin opposite the entry for 11 October, where the narrative of the discovery proper begins (see Figure 1, fol. 8r). The abbreviation *nō* ("note") is used frequently to highlight certain passages. Las Casas also highlights portions of text by copying words or short phrases in the margin to summarize important passages or simply scores the relevant text. A more evaluative or interpretive form of commentary ranges from a single word to several phrases (see Figure 1, fol. 55v). Sometimes the main text is simply scored in the left margin or underlined. Las Casas was careful to distinguish the commentary from his corrections to the main text by consistently placing the former in the left margin, while the revisions typically appear on the right-hand side.[9] The commentary usually appears boxed-off from the main text, further accentuating its presence and autonomy. The manuscript as a whole gives the impression of having been written with a careful hand, in reasonably clear and legible script.

The *Diario* and "Relación" were published for the first time in 1825 by Martín Fernández de Navarrete as part of his *Colección de los viages y descubrimientos que hicieron los españoles desde fines del siglo XVI*, a multivolume collection of writings about Spanish exploration. This edition appeared without most of Las Casas's annotations, however; nor was any mention made of the more than one thousand revisions to the primary text also contained in the margins and between the lines of the manuscript. In effect, Las Casas's pen was erased from the text, leaving the impression that the *Diario* and "Relación" had been achieved by the simple and straightforward transcription of Columbus's writings. All subsequent editions and translations of these texts between 1825 and 1892 were based on Fernández de Navarrete's; not until the Italian edition known as the *Raccolta* appeared in 1892 was the presence of Las Casas acknowledged, though only partially. This editor, Cesare de Lollis, returned to the original manuscript and included most, but not all, of the marginal commentary, without any explanation of the criteria employed in his selection.[10]

Most of the twentieth-century Spanish editions of the *Diario* and "Relación," and all the English translations I am aware of, also suppress in one way or another the presence of Las Casas's pen in the text.[11] Surprisingly, even the editor of the first facsimile edition, Carlos Sanz, silently omitted many of the marginal notes in his transcription. Recent editions and translations, beginning with Manuel Alvar's transcription in 1976, include most of Las Casas's commentary. But it is usually relegated to endnotes or footnotes, a practice that, at the very least, implies a statement on its subordinate status with respect to the main text.[12] The apparatus also makes it impossible for the reader to move from the main text to the marginal comments without interruption. Even the latest diplomatic edition and English translation, published in bilingual format by Oliver Dunn and James E. Kelley, omits the marginalia from the English half of the book. Thus demoted, isolated, and dismembered, the

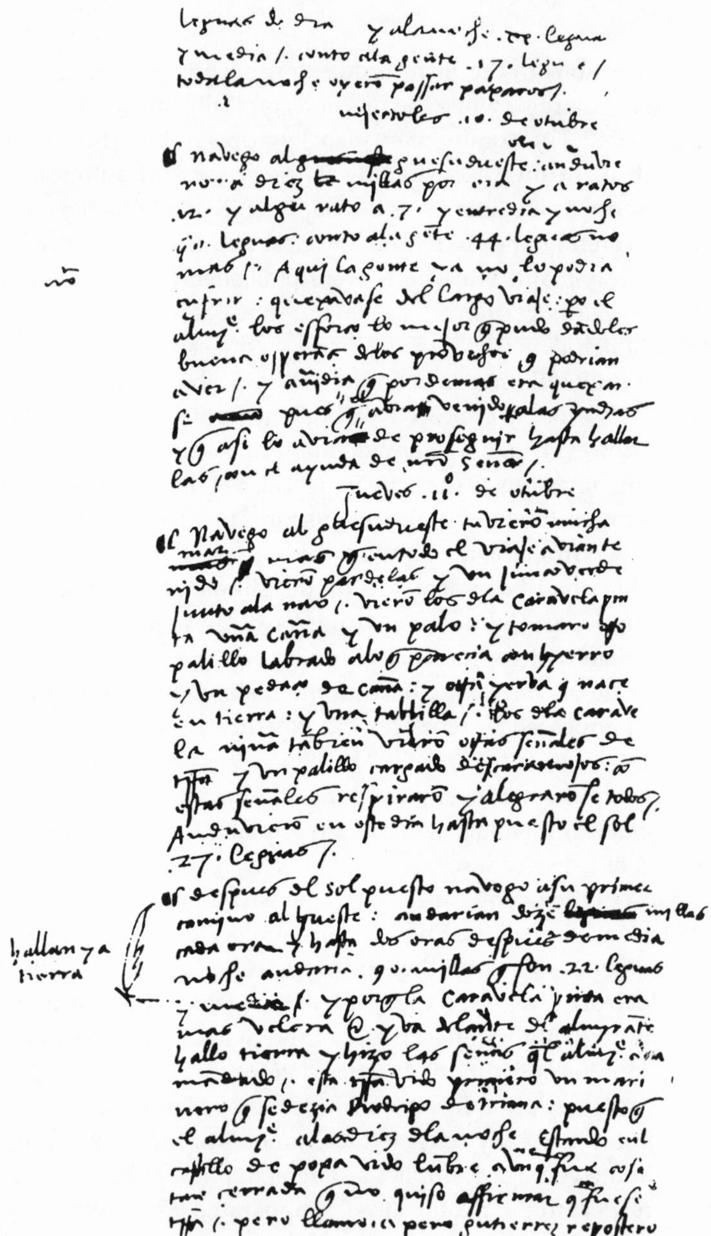

Figure 1. (*Above and opposite*) Pages from the "Libro de la primera navegación y descubrimiento de las Indias" (fols. 8r and 55v). From Carlos Sanz's facsimile edition, *Diario de Colón* (Madrid: Bibliotheca Americana Vetustissima, 1962).

commentary is no longer the integral part of the *Diario* and "Relación" Las Casas conceived it to be.

The physical integrity of the manuscript is fully respected only by Consuelo Varela, who recently edited it as part of an edition of Las Casas's collected works. Varela appears to hedge her bet in the introduction, however, when she anticipates the surprise that the inclusion of the *Diario* and the "Relación" in the works of Las Casas is likely to cause. Rather than affirm Las Casas's decisive mediation in the transmission of these texts, implicit in their inclusion in the collected works, Varela gingerly sidesteps her own bold implication—that Las Casas's pen and not Columbus's defines these texts—by affirming that the merits of the annotations alone justify their inclusion.[13]

As this brief survey suggests, our reading of the Columbian texts has been wholly defined by the institutionalization of an editorial fiction that creates the illusion of the pristineness and absolute authority of Columbus's voice by enforcing the wholesale suppression or manipulation of Las Casas's commentary. Each of the editors recognized the presence of Las Casas's pen in the margins of the manuscript and, openly or silently, each made value judgments about which marginal notes to include or eliminate, where to place them, and how to use them in the interpretation of difficult or obscure passages. Fernández de Navarrete, for instance, chose to include notes of a geographical character but not those critical of Columbus's words and conduct. The degree of premeditation that governed his selection is evidenced in the fact that his fair copy did not include certain annotations that nevertheless appear in the published edition.[14] One can only conclude that he must have gone back to the original specifically to consider the marginal text.

The real issue is not, then, whether the annotations are indeed a part of the *Diario* and "Relación," but how they are treated in established editorial practice.[15] The positivist belief that the past can be essentially reconstituted in the present through the study of documentary evidence has undoubtedly contributed in no small way to scholars' persistent reluctance to acknowledge that the most complete source we have on the first and third voyages is not a fair copy, or even a copy of a copy, but a highly manipulated version of a copy of whatever Columbus may have written.[16] Even those who acknowledge Las Casas's interventions typically feel obliged either to shield Columbus's integrity from the onus of the Lascasian violation by accusing Las Casas of fabrication or, conversely, to insist on Las Casas's absolute fidelity to the Admiral's ipsissima verba in the transcription of the first-person passages and to the substance, tone, and tenor of Columbus's lost original text in the paraphrases, which constitute some 80 percent of the *Diario*.[17] Although these two positions appear to represent opposite views with respect to Las Casas's handling of his source, they share a fundamental belief in the need to maintain the authority and integrity of the Columbian word. Both those who view Las Casas as a faithful and passive conduit for Columbus's voice and those who see him as a ventriloquist speaking his own mind through a Columbus-dummy ultimately maintain the privilege of the Admiral's testimony and the fiction that it is available to us in a fundamentally pristine text. Yet in the final analysis, neither those who chastise Las Casas nor those who hold him up as a model of editorial fidelity can afford to ignore the presence of his pen in his edition of the *Diario* and "Relación."

The unique physical appearance of the manuscript, with its ample margins and highlighted commentary, suggests that it not only served the likely purposes of aide-mémoire and citation source for Las Casas's treatises and histories, but that it was also intended for circulation among other readers. One thing is clear, Las Casas displayed the margins.[18] But the nature of the commentary itself is perhaps the strongest evidence that he was not writing for himself alone. While many of the annotations simply summarize or call attention to material contained in a particular portion of the main text, others correct Columbian errors (usually geographical or linguistic) or interpret passages of the main text on the basis of Las Casas's own experiences in the Indies. For example, a linguistic note on the Arawak word *bohío*, which Columbus apparently mistook as the proper name of an island, reads: "bohío llamavan los indios de aquellas islas a las casas y por eso creo que no entendía bien el Almirante, ante devía de dezir por la isla Española que llamavan Haití" (*Colección*, 76–77; The Indians of those islands called houses *bohío* and for this reason I believe that the Admiral did not understand correctly; he must have been referring to the island of Hispaniola, which they called Haiti). It seems unlikely that this type of

simple linguistic correction, of which there are many in the manuscript (e.g., *Diario* entries for 23 November, 26 November, 5 December), would have been intended for Las Casas's own edification.

More importantly, implicit in Las Casas's corrective stance with
respect to Columbus's linguistic incompetence is an ostentation of
the commentator's superior familiarity with the subject matter and
a questioning of the Admiral's perceptions and judgments. This
oneupmanship, as it were, induces readers of Las Casas's edition to
adopt a critical posture with respect to Columbus's testimony. Even
the Admiral's knowledge of geography is put in question, as in the
Diario entry for 1 November, which seems to have caught Las Casas's eye if the sheer quantity of notes is any indication. At the end
of the entry, after describing the Indians' willingness to repeat
Christian prayers taught to them by the Spaniards, Columbus
makes two of his most famous geographical blunders. He asserts
that Cuba is the Asiatic mainland and that he is now in the vicinity
of Zaitó and Quinsay, two of the great Tatar cities described by
Marco Polo in his *Travels*. Las Casas's comment is openly derisive,
"esta algaravía no entiendo yo" (*Colección*, 75; I do not understand
this gibberish). This is immediately followed by another correction
in the subsequent entry, this time for Columbus's preposterous location of Cuba at 42 degrees north latitude.

A close analysis of the main text shows, however, that not all the
commentary resides in the margins. Obviously anachronistic observations—some explanatory, others critical—are interpolated in
various places, sometimes in parentheses or, more disturbingly for
those concerned with the integrity of the Columbian word, embedded almost seamlessly in the paraphrase. Among the detectable interpolations are the concern expressed on 30 October about the integrity of the copy Las Casas was working with; the anachronistic
intrusion of the Arawak name of the island of Guanahaní (Columbus's "San Salvador") before the first contact with the natives from
whom Columbus could have learned it; the mention of Florida
many years before it was discovered; and the comical exclamations
of incredulity regarding the ephemeral islands Columbus was seeking in the vicinity of what later was to be known as the location of
Florida. In each instance, the editorial voice is affecting to speak
through Columbus, and the distinction between the author's enun-
ciation and the editor's has been effectively blurred. As I observed

in the essay preceding, we have no way of knowing on how many other occasions, now undetectable, the primary text has been violated, not only by the comparatively benign operation of paraphrasing, but by the physical invasion of the marginal discourse into the presumably unadulterated Columbian discourse itself.

As we have seen, in the physical disposition of Las Casas's manuscript the main text takes shape inside and in relation to the margins. It is in fact impossible to read the main text without also reading the marginalia—unless one physically manipulates the page to block out the commentary. The eye continually and ineluctably skips from the body text to the border and back. Las Casas's explanations, additions, corrections, and signals train the reader to depend on the marginal writing to understand the primary text. And before long one begins to sense that the text is simply not complete without the annotations. The commentary's very existence bespeaks the insufficiency of the main text, the necessity of the supplement. First and foremost, the marginalia situate the reader in a critical stance with respect to the primary text. To the extent that the commentary puts in question Columbus's judgments, interpretations, representations, and actions, it renders his authority relative in value. Beyond questioning the accuracy of the source, the commentary also makes its physical integrity a relative phenomenon. The commentary leads to the conclusion that the primary text is neither an infallible nor even a stable and complete entity. Ultimately, it argues for the need to question, criticize, and revise Columbus.

Las Casas's strongest criticism is reserved for Columbus's treatment of the Indians. The marginal text draws the reader's attention to those portions of the primary text that speak of Arawak generosity, intelligence, and diligence, and their peaceable and welcoming reception of the Christians. The marginal text, however, casts these passages in an ironic light, since Columbus frequently complements such encomiastic observations with an affirmation of the ease with which Spanish domination and exploitation could be established and maintained. In the margins the editorial voice provides an explicit critical counterpoint to Columbus's patently unchristian intentions, often in bitingly sarcastic or openly denunciatory terms. In the entry for 12 November, for example, Columbus states that the previous day six young Indian men in a canoe had come alongside the ship, and when five of the six boarded he ordered them to be detained. Las Casas remarks sardonically in the margin, "no fue lo mejor del mundo esto" (*Colección*, 81; this was not the best thing in the world). Columbus then says that he sent some of his crew ashore to take female captives so that the Indian men would behave better in Spain, having women from their own country along, and would be more agreeable to doing as they were told. Las Casas quips, "¡mira que maravilla!" (81; look how marvelous!) A few lines later Columbus relates that a sole man in a canoe had approached the ship later that evening and asked to be taken with the others, apparently because he was the husband of one of the captives and father of her three children, who were also being held on board. The marginal annotation demands, "porque [por qué] no le distes sus hijos" (81; why didn't you give him back his children?).

Indeed, Las Casas's harshest criticisms are expressed in the marginal commentary to passages where Columbus relates the capture of Indians to take back to Spain or makes observations regarding their exploitability. Las Casas categorically condemns the taking of any Indians against their will, for whatever purpose. In the entry for 15 January, Columbus tells of seizing four youths who had given him particularly good directions to nearby islands and making them guides for the return voyage. Las Casas's response is unequivocal: "fue muy mal hecho traerlos contra su voluntad" (*Colección*, 146; it was very wrong to take them against their will).

The entry for 16 December, which contains some of the *Diario*'s most lyrical descriptions of the land and people of the Indies, seems to have been of special interest to Las Casas, judging by the various notes ("nõ") that line the margins. It records a cordial meeting between the Admiral and a local *cacique* during which Columbus obtained information about the location of gold and elicited the full cooperation of his host. Columbus's closing remarks, however, turn to the suitability of the Indians for forced labor: "son buenos para les mandar y les hazer trabajar y sembrar y hazer todo lo otro que fuere menester, y que hagan villas y se enseñen a andar vestidos y a nuestras costumbres" (*Colección*, 111; they are fit to be ordered about and made to work, plant, and do everything else that may be needed, and build towns and be taught our customs, and to go about clothed, Dunn & Kelley, 237). This passage draws the follow-

ing comment from Las Casas: "algo más parece aquí entenderse [es-
tenderse] el Almirante de lo que devría" (111; the Admiral seems to
go farther here than he should).[19] In itself, the comment is strikingly
subdued. But its ironic intent and biting sarcasm are salient in the
context of the panegyric character of the rest of the entry, which accentuates the incongruity and the bad faith represented in these
closing observations. The meaning of the commentary lies precisely
in this contrast between idealization and exploitation, and in the
understated tone of the annotation within the larger context of the
entire entry, not just the closest passage. This is one of the clearest
examples of the integrality of the marginal and main texts in the Las
Casas edition.

On 25 December the *Santa María* ran aground and had to be abandoned. Columbus described at some length the invaluable help he
and his crew received from the local Indian *cacique*:

> El cual como lo supo dizen que lloró y enbió toda su gente de la
> villa con canoas muy grandes y muchas a descargar todo lo de la
> nao; y así se hizo y se descargó todo lo de las cubiertas en muy
> breve espacio; tanto fue el grande aviamiento y diligencia que aquel
> rey dio. Y él con su persona, con hermanos y parientes, estavan po-
> niendo diligençia, así en la nao como en la guarda de lo que se sa-
> cava a tierra, para que todo estuviese a muy buen recaudo. De
> cuando en cuando enbiava uno de sus parientes al Almirante llo-
> rando a lo consolar, diziendo que no rescibiese pena ni enojo, qu'él
> le daría cuanto tuviese.
>
> (*Colección*, 126)

> When he [the *cacique*] learned of it [the disabled ship], they said
> that he cried and sent all his people to unload everything from the
> ship. And thus it was done and in a very brief time everything
> from the decks was unloaded, so great was the care and diligence
> that king exercised. And he himself and his brothers and relatives
> were as diligent [unloading] the ship as in guarding what was
> taken to land in order that everything would be well cared for.
> From time to time he sent one of his relatives to the Admiral,
> weeping, to console him, saying that he should not be sorrowful
> or annoyed because he would give him all that he had.
>
> (Dunn & Kelley, 281)

Las Casas's marginal note reads, "nótese aquí la humanidad de los
indios contra los tiranos que los an estirpado" (note here the hu-

manity of the Indians in contrast to the tyrants who have extirpated them).

A few lines later in the main text Columbus affirms:

> son gente de amor y sin cudiçia y convenibles para toda cosa, que certifico a Vuestras Altezas que en el mundo creo que no hay mejor gente ni mejor tierra. Ellos aman a sus próximos como a sí mismos.

> they [are] a loving people, and without greed, and docile in everything. And I assure Your Highnesses that I believe that in the world there are no better people or a better land, they love their neighbors as themselves.

The first of Las Casas's marginal comments to this anecdote underscores the Indians' humanity but also establishes a significant contrast between Indian generosity and the Spaniards' subsequent tyranny—a point both alien and anachronistic with respect to Columbus's discourse. By interjecting the Spanish tyranny of the sixteenth century, the commentary affords readers a different vantage point from which to evaluate the events and words of 1492. The contrast intensifies the polarity: the kindness of the *cacique* and his people is enhanced in contrast to the later ingratitude of the Spaniards, and the Spaniards' genocidal crimes seem even worse in light of the Indians' generosity. The commentary thus sharpens the significance of the original anecdote ("in the world there are no better people") and uses it as a weapon by obliging the reader to consider the unwarranted violence of the Spanish conquest.

A second marginal note underscores Columbus's panegyric description of his hosts at the point where he affirms that the Indians followed the biblical commandment in their comportment. The criticism, by implication, is that the Christians did not. All of the above is written in the entry for 25 December, significantly identified by Las Casas (or Columbus?) in the section heading as "día de Navidad."

The image of the good Indians is the product ultimately of Las Casas's pen, not Columbus's; at best Columbus seems to have been ambivalent toward them. But Las Casas does not simply paint an edenic scene, the product of a bucolic nostalgia for a lost golden age. The marginal text lays bare the corrosive, subversive intentionality of the idealization.[20] Through contrastive, oppositional, polemical, and ultimately condemnatory annotations, Las Casas turns Columbus's own words against him, rendering his testimony a witness against itself. Read from the margins, the image of the beatified Indian becomes a component of a rhetorical strategy of contraposition that sets "the humanity of the Indians" against "the tyrants who have extirpated them," who consider themselves to be Christians.

Even those marginal notes that are not explicitly critical frequently point an accusatory finger at the main text. The irony of such passages is superseded only by the shamefulness of Spanish action they imply. The following description of a trading expedition to the domain of Guacanagarí, where Columbus built the ill-fated fort La Navidad and left thirty-nine Spaniards, is simply noted with a marginal abbreviation "nō" by Las Casas, without further commentary. His restraint seems justified, for the passage clearly speaks for itself:

> Después que fue tarde, dioles tras (sic) ánsares muy gordas el señor
> y unos pedaçitos de oro, y vinieron con ellos mucho número de
> gente, y les traían todas las cosas que allá avían resgatado, y ellos
> mismos porfiavan de traellos a cuestas, y de hecho lo hizieron por
> algunos ríos y por algunos lugares lodosos. El Almirante mandó
> dar al señor algunas cosas, y quedó él y toda su gente con gran
> contentamiento, creyendo verdadermente que avían venido del
> cielo, y en ver los cristianos se tenían por bien aventurados.
>
> (*Colección*, 121)

> Later, when it was afternoon, the lord gave them three very fat
> geese and a few small pieces of gold; and a large number of people
> came and carried for them everything that they had received in
> trade there; and they insisted on carrying the Spaniards on their
> backs; and in fact they did so through some rivers and muddy
> places. The Admiral ordered that they give the lord some things,
> and the lord and all his people, with great contentment, truly be-
> lieving that the Christians had come from the heavens, considered
> themselves very fortunate in seeing them.
>
> (Dunn & Kelley, 267)

The contrast between the helpfulness and reverence shown by the Indians toward the Spaniards and the implicit Spanish betrayal of their trust and goodwill are reminiscent of the discursive strategy employed by Las Casas in the denunciatory *Brevíssima relación de la destrucción de las Indias*, in which he painstakingly documents, island by island, region by region, the genocide perpetrated by the conquistadors against their peaceable and unsuspecting victims.

Las Casas's commentary continues throughout the *Diario* and into the "Relación." The annotations to the latter, however, excepting several corrections of fact, are rarely critical. One explanation for this change may be that the two sources are very different kinds of texts, different in form, content, and ideology. The *Diario* is the account of an exploration, predominantly narrational and replete with detailed nautical, geographical, and commercial observations. The "Relación" has an essentially hermeneutical objective, summarizing the third voyage and, especially, interpreting its spiritual significance in the context of the larger enterprise of the Discovery for a king and queen whose commitment to Columbus was palpably wavering.[21] Yet the physical integrity of the manuscript suggests that Las Casas transcribed these two texts to be read as if they composed a unit or whole. Clearly, their perceived coherence is not temporal, since there was an intervening second voyage (1493–94) with an accompanying *diario* (since lost) and at least four *cartas-relaciones*. Neither is it generic, since the "Relación" is not a day-by-day account. But Las Casas must have had access to the *diario* of the third voyage, for he seems to have used it together with the "Relación" to compose his account of that voyage in the *Historia*.[22]

Las Casas never stated his reasons for choosing the "Relación" over the journal account for his edition of the third voyage, and the choice warrants at least some speculation. A comparison of the fragments in the *Historia* that appear to have been extracted from the since-lost *diario* of the third voyage and those that clearly derive from the "Relación" shows that the distinguishing characteristic is the interpretative thrust of the latter, absent in the former. On the finding of the mainland, for example, this journallike fragment is jubilant, but quite literal and to the point:

> Volviendo al camino, el viernes, 17 de agosto anduvo 37 leguas, la mar llana; "a Dios, Nuestro Señor" (dice él) "sean dadas infinitas gracias." Dice que con no hallar ya islas le certifica que aquella tierra de donde viene sea gran tierra firme, o adonde está el Paraíso terrenal, "porque todos dizen," dice él, "que está en fin de Oriente, y es éste," dice él.
>
> (*Historia*, 394)
>
> Under sail again, on Friday, 17 August, he traveled thirty-seven leagues on a calm sea, "May thanks be given," says he, "to God

Our Lord." He says that since he no longer finds islands he certifies that that land from which he comes must be a great mainland, or where the terrestrial Paradise is located, "because everyone says," he says, "that it is at the end of the Orient and this is it," says he.

There is a simple, matter-of-fact sailor's straightforwardness about the astounding conclusions Columbus draws here from his observations of geographical phenomena: Since he no longer sees any more islands, the large land mass he has just discovered must be the mainland, and since it is located at the extreme Orient, it must of necessity be the site of the Terrestrial Paradise, because everyone (i.e., all the authorities on the subject) says that that is precisely where Paradise is located. Enough said on the question of Eden, the itinerary of the voyage moves on to the next day and the next place. On Saturday, 18 August, he traveled thirty-nine leagues; on Sunday, 19 August, he covered thirty-three leagues, arriving at Beata island, just off the coast of Española; and so on, as the *Historia* recounts by paraphrasing and probably summarizing its source.

The "Relación," in contrast, offers a convoluted erudite disquisition on the topic, which Las Casas transcribed verbatim or closely paraphrased. Paying special attention to the long interpretative sections concerning the nature and location of Paradise, Las Casas glosses Columbus carefully, adding authoritative references that support his interpretation of Paradise's location in the Indies over other competing sites because, as he puts it:

> experimentaba tanta frescura de tierras, y tan verdes y deleitosas arboledas, tanta clemencia y amenidad de sotiles aires, tanta y tan impetuosa grandeza y lago y ayuntamiento tan capaz y tan largo de tan delgadas y dulcísimas aguas, y allende todo esto, la bondad, liberalidad, simplicidad y mansedumbre de gentes, ¿qué podía otra cosa juzgar ni determinar, sino que allí o por allí, y aun cerca de allí, había la Divina Providencia constituído el Paraíso terrenal, y que aquel lago tan dulce era donde caía el río y fuente del Paraíso y de donde se originaban los cuatro ríos, Eúfrates, Ganges, Tigris e Nilo?
>
> (*Historia*, 389–90)

> he experienced such fresh lands, and such green and delightful groves, so much clemency and amenity in the subtle breezes, so much and such rapturous grandeur and [rapturous] lake and capacious and so large a union of such slender and sweet waters; and moreover, the goodness, generosity, simplicity, and gentleness of

the people. What else could he judge or conclude but that there, or around there, or even close to that place, the Divine Providence had constituted the Terrestrial Paradise, and that that freshwater lake was where the river and fountain of Paradise emptied and where the four rivers Euphrates, Ganges, Tigris, and Nile originated?

So obvious is the edenic character of the Indies to Las Casas that he closes this passage with the categorical affirmation that whoever experienced this splendor and did not arrive at the same conclusions as Columbus would deserve to be judged for an idiot ("de ser juzgado por mentecato fuera digno"). Moreover, the paradisiacal qualities of the Indies constitute positive proof of the favor in which God holds these lands and their peoples, and therefore confirms the natives' special aptness for evangelization.

Las Casas's rationale for uniting the *Diario* and "Relación" in one volume is to be found, I think, not in the texts' similarities but rather in their differences. Read as integral parts of an evolving historical argument and as a preliminary exercise in historiographical methodology, the two-part manuscript provides the skeleton for book 1 of the *Historia*. First, the *Diario* presents a fractured protagonist-narrator, a Columbus devoted to the Faith, cognizant of the Indians' suitability for evangelization, and committed to advocating a Christian mission before the Crown. But it also presents Columbus as *homo oeconomicus*, obsessed with finding gold and spices in order to secure for Ferdinand and Isabella a good return on their investment. Las Casas's concern, as expressed in the commentary, is how the Indians were exploited and enslaved by the mercantile Columbus, who during the first voyage repeatedly took Indian captives to serve as interpreters and guides, and for display to the Court as human samples. Las Casas recognized these actions as preliminaries to the slave trade Columbus was contemplating in the *Diario*, and which he undertook during the second voyage, and as the basic model for the system of forced labor known as the *encomienda*, which was approved by the Crown in the place of outright enslavement.[23] Every time the *Diario* relates the seizing of Indians, Las Casas condemns the action in a marginal comment.

The "Relación," in striking contrast, is devoted to establishing the paradisiacal nature of the new lands. Explicit economic concerns are subordinated to the spiritual value of the enterprise. Columbus relates the finding of the mainland, which he claimed was the site of the Terrestrial Paradise, as he had already predicted in the *Diario*. Many of Las Casas's marginal notes appear precisely opposite those passages in which Columbus interprets the edenic geography of the new lands. Typically, Las Casas here offers no commentary per se, but a short phrase flagging the passage and summarizing its content. On the only occasion when Columbus tells of taking Indians, Las Casas simply notes the fact in the margin. Apparently he was satisfied to underscore some notable passages but otherwise allow Columbus to speak for himself.

Read together, as Las Casas presented them in his manuscript, the *Diario* and the "Relación" suggest a development in Columbus's thinking and mode of diction, away from the profane concerns of commercial exploitation so evident in the various accounts of the first and second voyages, and toward a preoccupation with the spiritual significance of the enterprise. The gold sought after so fervently in the *Diario* (and even more so in the *relación* of 20 April 1494) is replaced in the "Relación" of the third voyage by the spiritual profit to be derived from the discovery of a land that, according to Columbus, was "más propincua y noble al cielo que otra" (*Colección*, 189; closer and more noble to heaven than any other). In the "Relación" Las Casas's and Columbus's voices seem finally to be in agreement, and the commentary loses its edge. Nonetheless, the commentary effectively makes Columbus a witness against his earlier self, while at the same time confirming the correctness of Las Casas's indictment.

It is in the context of Las Casas's discourse against the conquest that his critical reading of Columbus must be situated. Read from the margins of the *Diario* and "Relación," the image of the good Indians contained in these texts becomes a disturbing, haunting testimony not just, or even primarily, to the Indians' character, but to the Europeans' injustice. The marginal writing inscribes Las Casas's reproach into the image that, in turn, becomes an emblem of the condemnation.

One final document helps complete the picture of Las Casas's marginal discourse on the Discovery, which culminated in the *Historia de las Indias*. Las Casas's copy of Columbus's letter (c. autumn 1500) to doña Juana de la Torre, governess of the prince don Juan, is second only to the *Diario*/"Relación" manuscript in the number and quality of Las Casas's annotations.[24]

The letter to doña Juana is perhaps the most anguished of all of Columbus's writings. It was composed at the darkest hour of his career, between the third and fourth voyages, soon after he was brought back to Spain from Española in shackles, a prisoner of the Crown. It has all the earmarks of an apologia and a self-defense, composed for the sovereigns' benefit. Yet the addressee is not the Crown, nor one of the royal officials involved in overseeing the enterprise of the Indies, but a friend of Columbus's who was also close to Ferdinand and Isabella and therefore able to convey to them its sentiments. The tone of the letter is familiar, and Columbus openly acknowledges his bitterness and despair as well as his negative opinion of the Indians, who by then had rebelled against the Europeans on Española.

In the closing paragraphs of the letter, Columbus summarizes the difficulties he encountered and the benefits that accrued to Spain thanks to his labors. His words drew a series of sharp rebukes from Las Casas, comments that can be read as a synopsis of his views on the Discovery. The two short passages below, the focal point of his ire, are accompanied by no fewer than six marginal comments:

Yo debo de ser juzgado como capitán que fue d'España a conquistar fasta las Indias a gente belicosa y mucha y de costumbres y secta muy contraria, donde por voluntad divina, e puesto so el señorío del Rey e de la Reina, Nuestros Señores, otro mundo, y por donde la España que era dicha pobre es la más rica.

> no dezía el Almirante que era beliciosa cuando Guacanagarí le salvó la persona y hazienda, perdida su nao
>
> admirable fue la ignorancia del Almirante en esta materia
>
> voluntad permisiva, no agradable
>
> por esta riqueza injusta y de lo mal adquirido, verná a ser la más pobre del mundo

(Varela, 269–70)

I should be judged as a captain who set out from Spain to conquer, as far as the Indies, a very bellicose and numerous people with very foul customs and religion, which by divine will I have placed under the lordship of the King and Queen, Our Lords, an other world, thanks to which Spain, once called poor, is now the richest [of nations].

> the Admiral did not say they were bellicose when Guacanagarí saved his person and belongings when his ship was lost
>
> admirable was the Admiral's ignorance on this subject
>
> permissive, not consenting, will
>
> because of this unjust wealth and things acquired through ill deeds, [Spain] will be the poorest in the world

Del oro y perlas ya está abierta
la puerta, y cantidad de todo,
piedras preçiosas y espeçería y
de otras mill cosas se pueden
esperar firmemente. [. . .] Pareçe también qu'estas minas son
como las otras, que responden
en los días no igualmente. Las
minas son nuevas y los coge-
dores. El pareçer de todos es
que, aunque vaya ayá toda Castilla, que por torpe que sea la
persona, que no abaxará de un
castellano o dos cada día. . . .
Es verdad que tienen algún indio, mas el negoçio consiste en
el christiano.

no tenían uno sino muchos indios que sudaban y morían en
ello

consistir el negocio en el cris-
tiano era tenellos por fuerça y
dalles de palos y açotes, y no
aver misericordia d'ellos.

(Varela, 270)

The door to the gold and pearls
is now open, and all in great
quantity, precious stones and
spices and a thousand things
can be expected with confidence. [. . .] It also seems that
these mines are like the others,
they do not yield the same
every day. The mines are new
and so are the miners. Popular
opinion has it that, even if all
Castile goes there, no matter
how unskilled the person, he
will not make less than one or
two castellanos every day. . . .
It is true that they have [the
help of] an Indian, but the [suc-
cess of the] business lies with
the Christian.

they had not one but many Indians who sweated and died in
the endeavor

the [success of the] business
lying with the Christian meant
keeping the Indians by force
and beating and whipping
them, and having no mercy
on them.

Read in counterpoint with the main text voiced by Columbus, the
marginal commentary tells a story that goes something like this:
Calling the Indians warlike is hypocritical and ungrateful on the
Admiral's part; the truth of the matter is that he owed his life and

property to Guacanagarí, who, out of the goodness of his heart, helped him when he lost his ship. His ignorance regarding their customs and beliefs was astounding and therefore his (negative) opinions of them not to be trusted. God may have permitted the Spaniards to take possession of the Indies, but he did not sanction the way they went about it. He will punish Spain, rendering it the poorest of nations, for having enriched itself unjustly through the exploitation and abuse of the Indians. In fact, the Christian way of doing business was mercilessly to beat and whip the Indians into doing their work for them.

This reading strategy is no doubt self-serving, since Las Casas's authority is the direct beneficiary of the undermining of Columbus's. But it is more than that. It is consistent with the position Las Casas championed in all his written work and political advocacy: the negotiation for the Indians of a definitive and unassailable place at the center of the human community.[25] The ideological demarginalization Las Casas advocated for the Indians is mirrored in the interpretative strategy he applied to the Columbian texts, through a commentary that invades the primary text and ultimately transforms it. For Las Casas, writing in the margins of Columbus was a choice with profound ideological consequences. In the marginal text is Las Casas's reading of Columbus, an interpretation that becomes a creative act, fundamentally altering for future readers the text as it had existed.

III

Todo en este capítulo contenido lo es a la letra, con algunas palabras añadidas mías.

(Everything in this chapter is [written] word for word, with a few of my own words added.)
Las Casas, Historia de las Indias

Columbus's interpretation, as voiced in the "Relación," of the paradisiacal nature of the Indies becomes Las Casas's dominant theme in the *Historia*. He develops this topic by alternating between Columbus's testimony and his own experience, usually expressed in the form of commentary confirming an observation first made by the Admiral:

Dice [el Almirante] que era cosa de maravilla ver aquellos valles y los ríos y buenas aguas y las tierras para pan, para ganado de toda suerte de que [los indios] no tienen alguno, para huertas y para todas las cosas del mundo que el hombre sepa pedir.

(*Historia*, 184)

The Admiral says that it was a thing of wonder to see those valleys and rivers and good waters and lands for bread, for livestock of all sorts of which [the Indians] have none, for orchards and for all things in this world that man can ask for.

In confirming Columbus's observations by citing his own, Las Casas makes explicit and even intensifies the paradisiacal allusions in the Columbian text:

Todas estas son sus palabras y en todo dice gran verdad. Y puesto que por todas partes esta isla es un Paraíso terrenal, pero por esta de la Tortuga es cosa no creíble la hermosura suya, junta a la cual yo viví algunos años."

(184)

All these are his words and he speaks great truth in all he says. Because this island is everywhere a Terrestrial Paradise, but as for the one known as Tortuga, next to which I lived for some years, its beauty is unbelievable.

A few lines earlier, when the edenic quality of the island seems undermined by Columbus's offhand remark that it was quite cold, Las Casas immediately interjects a correction, "De ser felicísima dice bien, pero la frialdad no la tiene, sino frescor muy sin pena" (In saying that it is a most happy island he speaks correctly, but it is not cold, but rather refreshing without any discomfort). He then adds another explanation—that the wind and rain coupled with being at sea must have made it seem cold to the Admiral. When one checks his source for corroboration, however, one finds no mention in the text of rain during the days in question. Such a silent modification of the source suggests that Las Casas had as much or more at stake than did Columbus in maintaining the edenic image of the Indies.

Following his practice in the *Diario*, Las Casas usually transcribes verbatim in the *Historia* the idealizing passages, using the first-person singular. The marginal notes are frequently incorporated and expanded in the narrative itself or are carried over into the mar-

gins of the new text. Of the two practices, the former is most re-
vealing of Las Casas's tendency to turn the critical reading strategy
he employed in editing the *Diario* and "Relación," recorded in its
margins, into a critical rewriting of the history of the Discovery in
the *Historia*.

The entry for 16 December (which includes Columbus's lyrical
descriptions, the meeting with the *cacique*, and the prospects for
forced labor) is paraphrased or quoted integrally in the history. The
annotations, however, undergo various important transformations.
Three of the notes (marked by the abbreviation "nõ") remain in the
margin of the new text. But they become summary phrases that explicitly identify the specific aspects of the Columbian passages that
caught Las Casas's eye—the gentleness and generosity of the Indians, as well as their belief that the Christians had come from
heaven. Thus in the *Historia* one can verify what the *Diario* could
not show with any real precision: exactly which aspect of the main
text Las Casas intended to emphasize. In the passage describing the
edenic quality of the country, Las Casas's annotation loses the marginal indicator it had in the *Diario*, and the main text, which had
been paraphrased in the *Diario*, is expressed as a first-person quotation. Whether Las Casas recreated the "quote" from the paraphrase or still had access to his original source is unclear. Two other
notes in the *Diario*, one flagging a passage on indigenous agricul-
ture and breadmaking, the other a passage in which Columbus tells
the Indians about the greatness of his sovereigns, are not reproduced anywhere in the *Historia*.

Far more interesting, however, is the fate of the two critical annotations Las Casas made in the *Diario* entry for 16 December. Both
question the soundness of statements made by Columbus. The first
refers to a passage in which one of the Indian interpreters accompanying the Admiral explains to a *cacique* that the Spaniards came
from heaven and that they are seeking gold. Las Casas's marginal
comment in the *Diario* is in Latin, "satis improportionabiliter hec se
habent" (*Colección*, 110). In the *Historia* the comment is amplified
and translated into Spanish, and Las Casas removes it from the margin into the main text, where it appears in parentheses: "(harto im-
proporcionable cosa es venir del cielo y andar en busca de oro)"—
(*Historia*, 184; it is quite an incommensurate thing to come from
heaven and to go in search of gold). The new placement of the ex-

panded comment targets exactly what Las Casas found objection-
able—the mixing of gold and souls in the mission's objectives, as
stated by Columbus.

The closing lines of the entry are also annotated in the *Diario*,
with a reproachful comment on Columbus's observations regarding
the Indians' martial naiveté and suitability for forced labor ("algo
más parece aquí e[s]tenderse el Almirante de lo que devría"; the Admiral seems to go farther here than he should). In the *Historia* this
criticism is expanded and integrated into the main text to become a
condemnation of the *encomienda* and other abuses of the conquest.
Moreover, Las Casas holds Columbus responsible for having initiated the abuse through his misguided words:

> Dice aquí el Almirante: "Crean Vuestras Altezas . . . que esta isla y
> todas las otras son así suyas como Castilla, que aquí no falta salvo
> asiento y mandarles hacer lo que quisieren, porque yo con esta
> gente que traigo, que no son muchos, correría todas estas islas sin
> afrenta, porque ya he visto solo tres destos marineros descendir en
> tierra, y haber multitud destos indios, y todos huir sin que les quisie-
> sen hacer mal. Ellos no tienen armas, y son todos desnudos y de
> ningún ingenio en las armas, y muy cobardes, que mil no aguar-
> darán a tres; y así son buenos para les mandar y les hacer trabajar,
> sembrar y hacer todo lo que fuere menester, y que hagan villas, y
> se enseñen a andar vestidos y a nuestras costumbres." Estas son
> palabras formales del Almirante.
> Es aquí de notar, que la mansedumbre natural, simple, benigna
> y humilde condición de los indios, y carecer de armas, con andar
> desnudos, dió atrevimiento a los españoles a tenellos en poco, y
> ponellos en tan acerbísimos trabajos que los pusieron, y encarni-
> zarse para oprimillos y consumillos, como los consumieron.* Y
> cierto, aquí el Almirante más se extendió a hablar de lo que de-
> biera, y desto que aquí concibió y produjo por su boca, debía de to-
> mar origen el mal tractamiento que después en ellos hizo.
> *[Nota marginal] Nota: La causa por la cual tuvieron los españoles
> atrevimiento de supeditar y asolar estas gentes y esta fué la bondad
> y mansedumbre dellos.
>
> (*Historia*, 184–85)

> Here the Admiral says: "Your Highnesses must believe . . . that
> this island and all the others are as much yours as Castile, that
> there is nothing missing here save for a settlement and to order
> them to do whatever you may wish, because with the people I have
> with me, who are not many, I could overrun all this island without

resistance, because I have seen just three of these sailors land, and there being a multitude of these Indians, and all of them take flight without [the sailors] wishing to do them harm. They have no weapons, are all naked and without any skill in weaponry, and very cowardly, that a thousand will not stop three; and so they are good for ordering about and for forcing to work, to plant, and to do all that may be necessary, and to make them build towns, and to teach them to go about clothed and according to our customs." These are the formal words of the Admiral.

It should be noted here that the natural docileness, simple, benign and humble condition of the Indians, and their lack of weapons, together with their going naked, gave the Spaniards the audacity to hold them in low esteem, and put them to such harsh labor as they put them to, and to be relentless in their oppression and destruction of them, as they indeed destroyed them.* And certainly the Admiral said more here than he should have, and out of that which he conceived here and which came out of his mouth must have originated the bad treatment that he visited upon them afterwards.

*[Marginal note, in Las Casas's handwriting] Note: The reason the Spaniards dared to oppress and ravage these peoples; and that [reason] was their goodness and gentleness.

Through such fusions of the primary text and marginal commentary from his edition of the *Diario* and "Relación," Las Casas creates a new text in the *Historia*, a critical version of the history of Spain in the Indies. The discursive strategies mirror the ideological commitment the *Historia* promotes, as the once marginal comments on Indian virtue and Spanish bad faith are now firmly established at the center of the text. The purpose of Las Casas's historiographical method of transcription and commentary is not so much the accurate, objective representation of the events of the Discovery, as the orchestration of the prelude to an indictment of Spanish abuses and a revindication of the Indians in the context of a political campaign for reforms in colonial institutions and practices.[26] Dangerous words lead to reprehensible actions, he suggests in the final phrase of the passage. Through his critique of Columbus's words, he hoped to reform the text of history and, especially, to effect a change in the present and future course of events.

Earlier, we looked at Las Casas's comments in the *Diario* condemning Columbus's taking of Indians against their will. In the *Historia* two marginal comments accentuate these reprehensible actions: the seizing of five Indians who had approached the ship to trade on 12 November and the subsequent apprehension of seven women and their children to pacify the captives on board. The reconstitution of these passages in the *Historia* shows how Las Casas's critical reading of Columbus's words becomes a critique of historical action as it passes from the edition to the history. The passage is highlighted in the margins by comments that read "Nota unmalhecho del Almirante" (Note a bad deed of the Admiral's) and "Nota otro caso más feo" (Note another even uglier case). The entire passage, mostly paraphrased from the *Diario*, is framed between two first-person quotes concerning the innate goodness of the Indians, annotated approvingly in the margins. After laying out the particulars of the case, Las Casas comments:

> Cosa, cierto, que antes debiera padecer cualquier trabajo y peligro que hacerla, porque, en la verdad, no fué otra cosa sino violar tácita o interpretativamente las reglas del derecho natural y derecho de las gentes, que dictan y tienen que al que simple y confiadamente viene a contratar con otros, mayormente habiéndose ya confiado los unos de los otros y tratado amigablemente, lo dejen tornarse a su casa, sin daño de su persona ni de sus bienes, libre y desembargadamente. Agravia este hecho, haberlos rescebido en su tierra y en sus casas con tantas cerimonias y regocijos, adorándolos como a cosas divinas venidas del cielo, según ha parecido. ¿Qué sintiera el Almirante si a los dos cristianos que envió la tierra dentro, por fuerza los detuvieran?
>
> (*Historia*, 163)

> [It was] an action that [the Admiral] should have avoided at all costs, suffering whatever labor and danger [might have been necessary] rather than carrying it out, because, in truth, it was nothing other than a tacit or interpretative violation of precepts of natural law and the law of nations, which dictate that the person who comes simply and trustingly to trade with others, especially when confidence has already been established as a result of previous friendly contact, should be allowed to return to his home, without damage to his person or belongings, freely and unhindered. This deed is aggravated by the fact that the Indians received them in their lands and homes with so many ceremonies and jubilation, adoring them as if they were divine things coming from heaven, as already stated. How would the Admiral have felt if the two Christians he sent inland had been detained by force?

Las Casas goes on to comment that the Indians would have had just cause to wage war against the Spaniards for this violation of their natural rights and that, in any case, it put the Christians in a very bad light. For no matter what good end Columbus hoped to achieve, a bad deed, no matter how little or how much good might come from it, is never justifiable.

Las Casas then attacks Columbus for having taken the women and their children in hopes that their presence would placate the male captives. This action, he argues, only multiplied the earlier sin of seizing the men:

> Gentil excusa ha dado para colocar o justificar obra tan nefaria. Pudiérasele preguntar, ¿que si fué pecado y que tan grave, quitar o hurtar o robar con violencia las mujeres que tenían sus proprios maridos, pues el matrimonio es de derecho natural? . . . Item ¿Quién había de dar a Dios cuenta de los pecados de adulterio que cometieron los indios que llevó consigo, a quien dió por mujeres aquellas mujeres, y si quizá se añidió alguno de incesto, que es mayor que el adulterio, si por caso eran muy propincuos parientes? ¿Y los que cometerían también los maridos de aquéllas, casándose no pudiendo, prohibiéndolo la ley natural, con otras mujeres?
>
> (*Historia*, 164)

> He has given a genteel excuse to justify such a nefarious deed. One could ask of him if it wasn't a sin, and a very grave one indeed, to take, or steal, or rob with violence those women who had their own husbands, since matrimony is a natural right. . . . Likewise, who would be accountable before God for the sins of adultery committed by the Indians he took with him to whom he gave those women, or perhaps even the additional sin of incest, which is worse than adultery, if they happened to be closely related? And what about the sins of adultery committed by the husbands of those women, marrying other women without being able to, it being prohibited by natural law?

The link between reprehensible words, misdeeds, and their ever more nefarious consequences is established by Las Casas in the litany of sins that might hypothetically have been committed by the captives, and for which he holds the Admiral ultimately responsible. Also noteworthy is the excision from this passage, otherwise a close paraphrase of the *Diario*, of the offensive term *cabezas* (heads, as of livestock), which Columbus used to refer to the women captives (Varela, 56). It would seem that some of the Admiral's words were so offensive to Las Casas that his criticism of them could take no form other than tacit suppression.

Las Casas's condemnation of Columbus's words and conduct is projected into the future by the prophetic dimension of the *Historia*'s historical discourse. After all, the past itself cannot be rectified, only its interpretation and, thereby, actions in the future. In Las Casas's hands the Admiral becomes a symbol of the behavior of an entire nation, and the critique of his deeds an example for future generations. From this perspective, book 1 of the *Historia* appears not so much the biography of an individual as the reconstitution of an exemplary life to serve as an admonishment for others. The history closes with a contemplation of Columbus's fate: unjustly imprisoned and ultimately impoverished. But Las Casas is quick to point out in the closing chapter of book 1 that neither the Crown nor Bobadilla, the chief justice, was responsible for the Admiral's fate. Ultimately it was God's will: "determinó de le privar, como al cabo le privó, de todo su estado, no sólo en su persona, pero también en sus herederos y sucesores, como parecerá adelante (*Historia*, 489; [God] decided to deprive him, as he did deprive him, of all his estate, not only that pertaining to his own person, but also his heirs and successors, as will be seen ahead).

Las Casas knew the controversy his *Historia* would provoke, and in 1559 he forbade publication of the *Historia* until at least forty years after his death. Only in that way, he must have surmised, could his text reach posterity, his intended audience, free of the mediation and manipulation of his contemporaries. In his testament, dated 17 March 1564, Las Casas reaffirmed his intentions in having written the history to serve as an example and lesson for future generations: "Porque si Dios determinare destruir a España, se vea es por las destrucciones que habemos hecho en las Indias y parezca la razón de su justicia" (Because if God should decide to destroy Spain, it may be seen that it is because of the destruction we have wrought upon the Indies and the reason for his justice be made evident).[27]

In sum, Las Casas's marginal commentary does not constitute an accident suffered by the Columbian texts in the long history of their transmission. Rather, providing the commentary is the very reason that Las Casas initially undertook his editions of Columbus's writings. From the margins we come to understand how Las Casas read, and altered, the Columbian texts as well as the role those texts played in Las Casas's own version of the history of the Discovery.

Today, it is in most cases difficult, if not impossible, to separate Columbus's voice from that of his editor. Las Casas reconstituted and transformed his sources in such a way as to make his own text their indispensable supplement, placing his own marginal word at the center of the discourse on the Discovery. And yet, time and again, modern editors have silently censored or dismembered the marginal text to the point of illegibility in order to satisfy the need we have to believe that we possess a pristine text of Columbus's enterprise in his own words.

Las Casas's marginal writing does not oblige us to accept the version of the Discovery it promotes. It does, however, prevent us from reading Columbus unquestioningly. To read in the margins of Columbus requires that we assume a critical posture with respect to the text before us. Suppressing the marginal commentary cannot eradicate Las Casas's pen from the text. Such excisions serve only to obscure the most explicit aspect of a mediation that permeates the texts as they have been transmitted to us, and the only hard evidence we have to assess its effect on our readings. More importantly, to lose the editorial apparatus is to forfeit its critical intelligence. And, in so doing, we risk forgetting that the image of the Discovery that has endured in Western culture is not simply the product of an original, unmediated, monological word, but of a critical reading, a supplemental writing that questions, criticizes, corrects, protests, and finally condemns.

Voyage to Paradise

en passando de allí al Poniente, ya van los navíos alçándose
hazia el cielo suavemente, y entonces se goza de más suave
temperancia.

for in passing to the West, the ships go rising gently toward
the heavens, and then a milder climate is enjoyed.

Columbus, "Relación
del tercer viaje"

The fact that the historical event commonly referred to as the Discovery of America was necessarily conceived and carried out in the
form of a voyage has been studied extensively by scholars of maritime history and sailing enthusiasts alike. Among the aspects of the
Columbian enterprise that continue to figure prominently in the
discussions stimulated by the Quincentenary are Columbus's biography, his navigational abilities, the nature of the fleets and
crews, the reconstruction of the actual route, and the identification
of the precise landfall. It has been standard practice to plumb the
Columbian accounts for evidence to recreate the historical circumstances of the navigation. Yet there has been surprisingly little interest in the character of the texts themselves as accounts of travel.[1]

Though it seems too obvious to state, many of the Columbian
texts are travel literature. Individually and collectively, the accounts
of the voyages tell the Discovery as the story of a journey; that is,
they articulate the historical event of the navigation within the rhetorical bounds of the literature of travel available in Columbus's culture.

To consider the Discovery as a story in no way detracts from its
gravity as a historical event.[2] Such an approach does, however, shift
the focus from the events themselves to the way they are told, in
order to consider not the factual truth or accuracy of the accounting,
but the way the events are rendered meaningful to their intended
audience, in this case, the Spanish Crown. The importance of the
telling was recognized by Columbus himself in the so-called prologue to the *Diario* of the first voyage, where he noted that, as a discoverer, his obligation to the Catholic Monarchs was twofold: to

successfully conduct the voyage and to write about it, to tell its story (Dunn & Kelley, 19–21). By viewing the Discovery as the story of a kind of journey and by attending to the particular ways in which Columbus told that story, we can better understand how Columbus hoped his readers would assess the significance of his enterprise.

JOURNEYS

In *The Road to Botany Bay*, a recent book on the accounts of the exploration and settlement of Australia, Paul Carter proposes that those who wrote about their experiences did not record the journey so much as construct a figurative geography in which those historical actions would make sense. His study demonstrates how an unmarked geographical space comes into being as an object of knowledge through the onomastics of exploration as a metaphorical activity, or the "story" contained in the names of places:

> This was the justification of the explorer's record that, whether he found anything or not (whether he found, as it were, objects that already had names), his account of his route would serve to bring the country into historical being; it was a metaphorical equivalent, figuratively bringing distant things into relation with each other. In this sense, travelling was not primarily a physical activity: it was an epistemological strategy, a mode of knowing.[3]

While Carter's particular focus is on toponymy, the basic argument that names function in these texts as spatial metaphors that render the journey meaningful is also pertinent to other aspects of voyage narratives. Accounts of travel are, at heart, rhetorical vehicles for a hermeneutics of space, for an interpretive geo-graphy (writing the land) defining the relationship between the newly found country and the old.[4]

It is worth remembering that when Columbus set sail from Palos on 3 August 1492 he anticipated a voyage through uncharted waters in search of lands whose coastlines were etched in speculation, myth, legend, prophecy, and faith as much as in the solid lines of the mapmaker's pen. In recounting why the Admiral *believed* he could discover the Indies ("a creer que podía descubrir las Indias"), Ferdinand Columbus emphasized the speculative character of his father's enterprise, underscoring the important role that Columbus's own interpretations, informed by popular nautical lore and his readings of classical, Arabic, and Christian geographies, played in shaping and sustaining this belief (*Vida*, 42). Certainly one of Columbus's most pressing tasks was to place whatever lands he encountered in the context of the geographical notions of his time, by charting the course sailed and mapping whatever territory was found. Yet the Discovery as a geographical endeavor had an important interpretive dimension as well as an empirical one; it was defined by both ideological and practical epistemological objectives. Along with providing the maps and charts corresponding to a functional geography that explained how to get "there" and back, Columbus also had to respond to the demands of a cultural geography, predominantly hermeneutical in character, by offering an interpretation of the significance of the voyage. The texts narrating the Discovery can be read as verbal maps, as it were, that delineate the coastlines figuratively, supplementing and interpreting the charts and logs that traced the navigation and marked its spaces.

This textual figuration, at once a metaphor of the map and a metaphorical mapping, gave meaning to the geographical space traveled and the journey through which that space was experienced. Through the telling of the voyage, Columbus described a space and communicated the experience of it, thus defining a way of understanding it, of imagining it, of relating to it. In renaming the island the Indians called Guanahaní as San Salvador (island of the Holy Savior), Columbus made both an act of personal piety and an interpretation of the significance of the Atlantic crossing. The journey became an *imitatio Christi*, carried out not only in the name of Christ but in the same evangelical manner of traveling undertaken by the Savior himself. It was a pious offering to Christ and the figurative first step in a millenarian journey to carry the Word beyond the borders of Christendom to the farthest pagan realms. In the story of the voyage, the arrival at San Salvador becomes a synecdoche for the journey as an apostolic experience of space as it was described in the Scriptures. Christoferens, the name with which Columbus signed his writings from 1501 on, is the emblem of a journey undertaken not just on behalf of Christ but "in the manner of Christ."[5]

Columbus's writings of discovery did not appear in a vacuum, nor did they lack antecedents. The great geographical theories of Aristotle, Ptolemy, Marinus of Tyre, Strabo, Pliny, and others informed his work, to be sure. But the primary models were the more humble geographies of pilgrims, merchants, explorers, and missionaries, texts that comprised the bulk of popular medieval travel writing.[6] Each of these types of travel had unique modalities for articulating the journey and its goals. I want to consider Columbus's writings in relation to two of them, exploration and pilgrimage.

Michel Butor considers pilgrimage and exploration to be antithetical types of journeys in his typology of travel, or "iterology," as he calls it.[7] Although both types are round-trip journeys, Butor explains, pilgrims know exactly where they are going, while explorers set out for an unknown destination. There is another important difference between these two types of journeys, however. Both are voyages of "discovery," but in distinct senses of the term. In an exploration the destination is initially an enigma. It must be invented or created by the explorer-writer who brings it into cultural existence as an object of knowledge. Thus, as Butor notes, the tendency of exploration writings to repeat the Adamic gesture, untiringly (re)naming each identifiable site, practicing an onomastic cartography where coastlines are literally outlined by strings of names.[8] Pilgrimage destinations, on the other hand, are of necessity already named and therefore significant prior to the inception of the journey. The pilgrim-writer's task is not to describe new places, but to go to established sites to discover their hidden (albeit orthodox) spiritual significance. Pilgrimage, then, is essentially a hermeneutic practice.

Perhaps because modern usage favors the more pragmatic acceptation of discovery—the creation or invention of something new or the finding of something not previously thought to exist—we are inclined to think of the Columbian discovery as an exclusively empirical phenomenon.[9] The garden-variety dictionary typically designates the epistemological and spiritual acceptations of the term— "the revelation or disclosure of something hidden" and the related connotations of "becoming acquainted with" or "gaining understanding of"—as archaic definitions. Yet these senses of the term are at least as relevant to the Columbian notion of discovery as the empiricism prevalent in modern usage and conception. Pilgrimage and exploration are antithetical types of journeys, yet what distinguishes them is not so much the physical aspect of the actual journeys as the ways of thinking and writing about them. Pilgrimage

and exploration are distinct discursive modalities for the articulation of different ways of experiencing exotic spaces and interpreting
their significance. Indeed, one can also think of pilgrimage and exploration as ways of relating disparate spaces, of defining the relationship between the humdrum "here" and the exotic "there."

Broadly defined, pilgrimage is a spiritual journey whose purpose
is the personal discovery of the sacred significance of space. Two
other important subgenres are informed by pilgrimage's ideology
of travel as sacred quest, even as they exhibit their own unique characteristics, the crusade and the mission. Unlike pilgrimage proper,
both the crusade and the mission introduce an Other into the grammar of the journey, establishing relationships of persuasion or coer-
cion (i.e., evangelization) between the subject and the object of the
discovery. The crusade, then, can be seen as the spiritual equivalent
of military conquest insofar as both involve territorial expansion
through the use of force. The mission, on the other hand, is the spiritual counterpart of political conquest, the assimilation of commu-
nities or social spaces. Both these subgenres of travel as spiritual
quest inform Columbus's discourse of discovery in important ways,
as we shall see.

Defining the relationship between the long-known world and
the newly discovered one is precisely the purpose of Columbus's
discourse of discovery. The Columbian texts thus constitute metaphorical verbal maps establishing relations among distant and disparate places in order to create a coherent geo-graphical image. As
models for the articulation of particular types of journeys, pilgrimage and exploration provided Columbus with ways of conceiving
and representing the experience of space, ways of giving shape and
significance to the places he found.

CHRONOTOPES

Journeys may be thought of as geoepistemographical phenomena;
that is, as stories about knowing or experiencing space. To talk
about a journey as the subjective experience of space, or the story
about that experience, demands a broader definition of geography
than is customary. We must think of geography as describing not
just a physical space, but a spatiotemporal field where the subjective cognitive process of the traveler's individual consciousness ap-

prehends space in and through time. From the perspective of the traveler's experience, geography can be viewed as a spatiotemporal entity in which time and space are intrinsically related. Mikhail Bakhtin's term *chronotope* (borrowed from relativity theory and adapted for literary analysis) is a useful shorthand for the notion, fundamental to my argument, that "time-space," not space or time alone, determines meaning in the journey of discovery, that the meaning of a journey arises out of the relationship the narration of events establishes between the spatial and temporal aspects of the journey.[10]

What ultimately defines pilgrimage and exploration as distinct types of journeys, then, is not simply the nature of the destination as known or unknown, but the way in which each type conceptualizes the traveler's experience of spatiotemporal geography. The articulation of the character of the destination is a product of the way these genres construct the traveler's movement through time and space. As an epistemological activity, discovery "takes place," but also "makes place."[11] Although space takes shape through the traveler's experience of the journey, the spatiotemporal condition of the destination exists, already defined, at the journey's inception. It may change as a result of the experience or simply be confirmed by it, but an initial spatiotemporal paradigm is always present at the beginning of the journey, to set the traveler in motion. Moreover, a variety of chronotopes may appear throughout a given travel account, defining the journey experience in different ways at particular points in the story. Pilgrimage and exploration accounts are not necessarily monochronotopic, although specific types of spatiotemporal configurations predominate in their generic definitions.

Just as space can be of different kinds in travel accounts (e.g., known or unknown, sacred or secular), so can time be variously characterized. The nature of time is quite distinct in each of the genres at issue here. Yet in the spatiotemporal field of the chronotope, time-space is a homology. The activity of travel and the space traversed are defined reciprocally and are ideologically complementary. Thus, the story may be a hybrid comprised of several chronotopes, but each spatiotemporal event will be coherent in itself. The generic character of a given journey, then, is not necessarily determined by its spatiotemporal integrity or even the numerical predominance of a particular type of chronotope, but by the narrative grammar that dictates the hierarchical relations among the various chronotopes in the story. The following observations on the characteristics of pilgrimage and exploration as genres of travel, therefore, may not apply exactly in specific accounts.

Both pilgrimage and exploration deal with the extraordinary. In both modes the traveler embarks on a journey outside his or her quotidian world. Indeed, stories about exploration are a modality of the discourse of adventure, where the unexpected, the dangerous, the marvelous, and the unknown predominate. What determines the extraordinariness of exploration is the character of the space traversed: unknown and unmastered, the space dictates a challenge to the traveler and motivates the writing of the story of how that challenge was met. The encounter with space informs the nature of time, setting its significant intervals and contours, the pauses and movements of the journey. Pilgrimage, on the other hand, is temporally extraordinary: the places are known, but the experience of space is miraculous. Motivated by hope, remorse, conviction, or illumination, the pilgrim embarks on a voyage of spiritual purification whose ultimate goal is salvation. It is not so much the typical miraculous interventions by saints or deities (e.g., the supernatural calming of a terrible storm at sea so that the journey may be completed safely) that characterize the time of pilgrimage. The unearthly character of this time is in fact a constant rather than momentary irruption in the pilgrimage experience. The spiritual journey is carried out in history and eternity simultaneously; not only because the experience takes place within a providentialist temporal scheme in which earthly and sacred history are considered parts of the same continuum, but especially because every natural event refers to and becomes significant in the afterlife of eternity.

As Jacques Le Goff has noted in his study *Medieval Civilization*, Heaven and Earth were treated as a spatial continuity in the Middle Ages. A complementary coherence and uniformity is found in the relation between sacred and secular temporality in chronotopes informed by medieval Christian ideology. Le Goff adds that medieval chronology was not the ordering and dividing of a period of time into equal, exactly measurable units—what we would regard as objective or scientific time. Medieval chronology was made up of significant moments, temporal paradigms, rather than isochronal segments of time. These moments acquire their significance not through syntactical (chronological) relations with other moments in the sequence but by their paradigmatic relations with ideologically equivalent moments in the larger continuum of the history of salvation to which they ultimately refer. Thus in the pilgrimage accounts, the time-space of the journey can be read as a figure of sacred history: the pilgrim travels to Jerusalem in search of spiritual purification, just as the soul exiled on earth is a perpetual pilgrim on the road to the Heavenly Jerusalem (Paradise) and salvation.

Journeys of exploration, on the other hand, are described by a chronotope whose ideology of time-space is secular and pragmatic. Medieval accounts of exploratory travel are primarily concerned with the marking of distances, duration, direction, speed, and so on. They are also usually associated with the practical goals of commercial and political expansion. Such texts almost always constitute time and space literally and quantitatively rather than figuratively and paradigmatically. Despite the imprecision of the available measuring instruments, exploration texts exhibit a functional and pragmatic attitude toward time and space, quite unlike the transcendentalism of the genres of spiritual travel.[12] The chronotope of exploration responds to the practical materialism of the mercantilistic ideology that informs the journey. The promise of spiritual gain that defines the economy of pilgrimage finds its inverted reflection in the promise of new markets and profits that defines the economy of exploration.

CARTOGRAPHIES OF DISCOVERY

The etymological roots of *geography* suggest that this was a science born of writing—a way of knowing that was tied in the most intimate way to scriptural activity. Today, we are accustomed to thinking of geography as a discourse whose primary vehicle of expression is not the sentence but the figural language of maps. Yet cartography, from its origins in Antiquity through the Middle Ages and into the sixteenth century, has been ever an accessory to, and product of, geographical writing. Perhaps because their technical imprecision precluded them from "speaking for themselves," early maps typically served as visual images of the verbal descriptions of the world contained in books like Pierre d'Ailly's *Ymago Mundi* (1480 or 1483), a work Columbus owned and annotated prolifically.[13] Cartography, then, was not an independent and autonomous form of geographical discourse but an illustrative art, supplemental to geographical writing. With the rise of Christianity and its dogmatic geography, which privileged the authority of Sacred Scripture over empirical observation, European cartography became primarily a hermeneutical practice devoted to the visual interpretation of the spiritual significance of the physical world as defined by Christian Scripture.

A brief consideration of the cartographic consequences of the rise of Christian geography is instructive on this point. Ptolemaic maps organized the world on a grid. Trapezoidal in shape, these maps have no focal points and are centered only to allow the *oikoumene*, the "known world," to be fully spread out within the confines of the grid. Samuel Edgerton puts it this way:

> No part of Ptolemy's map was emphasized as having ideological significance. It was completely ecumenical and nonmystical. Whereas Ptolemy assumed the central meridian to pass through Syene, in later versions it was moved slightly eastward, though the map center itself remained on the latitude of the Tropic of Cancer, which ran through Syene. One might even say that, aesthetically, Ptolemy's design was "positional attenuating," since it deemphasizes the center and stresses instead the spreading of the grid in all directions from the perimeter.[14]

The Ptolemaic world map reproduced here (Figure 2) is from a Latin edition of Ptolemy's *Geographia* (Rome, 1472). Columbus studied and annotated the 1478 edition of the work. The *Geographia* was not known in Europe until the 1470s, and although it exerted a profound influence on the geographical thought of the waning Middle Ages, Columbus's attitude toward it was somewhat critical.[15]

Christian geography, on the other hand, placed Jerusalem at the center of the world, reflecting its ideological privilege as Center of the Faith. The earliest Christian maps often did little more than interpret figurally and schematically the teachings of the Church, rendering Jerusalem as *umbilicus regionis totius* surrounded by Asia, Europe, and Africa, all within a circle or *rota*. These "wheel" maps, also known as the T-O *mappaemundi* (Figure 3), situated the East, thought to be the location of the Terrestrial Paradise, at the upper

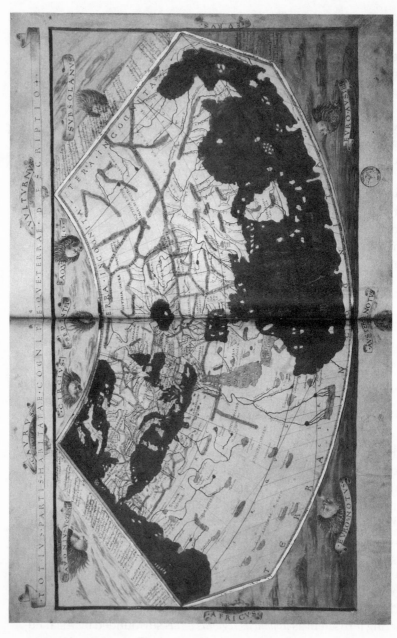

Figure 2. Claudius Ptolemy, world map. From the *Geographia* (Rome, 1472). Courtesy of the American Geographical Society Collection, Milwaukee, Wisconsin.

Figure 3.   Isidore of Seville, T-O *mappamundi*, 1472. Courtesy of the Newberry Library, Chicago.

extremity, instead of the North. The T, which crossed at Jerusalem, represented the rivers and seas separating the three known continents. The image was oriented vertically, with its ideological meridian connecting the center at Jerusalem with the Earthly Paradise at the apex of the map. A more elaborate variation of the T-O model is the Ebstorf map (c. 1240) which shows Jerusalem at the center, highlighted by the image of Christ, a patch of gold leaf, and the Terrestrial Paradise at the top (Figure 4). A unique feature of this map is the inscription of Jesus' head, hands, and feet at the four cardinal points. The symbolism is clear: the world is Christ's crucified body, Jerusalem his navel, and the limits of the world are bounded and defined by his reach. As David Woodward has noted, the hermeneutical function of the *mappaemundi* appears to have grown increasingly important and complex.[16] Once simple book illustrations, the maps were, by the fifteenth and sixteenth centuries, placed on the first or second page of a codex, perhaps reflecting the heightened role cartography played in giving the reader an ideological

Figure 4.   Ebstorf *mappamundi*, c. 1240. Courtesy of the William L. Clements Library, University of Michigan.

preview of the written text. In any case, the relationship between text and map was an intimate one: the text was the source relied on for the verbal directions used to create the map, and the map in turn functioned as a figure of the text.

In this respect *mappaemundi* were not significantly different from the other medieval cartographic genre, the portolan chart, a term derived from *portolano*, the Italian word for the written sailing directions. The *portolanos* are generally considered to be the precursors of the late-fifteenth- and sixteenth-century *roteiros* (rutters).[17]

The portolan charts were companion pieces to the written directions, which recorded coastal features, ports, islands, winds, currents, distances, and the like, based on practical knowledge obtained through actual travel experience. Like the *mappaemundi*, the portolan charts were intimately related to geographical writing, and each cartographic genre's pictorial mode of representing geographical objects illuminates the modalities of textual geographies and the travel genres that are informed by them.

Most scholars today assume that written directions guided the drawing of maps. The complementary relation between writing and cartography was underscored by Columbus when he proudly announced to the Crown that he would deliver text and maps representing and confirming his discoveries. He makes his most explicit statement on the twin aspects of the geographer's task in the "Relación del tercer viaje," when he refers to the authorities he consulted in the formulation of his geographical theories as "aquellos qu'escribieron e situaron el mundo" (Varela, 203; those who wrote about and situated the world). To understand the cartographic tradition that informed Columbian geography, we must take a few moments to examine the two cartographic genres—the *mappaemundi* and the portolan chart—and their ideological and formal differences.

Tony Campbell identifies the main characteristics of portolan cartography as spatial precision, realism, and historical accuracy.[18] The oldest surviving charts, attributable to Genoese mapmakers of the thirteenth century, already demonstrate the desacralized materialistic conception of space that typifies the genre. Both the historical moment in which these charts proliferated (late 1200s to the early 1500s) and their character suggest that they were drawn to satisfy the practical needs of sailors and merchants involved in the increasingly intensive trading activity along the Atlantic coasts of Europe, northwestern Africa, and the Mediterranean and Black seas. They are composed of a single bold and unbroken line which traces the coastal features with such precision that even the oldest charts very closely approximate the actual outlines of the Mediterranean and Black seas. The extant charts are striking in the clarity and exquisiteness with which they depict their intricate coastal geographies. Strings of place-names also helped define toponymically the political and economic contours of the geography. Political jurisdiction and economic importance were highlighted through changes in the color of ink and the use of flags. In this way, portolan cartography was responsive to historical change as well as to the expansion of hydrographic knowledge. Its range continually widened to accommodate new discoveries and revised content as fresh information became available; in this way, the charts acknowledged time as a dimension in the experience of geographical space.

Although portolan charts vary considerably in the degree of decorative detail they contain, they consistently exhibit an austere realism with respect to their primary objective, the depiction of coastal geography. Decoration typically was limited to internal or marginal areas of the map that contain little geographical information. Decorative elements seem to function simply as embellishment or highlighting, unlike the *mappaemundi*, where decoration was usually at the behest of an intense geographical symbolism.

The portolan cartographers also depicted imaginary or legendary islands in the Atlantic with the same straightforwardness. Such fabulous names as Legname, Corvi Marini, San Zorzi, St. Brendan's Isles, Brazil, and so forth often appear in the vicinity of known islands like the Canaries and the Azores. Some early rutters even give distances to some of these mythic islands, underscoring the literal way in which these maps were interpreted. An especially striking example of this imaginary insular geography is found on the Pizzigano Chart of 1424 (Figure 5). Starkly functional in appearance and among the least ornamental of portolan charts, the document's portable size and shape, even the way it was rolled for storage, suggest that it was intended for regular practical use, not for display. The Pizzigano Chart was almost certainly created for use in Atlantic navigation, since only those coasts and the westernmost portion of the Mediterranean are represented. Nevertheless, it prominently situates several fantastic islands in the western Atlantic (Antilla, Satanazes, Brazil, Ymana, etc.) in a matter-of-fact fashion difficult to distinguish from that used to depict the real insular geography.

The Canepa Chart of 1489 (Figure 6), as geographically complete and sophisticated as any of its contemporaries, also depicts a legendary insular geography in the Atlantic without distinguishing it from the known islands. According to Ferdinand Columbus, it was precisely the belief in the existence of such islands that reassured his father about the feasibility of the long transoceanic passage (*Vida*, 51). It is very probable that Columbus employed just such a chart to plan his navigation and illustrate his proposal at court. In fact, the only cartographic drawing we have from his hand, of the

Figure 5. Zuane Pizzigano, portolan chart, 1424. Courtesy of the James Ford Bell Library, University of Minnesota.

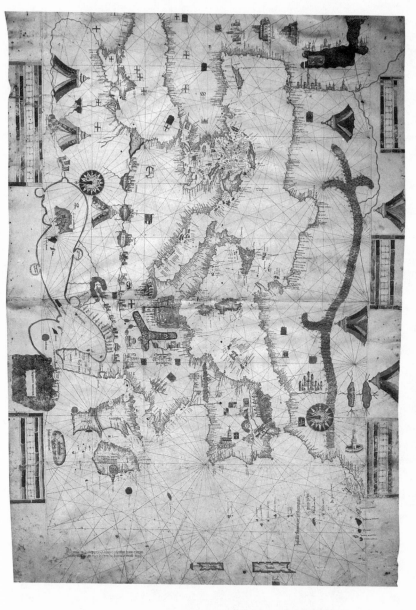

Figure 6. Albino de Canepa, portolan chart, 1489. Courtesy of the James Ford Bell Library, University of Minnesota

northwest coast of Española (Haiti), appears to be a preliminary sketch for an eventual chart and is informed by portolan functionalism, realism, and accuracy.[19] A detailed description of a map of the discoveries composed for the Crown by Columbus has survived in a *carta-relación* of the second voyage, dated January 1494:

> Verán Vuestras Altezas la tierra d'España y Africa y, en frente dellas, todas las yslas halladas y descubiertas este viaje y el otro; las rraias que ban en largo amuestran la ystançia de oriente a Oçidente, las otras questán de través amuestran la ystançia de setentrión en ahustro. Los espaçios de cada rraia significan un grado, que e contado çinqueta y seis millas y dos terçios que rresponden destas nuestras leguas de la mar, catorze leguas e un sesto; y ansí pueden contar de oçidente a oriente como de setentrión en ahustro el dicho número de leguas. . . . E para que podrán ver la distançia del camino ques d'España al comienço o fin de las Yndias, y verán en quál distançia las unas tierras de las otras rresponden, berán en la dicha carta una rraia que pasa de setentrión en austro, ques vermeja, y pasa por çima de la ysla Ysavela sobrel Tín d'España, allende del qual están las tierras descubiertas el otro viaje, y las otras de agora, de acá de la rraia, se entiende; y espero en Nuestro Señor que cada año mucho abremos de acreçentar en la pintura porque descubrirá continamente.
>
> (Rumeu, 2: 451–52)

Your Highnesses will see the land of Spain and Africa and, in front of them, all of the islands found and discovered on this voyage and the other one; the lines that run lengthwise show the distance from east to west, the others that run horizontally show the distance from north to south. The spaces between each line represent one degree, which is comprised of fifty-six and two-thirds miles that correspond to fourteen and one-sixth of our sea leagues; and thus you can count from west to east, like from north to south, the said number of leagues. . . . And so that you can see the distance of the route from Spain to the beginning or end of the Indies and see the distance between particular lands, you will find on said chart a red line that runs from north to south and passes over the island of Isabela on top of Tín d'España, beyond which line are the lands discovered on the other voyage, and on this side of the line lie the other ones from [this voyage]; and I have hope in Our Lord that each year we will have to enlarge the map because he will continuously discover [new lands].

What Columbus describes was probably a portolan-style map, similar to the well-known Juan de la Cosa Map (c. 1500), oriented toward the Atlantic from the west coasts of Europe and Africa, and including all of the already-discovered insular geography in the western Ocean Sea, a region that on pre-Discovery charts had also been depicted, but only hypothetically.[20] Columbus's chart included lines of longitude and latitude, according to his description, that facilitate a more accurate assessment of distances, and a red line passing through Isabela marks the boundary between the discoveries of the first and second voyages. Just as portolan charts expanded and evolved in response to new information, so Columbus's map, he anticipates, will grow yearly when new discoveries come to light.

In contrast to the realism of the portolan genre, the cartographic discourse of the *mappaemundi* is characterized by its figurative dimension. A rubric on the Ebstorf map illuminates this aspect, underscoring the image's anagogical significance: "A map is called a figure, whence *mappamundi* is a figure of the world."[21] The body of Jesus inscribed on this map is a particularly clear example of this function: the disk containing the world, which is in turn contained by the body of Jesus, can be interpreted iconically as the Host, symbolizing the communion of all nations in the body of Christ. Whatever real geographic information these maps may contain, their primary function is hermeneutical; the representation of geographical reality is subordinated to the promotion of a particular spiritual interpretation of the world.

Mappaemundi also appear to have played an important role in the motivation of spiritual forms of travel. The Haldingham map in the Hereford Cathedral was periodically expanded by its makers, who added place-names taken from various written itineraries of religious travelers. Such a map could have served both the commemorative purpose of recording actual pilgrimages and the rhetorical one of stimulating new travelers to undertake a like journey by providing a model for emulation and planning. Whatever the purposes of such emendations, the map itself is a figure of the spiritual goals and significance of the journey. *Mappaemundi* defined a geography whose essentially figurative, schematic, ahistorical character could hardly have served the traveler's practical needs for precise directions or distances. Yet the promise of redemption they proclaimed in their metaphorical ordering of spaces—for example, situating the favored destinations of real and mystical pilgrimages (Rome, Jerusalem, and the Terrestrial Paradise) on the same ideological meridian—encouraged the traveler toward his or her destination, itself a figure of the spiritual goal. These maps, although they may appear absurdly fanciful to the modern viewer, were responsive to the purposes for which they were designed: the promotion of a Christian ideology of space and the stimulation of real and imaginary spiritual voyages which would enact that ideology through actual or imaginative experience.

Although cartography may seem the most static and atemporal of discourses, maps are nevertheless profoundly chronotopical; they represent time-space in an ideologically coherent image of the world (understood as a spatiotemporal reality, as in the phrase "the end of the world"). For example, portolan geography is so inscribed in a particular historical moment that the temporal coordinates of undated portolan charts usually can be approximated with a considerable degree of accuracy. Moreover, their historical realism and toponymic specificity mirrors the literalism of the *portolano* and the temporal exactingness of later rutters. When these maps are read in conjunction with the written record of the voyage they were intended to complement, their functional temporal character intensifies as each location on the map acquires a concrete time value in relation to every other relevant point on the trajectory. From this perspective, every location becomes a time-space coordinate of the navigation as well as a place existing at, and significant at, a specific historical moment. *Mappaemundi* are equally, although distinctively, chronotopic. In contrast to the functionalism and materialism of portolan charts, they represent a metaphysical view of time-space, a spiritual chronotope, that is defined by the spatial continuity between Earth and the Other World (Heaven or Hell) and the secular-sacred temporal continuum that is the history of salvation. Time and space are conceptualized as essentially limitless, bounded only by the figure of Christ, the measure of whose infinite and eternal reach defines the spatiotemporal contours of the Ebstorf map.

The term *mappamundi* was also used generically well into the eighteenth century to mean a verbal geography, a usage that further blurs the distinction between text and map. In implying that the geographical text is like a map, the metaphorical acceptation suggests that just as writing helped define cartographic images, so did maps influence the articulation of spatiotemporal fields in texts. From this point on, I will use the term "textual cartography" as shorthand for the notion that maps informed the chronotopes of geographical writings, just as writing informed the chronotopes of cartography, from the Middle Ages and into the modern period.[22] To put it another way, geographical texts construct time-space much in the way maps do, and in their articulation of space, journeys reflect the particular cartographies that inform them. Map and text are thus complementary and even indispensable modalities for articulating the discovery experience.

Approaching the Columbian texts from this perspective offers two important advantages. First, by conceiving the geographical image as the product of a particular type of experience, we can discuss the geographical and epistemological aspects of the Discovery as related issues. Second, this reading strategy, akin to the practice of placing maps in the opening pages of a book to guide the reader through the textual cartography beyond, matches the strategy of representation favored by Columbus in the prologue to the *Diario*:

> También, Señores Prínçipes, allende de escrevir cada noche lo qu'el día passare y el día lo que la noche navegare, tengo propósito de hazer carta nueva de navegar, en la cual situaré toda la mar e tierras del mar Occéano en sus proprios lugares, debaxo su viento, y más componer un libro y poner todo por el semejante por pintura, por latitud del equinocial y longitud del Occidente.
>
> (Varela, 17)

> Also, my Lord Princes, besides writing down each night whatever I experience during the day and each day what I sail during the night, I intend to make a new sailing chart. In it I will locate all of the sea and the lands of the Ocean Sea in their proper places under their compass bearings and, moreover, compose a book and similarly record all of the same in a drawing, by latitude from the equinoctial line and by longitude from the west.
>
> (Dunn & Kelley, 21)

Once a mapmaker by trade, Columbus took pride in his cartographic skills long after his successes as a mariner and discoverer had made him a name.[23] In a letter addressed to the Catholic Monarchs (1501) included in the *Libro de las profecías*, he boasted of his God-given abilities:

A este mi deseo fallé a Nuestro Señor muy propicio y ove d'El para
ello espíritu de inteligençia. En la marinería me fiso abondoso, de
astrología me dio lo que abastava y ansí de geometría y arismética y
engenio en el ánima y manos para debusar espera, y en ella las çib-
dades, ríos y montañas, islas y puertos, todo en su propio sitio.

(Varela, 277)

For this my purpose I found Our Lord very favorable and he gave
me the intellectual enlightenment for it. In seamanship he endowed me generously, in astrology he gave me what was necessary
and likewise in geometry and arithmetic, and the talent and hands
to draw a sphere and upon it cities, rivers and mountains, islands
and ports, all in their proper place.

That Columbus consulted maps of various kinds to plan and
carry out his navigations is obvious, but it is also quite likely, as Paolo Revelli has noted, that aboard his vessels were both portolan
charts of the eastern Atlantic and *mappaemundi* depicting the uncharted Asiatic geography of the western Ocean.[24] In any case, numerous references by Columbus to both of these cartographic
genres in the accounts of the voyages confirm that he sailed with
two very different cartographic images in mind: a portolan one,
which guided the navigation, and a hermeneutical one, which
aided him in interpreting the nature and significance of the new geography he was encountering. The two following passages concern
the same insular geography, but the first is informed by a practical
portolan cartography, the second by the spiritual paradigms of the
mappaemundi:

Este día ovo mucha calma y después ventó, y fueron su camino al
Güeste hasta la noche. Iva hablando el Almirante con Martín
Alonso Pinçón, capitán de la otra caravela Pinta, sobre una carta
que le avía enbiado tres días avía a la caravela, donde, segund pareçe, tenía pintadas el Almirante ciertas islas por aquella mar, y dezía el Martín Alonso que estavan en aquella comarca, y respondía
el Almirante que así le pareçía a él; pero puesto que no oviesen
dado con ellas lo devían de aver causado las corrientes, que
siempre avían echado los navíos al Nordeste, y que no avían andado tanto como los pilotos dezían. Y estando en esto, díxole el Almirante que le enbiase la carta dicha, y enbiada con alguna cuerda,
començo el Almirante a cartear en ella con su piloto y marineros.

(Varela, 24)

This day there was much calm and later it blew and they went on their way west until night. The Admiral began talking to Martín Alonso Pinzón, captain of the other caravel, Pinta, about a chart that he had sent to him on the caravel three days before, on which the Admiral had apparently drawn certain islands in that sea; and Martín Alonso said that they were in that region and the Admiral answered that so it seemed to him, but since they had not encountered them it must have been caused by the currents which always had driven the vessels northeast and that they had not traveled as far as the pilots said. And at this point the Admiral said to send the said chart to him. And it having been sent over by means of some cord, the Admiral began to plot their position on it with his pilot and sailors.

(Dunn & Kelley, 41–43)

Maravillóse en gran manera de ver tantas islas y tan altas y çertifica a los Reyes que desde las montañas que desde antier a visto por estas costas y las d'estas islas, que le pareçe que no las ay más altas en el mundo ni tan hermosas y claras, sin niebla y nieve, y al pie d'ellas grandíssimo fondo; y dize que cree que estas islas son aquellas innumerables que en los mapamundos en fin de Oriente se ponen. Y dixo que creía que avía grandíssimas riquezas y piedras preçiosas y espeçería en ellas, y que duran muy mucho al Sur y se ensanchan a toda parte. Púsoles nombre la mar de Nuestra Señora. Dize tantas y tales cosas de la fertilidad y hermosura y altura d'estas islas que halló en este puerto, que dize a los Reyes que no se maravillen de encareçellas tanto, porque les çertifica que no dize la çentessima parte: algunas d'ellas que pareçía que llegan al çielo y hechas como puntas de diamantes.

(Varela, 57–58)

He marveled greatly to see so many and such high islands, and he assures the sovereigns that it seems to him that there are no higher mountains in the world than those he has seen since day before yesterday along these coasts and on these islands, nor so beautiful and clear, without mist or snow; and at their feet very great depth. And he says that he believes these islands are those innumerable ones that in the maps of the world are put at the eastern end. And he said he believed that there were great riches and precious stones and spices in them, and that they extend very far south and spread out in all directions. He gave them the name Mar de Nuestra Señora . . . [In contrast to Varela, Dunn and Kelley insert a note from the margin in the text proper at this point.] He says so many and such things about the fertility and beauty and height of these is-

lands that he found in this harbor that he says to the sovereigns
that they should not marvel that he praises them so much, because
he assures them that he believes he does not tell a hundredth part.
Some of them appear to reach the heavens and are formed like
points of diamonds.

(Dunn & Kelley, 153–55)

These two passages exemplify the conceptual cartographic models
available to Columbus for describing geographical spaces and the
discursive transformation that takes place when one cartographic
genre or the other informs the representation of the new geography.
In the first passage, the articulation is informed by a navigational
cartography, akin to that of the portolan chart on which the Admiral
was plotting the fleet's course in order to find landfall. In the second
passage, Columbus is relating to the Crown his interpretation of the
significance of the geography he has experienced. The newly
sighted islands are identified with the innumerable (hypothetical)
islands that the *mappaemundi* situate at the end of the Orient. Consequently they are endowed with the poetic and spiritual inflections
that characterize Christian orientalist geographical discourse. They
are islands of ineffable wealth, beauty, and fertility, so extraordinary
that a literal description does not suffice and the islands assume the
metaphorical shape of diamonds rising toward heaven. Their spiritual value is inscribed symbolically in the name he gives them, Mar
de Nuestra Señora (Sea of Our Lady), as he practices an onomastic
cartography, tracing the route of the voyage through a figuratively
Christian landscape that marks the continuity between this world
and the Other.

EXPLORATION

Samuel Eliot Morison, following Las Casas and Ferdinand Columbus, called attention to the importance of the Portuguese precedent
in the early conceptualization and formulation of the enterprise of
the Indies.[25] It was Las Casas, however, who provided perhaps the
strongest evidence for the idea that Portugal's early explorations in
the eastern Atlantic were intellectually decisive and provided the
practical motivation for Columbus's enterprise. As Las Casas tells
it in the *Historia* (bk. 1, chap. 13), the story Columbus heard from
Pedro de Velasco, a Portuguese pilot who told of lands he had

sighted to the west of Ireland, provided a decisive stimulus for the first voyage. Biographers have often discussed Columbus's years in Portugal (1478–c. 1485) and his service on Portuguese commercial expeditions along the African littoral in search of an eastern sea route to India as the inspiration for his idea to sail west to reach India faster. Morison, in particular, has noted the knowledge of westerly winds and currents Columbus must have obtained on those African voyages, knowledge that made his Atlantic crossing a success where others had failed. Yet the relevance of Portuguese nautical and maritime writings to Columbus's articulation of the voyages to the Indies has received little attention. Scholarship on the Discovery typically has ignored the Columbian texts' important place in the history of travel literature even while focusing on their contribution to the history of travel.

João Rocha Pinto, in his study *A viagem: Memória e espaço*, has shown that Portuguese maritime travel literature of the so-called Age of Discovery, roughly encompassing the fifteenth and sixteenth centuries, employed a variety of distinct forms, ranging from listlike and highly technical writings (e.g., sailing directions, rutters, navigation manuals and guides) concerned with navigation as spatial displacement or movement (how to get from here to there) to more narrative and descriptive forms (e.g., relations, letters, voyage diaries) concerned with the voyage as an experience. Rocha Pinto suggests that the earlier forms emphasized the spatial aspects of the journey, while the most temporally oriented of forms, the *diario de bordo*, he argues, did not appear until the mid-sixteenth century.

The earliest Portuguese navigation guides, the *roteiros* (rutters), were composed of concrete technical directions on the route, astronomical observations, winds and currents, compass readings, coastal features, and so on. Some *roteiros* of specific voyages (e.g., "Roteiro da viagem que Dom Jhoão de Castro fez a primeira vez que foy a India no ano de 1538") began to follow a systematic chronology in the recording of the voyage. In contrast, more traditional rutters, like the Spanish "derrotero general" found in Alonso de Chaves's "Espejo de navegantes" (c. 1537), which has been described as a navigational chart in prose, contained virtually no temporal elements.[26] Like the charts they accompanied on board exploration vessels, traditional rutters served the practical needs of navigators for tracing the coordinates of the route and the contours of the geography traversed.[27] The "how-to" quality and the systematic, detailed character of the entries describe a rigorous verbal map of the navigation that renders each location on the itinerary significant in relation to the trajectory of the journey as a whole.

By the late sixteenth century the temporalization of space in the writings generated by the voyages of exploration was fully achieved, as Adriaen Veen's instructions for composing a *roteiro* (1597) make clear. Among the genre's essential components, Veen lists the recording of the year, the month, the day, the time of day, as well as the transitions from one to the next; for example, from ante to post meridian).[28]

While Rocha Pinto seems to be correct in asserting that rigorous chronology was not introduced into European nautical literature until later in the sixteenth century, it does not necessarily follow that earlier works were not temporally sensitive. The earliest surviving *roteiros* of Portuguese exploration of the African Atlantic, dating from the late fifteenth century, were indeed essentially devoid of temporality. They were typically not intended as accounts of specific navigations, but as directions to be followed by future mariners. Once narrative elements enter the accounts, however, so too does time, for narration is, by definition, an intensely temporal form of writing, establishing meaningful sequences and relations among a series of events or experiences.

Narrative, however, is a rare commodity among the early writings of European maritime exploration. The oldest Portuguese nautical texts, such as the one known today as "Este livro é a rotear . . . ," collected by Valentim Fernandes in the early sixteenth century, or the "Roteiro de Flandres," collected in João de Lisboa's *Livro de Marinharia* later in that same century, exhibit only the most rudimentary of narrative qualities in order to represent the succession of noteworthy geographical and hydrographic phenomena.[29] The same can be said of the oldest surviving French *routier*, written by Pierre Garcie in 1483–84.[30] To call them narratives, however, would be to stretch to the breaking point the limits of the definition. Yet there are important examples of narrativization among the earliest writings associated with the Portuguese voyages of exploration of the African littoral. For narrativization (and therefore temporalization) is a fundamental characteristic of any travel literature whose purpose is to relate the subject's experience of geographical space, rather than just describe the existence of places independent of the writer.[31] The Valentim Fernandes collection (c. 1506–1508) contains descriptions and a chronicle of the African discoveries. Duarte Pacheco Pereira's *Esmeraldo de situ orbis* (c. 1505–1508) and two mid-fifteenth-century accounts of the African voyages by Italians who sailed with the Portuguese, Alvise Ca' da Mosto and Antonioto Usodimare, all represent not only the physical contours of space but, especially, the subject's experience of it.[32]

The *Esmeraldo* is a particularly interesting case, for although it has been described as primarily a *roteiro*, Pacheco blends a variety of genres to constitute space through his own experience of seascape and landscape. His text reads variously like history, a treatise on cosmography, a book of seamanship, an ethnographic description, and a commercial journal, all of which have been inscribed onto the basic structure of the nautical guidebook.[33] It is not always clear to what extent Pacheco is reporting his own experiences or giving secondhand reports, but throughout he subjectifies the atemporality and strict objectivity of the *roteiro* to represent a geography mediated by the intervention of the human consciousness that renders it meaningful.[34]

The increasing tendency to temporalize space had profound implications for the relation of exploratory travel to knowledge, and for exploration as an epistemological phenomenon.[35] Not only did it represent a shift from writing the voyage as charting or marking the boundaries of an unknown space to telling the story of the voyage as a narrative sequence of events (a historical phenomenon); it further implied that maritime exploratory travel writing had become a way of relating the explorer's experience (in time) of space— of becoming familiar with, of interacting with, of knowing a previously unknown space.[36] Ultimately, the temporalization of space in exploratory travel writing rendered it fully chronotopic, thereby transforming it from a technical to a cultural discourse.

The chronotopic values that characterize portolan cartography— spatial precision, realism, and temporal accuracy—have their scriptural counterparts in the *roteiros, diarios de bordo*, and *relaçãos* of the Age of Discovery. Just as exploration produced maps that defined the historical and physical outlines of previously unknown spaces, the written texts fully constituted a spatiotemporal field that gave meaning to the explorer's unprecedented experience of the journey through the new geography. Perhaps the earliest surviving navigation account with these characteristics is Alvise Ca' da Mosto's (1433–77) account of his voyages to Guinea with Portuguese expeditions in the mid-fifteenth century. In the preface to the journey narrative proper, Ca' da Mosto explains the purpose of writing: to record his experiences of the unknown Ocean and lands of "Lower Ethiopia" beyond the Strait of Gibraltar, which had never before been visited by Europeans.[37] The new lands are compared to the world familiar to his readers so that, as he puts it, his descendants may know his reasons for seeking diverse things in various and new places. As one reads a bit further, it becomes clear that Ca' da Mosto's "discovery" is motivated both by curiosity (the desire to see the marvels of strange lands and peoples) and by the promise of economic profit (the spices, gold, and other valuable things potentially to be found there). The experience of discovery is inscribed by Ca' da Mosto in the discourses of mercantilism and exploration, structured within a journey whose spatiotemporal field is represented as realistically as possible—wholly appropriate to an author who is credited with composing the oldest surviving *portolano*, printed in Venice in 1490. The text is characterized by a pragmatic, materialistic, quantitative mode of diction that strives to render the experience specifically, concretely, and objectively.

In the Columbian corpus, the *Diario* of the first voyage stands out as the most typical exploratory nautical writing. Las Casas's undeniable hand in the shaping of the text that has come down to us notwithstanding, the basic structure and diction of the *Diario* are closely related in form and function to the *roteiro* genre.[38] For the first forty-two days of the voyage, the text records technical navigational information regarding direction, speed, winds, currents, and other maritime phenomena relevant to the successful completion of the voyage. These data, organized in listlike fashion, provide the framework for a basic chronology of daily entries. The predominant organizational principle within these segments, however, is spatial, responding to the practical necessity of keeping a precise record of the distances traveled by the fleet. The daily subdivisions no doubt reflected the expectation that the fleet would be sailing out of sight of land for long intervals. Navigation on the high seas required a systematic recording of location in relation to fixed points, but astronomical navigation was still only an embryonic science at best.

In the absence of a topography against which to establish position, elapsed time was the only way to record the route. Such a record was especially important for the first voyage since Columbus anticipated sailing in uncharted waters and thus his own observations would be the only guide available for the return course.

With the landfall entry of 11 October 1492, however, the *Diario* increasingly emphasizes the temporal dimension of the journey. Although the entries continue to record the route, they begin to focus, like Ca' da Mosto's account, on the events of the voyage as the coherent experience of the individual consciousness of the narrator-navigator. Each day's entry is no longer a mere collection of navigational data marking a particular point on an itinerary, but a spatiotemporal field where the journey as process and event unfolds. Each entry is a narrative segment, a portion of the story of the voyage that not only tells where Columbus happened to be and the route he followed to get there, but also places the significance of that particular geography (i.e., what occurred there) in the context of the unfolding larger voyage experience.

The organization of information along chronological lines, even in highly sophisticated chronologies, does not constitute in and of itself a radical departure from writing as enumeration, characteristic of the *Diario* up to 11 October, and the technical nautical genres that inform such writing. The temporalization of space is accomplished not by the simple addition of temporal units to the spatial record but, as I noted earlier, by the narrativization of the accounting of the voyage. Mary B. Campbell's observations regarding a similar development in the pilgrimage travel literature of the early Middle Ages may help to clarify this distinction. Referring to the listlike itineraries of pilgrimage to the Holy Land, Campbell notes that "In the list all the places are simultaneous and perpetual. They bear no relation to the traveler, and only the spatial relation of distance to each other. The list is in no sense literature; it is an aggregation of data. Literature, anonymous or signed, 'popular' or 'serious,' is the imprint of a human mind on such data, an imprint that imposes a pattern of relations, attempts to make sense."[39]

In narrativizing technical nautical writing, the *Diario* imposes a pattern of relations among the geographies of "here" and "there," New World and Old. Thus, the reader encounters not so much a "navigational chart in prose," as a culturally inflected discourse whose purpose is to give meaning to the voyage by relating the narrator's subjective experience of it. The shift from enumeration to narration in the entries after the landfall not only reflects the more complex information to be recorded once the fleet sighted the island of Guanahaní (San Salvador) but also marks a fundamental change in the way the voyage was conceptualized. To discover was no longer simply to find something and record its location; discovery had become a way of knowing what was found.[40]

The reactions of some of the earliest and most interested readers of Columbus, the Catholic Monarchs and Bartolomé de Las Casas, suggest that the text before them was not quite what was expected from the Admiral. Isabella wrote to Columbus in September 1493 requesting the "carta de navegar" and "pintura" he had promised to send with the written account of the first voyage. That what Columbus had presented was deemed unsatisfactory and somewhat baffling is confirmed by another letter dated the same day, this time from both Ferdinand and Isabella, asking for additional navigational information "para bien entenderse mejor este vuestro libro" (so that this book of yours might be better understood).[41]

Another clue to the text's irregularity vis-à-vis traditional nautical genres is found in the unusual nomenclature Las Casas employed in referring to it.[42] In his editorial remarks introducing the narrative portion of the *Diario* (beginning with the 11 October entry), Las Casas refers to his source as the "libro de su primera navegaçión y descubrimiento d'estas Indias." The use of the adjective "estas" (these) is often quoted to support the argument that Las Casas transcribed the text while living in the Indies. More striking, to my mind, is the peculiar phrasing, which suggests that navigation and discovery were different activities, or distinct genres, in Las Casas's mind. That he added the qualifier "y descubrimiento" suggests that the traditional nautical genre "libro de navegación" was too narrow a category for what Columbus had written.

The typical *diario de bordo*, according to Rocha Pinto, was completely divorced from the general voyage experience.[43] He describes the *diario de bordo* as a specialized genre, concerned with organizing the writing of the voyage along strict chronological lines and with recording practical, technical, and scientific information related exclusively to the navigation proper, such as winds, currents, atmospheric phenomena, distances and directions, compass variations, coastal topography, and latitudes and longitudes. The *Diario* of Columbus's first voyage includes all the above, and much more.[44] The text tells at least two different, yet related stories: one about exploration and demarcation of a previously unknown and uncharted geographical space, and another about the significance of the voyage to a destination constituted in the text as familiar (already known). It articulates navigation and discovery, as Las Casas recognized, as distinct operations. That the "unknown" space in question was the route, and not the destination, is made clear in the prologue:

> Vuestras Altezas . . . pensaron de enbiarme a mí, Cristóval Colón, a las dichas partidas de India para ver los dichos prínçipes . . . y ordenaron que yo no fuese por tierra al Oriente, *por donde se costumbra de andar*, salvo por el camino de Occidente, *por donde hasta oy no sabemos por cierta fe que aya passado nadie.*
>
> (Varela, 15–16; emphasis added)

> Your Highnesses . . . thought of sending me, Christóbal Colón, to the said regions of India to see the said princes . . . and you commanded me that I should not go to the East by land, *by which way it is customary to go*, but by the route of the West, *by which route we do not know for certain that anyone previously has passed.*
>
> (Dunn & Kelley, 19; emphasis added)

Rocha Pinto's observation that the temporalization of space in nautical literature was not fully achieved until at least the mid-sixteenth century further underscores the novelty of Columbus's account of the first navigation.[45] Moreover, unlike the typical *diario*, which Rocha Pinto describes as a strictly technical writing, the Columbian *Diario* blends an account of the navigation with the Admiral's testimony of the subjective experience of the space encountered. To my mind, it is precisely such testimony that makes it, as Las Casas labeled it, a book about navigation *and* discovery. What renders the particular geography of the Discovery meaningful is not its precise navigational coordinates, but the relations established by the narrator between "here" and "there." The "libro" Columbus sent to the Crown, as the sovereigns' requests for more geographical and navigational information appear to confirm, was not exclusively (perhaps not even primarily) concerned with the accurate marking of the route within the precise contours of a *roteiro*-like geography. It has been argued that the Crown's requests and the journal's deficiency with respect to technical information suggest duplicity on Columbus's part: that he purposely suppressed such information in order to keep knowledge of the route, and thereby any subsequent voyages, for himself alone. Yet analysis of Columbian discourse shows that the first voyage through the Indies is articulated as the experience of a geography profoundly resonant with the cultural, political, and economic ideologies of the late fifteenth century.[46] Starting with the entry of 11 October 1492, the *Diario* increasingly subordinates technical nautical modes of discourse in favor of modes that emphasize the subjective experience of space.

In the texts relating the first and second voyages, the qualities that describe the journey experience are predominantly sensorial, practical, and secular, as we have seen. The names with which Columbus marks the surface of his verbal map may be of a religious origin, but they usually represent physical similarities between known and new things rather than spiritual affinities or significances:

> Desta ysla vine a la otra de Santa María de Monsarrate, que era a la distançia de çinco leguas, tierra es mui alta y conforme a Monsarrate [sic, for Montserrat], y desta vine de una en otra corriendo a mi camino, poniéndoles a cada una nombre, y porque asçinden a gran número, a todas juntamente las nombré de Todos los Santos.
>
> (Rumeu 2:450)

> From this island I went to the other one named Santa María de Monsarrate, which was at a distance of five leagues, the land is very mountainous and similar to Monsarrate, and from this one I went from one to the next following my route, and to each I gave a name, and because their number climbed to so many, to the lot I gave the name of All Saints.

Though the European Montserrat, a jagged mountain northwest of Barcelona, was a place of profound spiritual importance—the site of a Benedictine monastery erected to commemorate a miraculous appearance of the Virgin and a popular destination of pilgrims seeking the Virgin's intercession—Columbus's explanation for naming the Caribbean island after Montserrat is only that its peaks physically resemble those of the Catalonian mountain. Likewise, he names the group of islands All Saints simply because there are so many of them. Not only is there no spiritual significance in this use of religious names, but the very suggestion that the pantheon of Catholic saints is so large as to resemble the proliferating islands in Columbus's path borders on irreverence.

The motivation for the journey as expressed in these early accounts is often unabashedly practical and profane: to find gold, spices, and other commodities. Consequently, the route and map Columbus traces is the one he believes will most likely lead to those resources. In the *carta-relación* of January 1494 he explains why he pursued a particular route of exploration on the second voyage:

> Yo me acuerdo quel año pasado un yndio viejo, aquí en esta ysla Ysavela, me dixo que en estas partes de los caníbales avía una ysla pequeña y que los tres quartos eran oro, y agora conforma, porque yo beo la tierra para ello dispuestas [sic].
>
> Todas estas islas, que agora se an fallado, enbío por pintura con las otras del año pasado y todo en una carta que yo conpuse, bien con harto travajo por las grandes mis ocupaçiones del asiento que acá se faze de la villa.
>
> (Rumeu 2:451)

> I recall that last year an old Indian, here on this island of Ysavela, told me that in this region of the cannibals there was a small island and that three-quarters of it was of gold, and now it all makes sense because I see the land disposed to it.
>
> All these islands which have now been found I am sending you in a drawing along with last year's, all of them together on a chart I made, with quite a lot of effort owing to my many responsibilities pertaining to the foundation of the town that is underway here.

The desire to seek out the islands of the Carib Indians ("caníbales"), notorious for their anthropophagy, is none other than that they were reputed to be gold-bearing, as Columbus understood it from a *cacique* during the first voyage. Indeed, almost without exception, the actions undertaken during the second voyage are related to this materialistic quest. Even the capture of Cahonaboa, the *cacique* reputed to own the largest pieces of gold on Española and suspected to have been responsible for the deaths of some of the Spaniards left at La Navidad on the first voyage, is ultimately motivated by the search for gold, "porque sabremos dél toda la verdad y de toda la ysla y de oro" (Rumeu, 2:481; because we will learn the whole truth from him and about the entire island and the gold).

The journey of exploration is thus propelled by the worldly goals of the enterprise—to establish a colony for the exploitation of indigenous resources. And the resulting verbal "chart" marks the route of gold through a textual geography that literally is "mined" with references to its potential wealth: "Ya dixe que las tierras, queste viaje se an descubierto, son tantas y más quel año pasado y no de menos preçio como la pintura hará manifiesto" (Rumeu, 2: 462; I already said that the lands discovered on this voyage are as many and more than last year and no less valuable, as the map will show).[47]

Even from a cursory glance at Rocha Pinto's typological synopsis of Portuguese voyage literature, one easily recognizes the filiation of Columbus's writings. The generic models Columbus would have had most immediately in mind were undoubtedly those he became familiar with aboard Portuguese commercial vessels and through other activities related to his African voyages of the 1480s, or perhaps even earlier in the chartmaking business he operated with his brother Bartolomé in Lisbon in the late 1470s. As Ferdinand tells it, Columbus's Portuguese mother-in-law was an early source of maritime writings, charts, and maps for the future Admiral of the Ocean Sea. Dona Isabel's deceased husband, Bartolomeu Perestrello, had held the hereditary captaincy of the island of Porto Santo near Madeira. According to Ferdinand, Perestrello's collection of sea charts and texts was given to Columbus by Dona Isabel when she learned of his interest in navigation.

Columbus's own writings, however, move well beyond such technical nautical genres as the *roteiro*, the *livro de marinharia* (book of seamanship), and the *livro de armação* (book of chandlery).[48] Strong narrational and descriptive qualities link the Columbian texts to relations, letters, memoirs, and journals—genres that did not flourish until later in the Age of Discovery—and the texts also incorporate various judicial forms (contracts, testaments, instructions, petitions, etc.), not to narrate the voyage experience itself, but to complement the pragmatics and ideology of the voyages and articulate the larger enterprise of discovery.

The first voyage, as recounted in the *Diario*, could be described as a hybrid composed of characteristic elements of such genres as the rutter, the relation, the memoir, and the navigation logbook, and often blending technical nautical, geographical, economic, ethnographic, judicial, and religious modes of diction.[49] Two other versions of that voyage are found in the "Carta a Luis de Santángel" (15 February 1493) and the "Carta a los Reyes," both of which offer similar accounts. The letters have much in common with the *Diario*, yet they are clearly of very different filiation since they forego the technical nautical elements and strict chronology evident in the *Diario* in favor of a general descriptive content.[50] The letters strike the tone and tenor of a personal epistle geared to the nonspecialist. Their primary purpose appears to be promotional, announcing triumphantly the completion of the voyage by highlighting its most notable and least technical aspects.

Rumeu de Armas's recent publication of Columbus's *Libro Copiador* has made available for the first time to modern readers Columbian accounts of the second voyage (1493–96).[51] In four *relaciones* addressed to Ferdinand and Isabella, Columbus records in considerable detail his thoughts and experiences concerning the establishment of the colony on Española, the exploitation of the Indians and the islands' natural wealth, the continuing search for the empire of the Grand Khan, relations among the Christians and between them and the Indians (including the capture of the *cacique* Cahonaboa and the skirmishes between his people and the Spaniards), the disastrous fate of La Navidad, and, especially, the obsessive search for gold. Another surviving text of this voyage is Columbus's "Instrucción a Mosén Pedro Margarite" (9 April 1494), his instructions to the head of a scouting party charged with the reconnaissance of the interior of Española. The instructions to Margarite, akin to those Columbus himself received from the Crown for each of the voyages, set forth the Admiral's orders and the practical manner in which they should be carried out.[52]

The third voyage is told primarily in the "Relación del tercer viaje," addressed to the Crown, and in a portion (30 May–31 August 1498) of a since lost *diario* of the same voyage excerpted by Las Casas in his *Historia de las Indias*. (Another version of the "Relación" of the third voyage appears in the *Libro Copiador*.) Also pertinent to this voyage are the "Carta a doña Juana de la Torre" (c. autumn 1500), governess of the prince don Juan, and the "Carta a los Reyes" (1501), which serves as an introduction to the *Libro de las profecías*. Parts of the "Relación" appear to have been derived from the missing *diario* transcribed by Las Casas, but the thrust of the letter is less to relate the voyage than to interpret its significance, and Columbus quickly moves on from relating the navigation to an impassioned defense of his achievements and a treatiselike interpretation of the ultimate significance of his enterprise. The other letters are highly polemical pieces in which Columbus seeks to establish the merits of his endeavor and to defend himself from the accusations of his ever more numerous detractors. Considered as a group, the letters pertaining to the third voyage could be viewed both as personal epistles recounting Columbus's experiences and as manifestoes that attempt to carve out an ideology of discovery within which Columbus's particular achievements are set and then interpreted. From the third voyage to the end of his life, as he became increasingly embattled with the Crown over his performance, titles, and privileges, Columbus also became quite prolific in producing letters and legal documents to complement the accounts of his voyages.

Together the later texts yield a picture of a disillusioned and persecuted man struggling to be recognized for his achievements and trying to put his affairs in order before death overtakes him. In the "Relación del cuarto viaje" (7 July 1503), also known as the "Lettera rarissima," Columbus addresses Isabella and Ferdinand from Jamaica, where the sea-battered remains of his fleet had taken refuge at the end of the most difficult and dangerous of his expeditions. The letter's pretext is to report on the voyage and therefore it pays lip service to the forensic-testimonial quality of the *relación* genre, but it quickly assumes an overwhelmingly plaintive and confessional tone. An anguished petition for recognition and compensation, this *relación* presents the voyage as a mystical experience with strong messianic and prophetic overtones. The discursive character of these later texts suggests that the generic models of nautical exploration and commerce associated with portolan cartography were superseded in Columbian writing by a quite different textual geography, to which I now turn.

AMERICA TWICE-DISCOVERED:
COLUMBUS VERSUS VESPUCCI

In the opening sections of this essay, I drew a distinction between writing about journeys to known places versus unknown destinations. Known places are those already inscribed in the body of knowledge, sites for which ideological (if not cartographical) coordinates are already in place. In contrast, unknown destinations are those whose semantic field is sparse or empty, a condition by no means restricted to places not even suspected to exist. Yet the designation of a site as "known" is at least as much a function of the way it is articulated as of its objective status. A site's cultural significance, its place and role in the body of knowledge, is ultimately constituted through the very act of writing or mapping it. While different genres may be deemed appropriate to known or unknown places, the choice of rhetorical vehicle is ultimately not imposed from outside the act of writing but from within it. In the final analysis, geographical space is always constituted discursively, *as if* it were either known or unknown. That is, its discursive character does not guarantee its empirical status. Discourse is, even in its most realistic or factual forms, a position-taking with respect to its object, shaping its meanings and cultural significance beyond its objective condition.

European travel in the fifteenth and sixteenth centuries was usually carried out in regions considered known, not necessarily through the actual experience of travelers, but because the areas had been mentioned in the writings of the *auctoritates* of classical and Christian antiquity. This was the case with both the Portuguese voyages of exploration along the African littoral and the eastern Atlantic, as well as the so-called New World discoveries, which were not universally considered "new." However, the various rhetorical vehicles available for the articulation of geographical space ultimately responded not so much to the pragmatics and ideology of the voyage as a historical event, but to the scriptural "event" through which the voyage subsequently was interpreted.

The claim of America's novelty, its "discovery" in the modern sense, was the product of a rhetorical tour de force, not of an empirical observation. The dubious honor belongs, as is well known, to Amerigo Vespucci, who in a letter to Lorenzo Pietro Francesco de Medici in the spring of 1503 described the South American mainland as a new world because "none of these countries were known to our ancestors and to all who hear about them they will be entirely new," and even if "they have affirmed that any continent is there, they have given many reasons for denying it is inhabited."[53] Vespucci's claim to the discovery, then, rested not on actually finding the new continent (although his subsequent phrasing is ambiguous enough to suggest he had), but on the assertion that the ancients had not known its true nature whereas he now did—"But this opinion is false, and entirely opposed to the truth. My last voyage has proved it, for I have found a continent in that southern part; more populous and more full of animals than our Europe, or Asia, or Africa, and even more temperate than any other region known to us, as will be explained further on." The semicolon in the English translation, however, resolves an ambiguity that inheres in the Italian original: whether Vespucci is claiming to have found a new continent altogether or merely a continent more populous than originally thought.[54]

Five years before Vespucci or any other European, Columbus had noted the temperateness of this same mainland and the quantity and quality of its inhabitants.[55] For him, however, it was not a "new" world but an "other" world ("otro mundo"). As he explained in 1498 in a letter to Ferdinand, *terra firma* is a place "well known to the ancients, and not unknown as the envious and ignorant would have it."[56] The implications of this position are many, not the least important of which is the apparent recognition by Columbus of a fundamental otherness or difference in the physical and cultural landscape he encountered, a question I discuss in the essay that follows, "Gender and Discovery." For the present argument, however, it is necessary to observe that Vespucci's sense of discovery is diametrically opposed to Columbus's position, and it does not seem too farfetched to suggest that it may have been so intentionally and self-servingly. For Vespucci, *retrovare* meant to discover something previously unknown, at least in the sense that its true nature, if not its existence, had previously been unsuspected. For Columbus, on the other hand, "the Indies" could not be considered new in any sense since many before him had written extensively about it. This land was "other" with respect to the world he and his readers were familiar with; that is, the explored parts of Europe, Asia, and Africa, but it was certainly a world familiar to the writers of classical and Christian antiquity.

This does not mean, of course, that Vespucci and not Columbus discovered America, as some have argued.[57] It does suggest, however, that Columbus "discovered" the territory in a way quite different from Vespucci. Columbus's and Vespucci's respective discoveries were ultimately defined by how they were articulated rather than how they were actually carried out or what they yielded. If Vespucci has been given much of the credit for discovering America, certainly it is not because he was the first European to find it or even to write about it (Columbus was), but because he was the first to express it as a new geographical entity; that is, he wrote of his voyage as the story of a journey to a place unknown. The scientific merits of this interpretation were minimal. Were it not for the existence of the Bering Strait, Columbus would have been as "correct" in his basic geographical premise—that he had reached the extreme Orient—as Vespucci turned out to be in his. Neither explorer made a definitive contribution to our knowledge of the true configuration of post-Discovery geography. Yet each made a profound contribution to the ways in which we think about the world. Through his writing, Columbus brought his discovery into cultural being by assigning significance to the journey and its spaces as a voyage to a place already known.

THE GRAMMAR OF DISCOVERY

Vespucci's sense of discovery as the finding of something new, not previously known to exist, is much closer to the prevailing modern sense than Columbus's notion that the Discovery involved the revelation of something already known but somehow concealed. Columbus's usage, which is deemed an archaism in common speech today, is nonetheless alive in popular symbolic language. The recent tourism slogan "Discover the U.S. Virgin Islands: America's Paradise" defines the modern West Indies by invoking a geographical symbolism that shares some important similarities with Columbus's representation of the *Indias Occidentales*, the "end of the Orient," as the site of the Terrestrial Paradise.[58] The slogan suggests a way of reading the Columbian texts that runs counter to the tendencies of recent scholarship and is foreign to the prevalent contemporary notion of the Discovery.

The winter-weary resident of northern latitudes is especially susceptible to the allure of the physical pleasures embodied in the slogan's metaphor—perhaps in much the same way as the ocean-weary veteran of an Atlantic crossing might have felt at the close of the fifteenth century. To travel to the West Indies, the slogan implies, is to indulge the senses. Yet the metaphor also promises the traveler a more profound sense of well-being that transcends bodily pleasure to approach a mystical or spiritual rapture. A journey to the paradise of the West Indies promises not only relief from the harshness of winter but a regenerating, purifying experience that will improve the traveler's life, physically and spiritually, after returning home.

Both the slogan and Columbian writing propose a destination of profound symbolic significance and a way of traveling. In each context "discovery" is not so much the locating of an entity (the thing discovered) as a type of activity, not so much a place as a particular kind of experience of place. What defines the discovery in each case is how the traveler relates to his or her destination, the interaction that not only happens there but also helps create the place as a result.[59] The noun *descubrimiento* does not appear even once in any of Columbus's accounts of the first navigation, though forms of the verb *descubrir* appear repeatedly.[60] In the slogan, "discovery" assumes the form of an imperative verb, urging the traveler into the experience.

Verbal persuasion—the intention to convince the reader of the merits and benefits of the journey—is another point of equivalence between the slogan and Columbian writing. Both are fundamentally rhetorical vehicles. As Ferdinand Columbus, the man most likely to have been privy to his father's intimate intentions, later explained, his father had called the lands he discovered the Indies, "because he knew all men had heard of the great fame and wealth of India; and by using that name he hoped to arouse the interest of the Catholic Sovereigns (who were doubtful of his enterprise)."[61] The strength of both the slogan's and Columbus's articulation of discovery hinges on the symbolic force inherent in the metaphorical transformation of the West Indies into Eden: the syntactical linking of "discovering" and "Paradise" plays on the reader's imagination. Yet the effect of such phrasing is most immediately to motivate us to imagine a journey (which only later may—or not—lead to actual travel) whose itinerary is figurative rather than literal.

This imaginary journey, a product of the act of reading, is perhaps the most instructive parallel that can be drawn from the analogy. Neither the slogan nor the Columbian texts articulates "discovery" as an empirical feat. In each case "to discover" is to reveal a recondite significance, in the hermeneutical sense of uncovering a symbolic meaning, not to find a place unknown, since in each case the destination's location is "known" (Paradise appeared on medieval *mappaemundi* just as certainly as the Virgin Islands do on modern maps). That Columbus's contemporaries understood his discovery in this sense is borne out in the first article of the "Instructions from the Sovereigns to Columbus" (29 May 1493) issued in preparation for the second voyage—"it pleased our Lord God in His blessed mercy to discover the aforesaid islands and mainlands . . . by the efforts of the aforesaid Christopher Columbus . . . who has made [the islands and mainlands] known to Their Highnesses."[62]

The journey of discovery, then, is first and foremost an imaginative voyage. The traveler to Paradise must move through a symbolic cultural space in order to reach the longed-for destination. By linking discovery and Paradise, the slogan, like Columbian writing, invites us to perform a tropological reading in which the literal sense (Go to the Virgin Islands) is subordinated to the metaphorical spiritual signification (Discover Paradise).[63]

PILGRIMAGE

If Paradise did exist on this earth of ours, many a man among those who are keen to enquire into all kinds of subjects would think he could not be too quick in getting there: for if there be some who to procure silk for the miserable gains of commerce, hesitate not to travel to the uttermost ends of the earth, how should they hesitate to go where they would gain a sight of Paradise itself?

These words, written by Cosmas Indicopleustes (i.e., Indian sea traveler) in the mid-sixth-century *Christian Topography*, represent one of the earliest expressions of two fundamental themes of the Columbian discourse of Discovery—commerce and Paradise—significantly linked and valuated by Cosmas to favor the mystical component.[64] I do not intend to argue whether the *Christian Topography* directly influenced Columbus's writing, but to underscore the strength and durability of these important medieval travel topoi. Commerce and Paradise were still the great motivators of European exotic travel in 1492. Columbus's choice of the term *negocio* (business) to refer to his enterprise is telling, for it simultaneously alludes metaphorically to the spiritual dimension of the project (i.e., *negotium crucis*) and literally to its commercial dimension.[65] In identifying economic and spiritual goals as the great motivators of his journey, Columbus was expressing a cardinal aspect of the medieval world view: the interrelatedness of the profane and the sacred, of gold and God.

Travel literature of the period appears to confirm this nexus. As Raymond Beazley has shown in *The Dawn of Modern Geography*, European travel abroad during much of the Middle Ages was undertaken primarily by Christian pilgrims, missionaries, and merchants. Among the earliest extant works relating a journey beyond the borders of Europe are the fourth-century anonymous "Itinerary from Bordeaux to Jerusalem" and the *Peregrinatio ad Terram Sanctam* of Egeria. These texts initiate the genre of religious travel literature, known as *peregrinationes*, focused on the pilgrimage experience. The *peregrinationes* are roughly of two types: narrations of travel to earthly places of religious import (the Holy Land, Rome, Santiago de Compostela) and mystical voyages to otherworldly sites such as Hell, Purgatory, or Paradise. Although modern readers differentiate the destinations as actual or imaginary, the medieval accounts typically presented both types of pilgrimages as the real experiences of men and women traveling through concrete geographical spaces— in this world or the other—to destinations whose spiritual significance was deemed complementary to the goals of the journey. Paradise and Jerusalem (and often Rome as well) were situated on the same ideological meridian in medieval *mappaemundi*. The twelfth-century accounts of the pilgrimages made by Saint Brendan and Owein, for example, involve visits to Hell and the Terrestrial Paradise that are articulated as actual voyages through a specific Atlantic geography. Such a blending of mystical experience and real geography became an increasingly important tendency in medieval travel narratives of journeys to the Other World.[66]

As Cesare Segre has observed, the pilgrimages to the Other World often were voyages of discovery, at once physical and spiritual experiences representing the search for self-purification and redemption through practical knowledge of a geography conceived of as simultaneously mystical and real.[67] The Garden of Eden, as Genesis tells us, is located in this world. Its inaccessibility is not due to geographical remoteness but to the divine sanction against Adam and Eve and their progeny. In the medieval voyage narratives, entrance to Paradise is a reward granted as a special favor by God to the pilgrim in recognition of a special spiritual achievement.

Even Cosmas, once a merchant-traveler by trade and one of the most prominent figures in the story of early medieval commerce, represented his experience of geography as nevertheless predominantly spiritual. The *Christian Topography*, written after he became a monk, is instructive for the geographical paradigm it presents as well as for its conception of exotic travel, despite his archaic flat-earth cosmography. Cosmas's attempt to harmonize "science" with religious belief to explain the nature of the world resonates in the Columbian hermeneutics of discovery, and remnants of the mystical semiotics of space depicted in Cosmas's cartographical drawings (among the oldest Christian "maps" to have survived) are evident in Columbian imagery. In Cosmas's highly allegorical sketches, Heaven is represented in the figure of Moses' tabernacle enclosing an earth shaped like a mountain reaching up to the firmament.[68] For Cosmas, the geographer, the ultimate journey was to Paradise, and the true geography was that which interpreted empirical knowledge of the world in light of the authority of the Scriptures.

The two great motivators of medieval travel, although definitely hierarchized, are related geographically and ideologically. According to Cosmas, Paradise was both a place and a symbol of spiritual fulfillment, just as silk was a metonymy for material wealth. Both were traditionally found in the East. Thus Oriental geography was associated with the achievement of spiritual and worldly states of plenitude alike. This association is found already in the earliest articulation of Judeo-Christian geography in Genesis 2:10–12, where the great river that nourishes the bountiful Garden of Eden is also the source of the river Pison, which encircles the gold-bearing land of Havilah "and the gold of that land is good."

The biblical prelapsarian Paradise is of this world and, accordingly, it provides generously for the well-being of human spirit and body alike. The defining characteristic of prelapsarian existence in the Garden is the unproblematic, indeed complementary, relationship between bodily and spiritual gratification. Columbian writing is replete with resonances of this complementary valuation. In the account of the fourth voyage, for example, gold and wealth, presumably through alms and charitable acts, are described as capable of facilitating the entrance into Paradise of souls condemned to purgatory: "El oro es excelentíssimo; del oro se hace tesoro, y con él, quien lo tiene, haçe cuanto quiere en el mundo, y llega a que echa las ánimas al Paraíso" (Varela, 327; Gold is a most excellent thing; gold constitutes treasure, and with it, whosoever possesses it, can do whatever he wishes in this world, even sending souls to Paradise).

The tragedy of life after Eden is not only, or even primarily, that it becomes a struggle for survival in a suddenly hostile world, but especially that it is the struggle of a self suddenly divided against itself, flesh against spirit. For the physical indulgences associated with sinfulness in a postlapsarian world (e.g., lust, greed) had once complemented and enhanced Adam and Eve's spiritual beatitude. The dual spiritual and commercial goals of the Columbian enterprise—to convert new souls to Christianity and liberate the Holy Land with the riches extracted from the Indies—appear to respond to the Christian millenarian yearning for the end of the world and the concomitant restoration of humankind's prelapsarian integrity.

Columbus's conceptualization of his journey to the Orient to spread the Faith and return with gold, spices, and precious stones to help restore Jerusalem no doubt conformed ideologically to this cultural ideal of spiritual and material plenitude associated with the East. The paradisiacal note sounded in the *Diario* of the first voyage becomes a dominant theme, culminating in the proclaimed discovery of the precise location of the Terrestrial Paradise during the third voyage. This peculiar claim, and the often intensely mystical terms in which it was expressed, has led some modern readers to dismiss it as the product of illness or madness.[69] Yet this theme and Columbus's diction are consistent with both his stated goals for the enterprise and the cultural horizons within which the Discovery took shape.[70] It was no coincidence that after years of advocating his project at various European courts, Columbus was successful at last with the Catholic Monarchs, the self-styled defenders of Christian ideals on the international political stage of late-medieval Europe.

The ideological appeal of Columbus's project for the Catholic Monarchs must have been very strong, for it was known to be technically flawed, as several commissions of experts who considered his proposal repeatedly pointed out.[71] Among the various arguments and rationales that convinced Ferdinand and Isabella to support the plan must have been the economic and political circumstances in which Spain found itself at the end of the fifteenth century. The possibility of forming an alliance with the Mongols against Islam had been a feature of Christian policy throughout much of the Middle Ages, as the papal embassies of Plano Carpini, Rubruck, Monte Corvino, and Pordenone in the thirteenth and fourteenth centuries indicate. Spanish political relations with the Far East date from the early fifteenth century, when Henry III of Castile sent his own emissaries on an overland mission to the Tatar emperor Timur. Ruy González de Clavijo, in an account of his own journey in 1403–1406 through the Tatar realm on behalf of the sovereign, writes of the friendliness with which he and the other Castilians in his party were greeted. There is no evidence, however, that any concrete plans for an alliance were ever made. Yet the possibility of such an association remained a feature of Spanish policy until the beginning of modern history. In the letter that has come to serve as the prologue to the *Diario*, Columbus explicitly affirms that establishing relations with Oriental princes was an important component of the political agenda of his first voyage. Such relations, as would be expected, implied the conversion to Christianity of the princes in question—not by force, Columbus was careful to note, but by request.

The ideological boundaries of the enterprise explicitly outlined in the prologue situate the Columbian enterprise squarely within the Iberian reconquest project, which after over seven centuries had just culminated in the successful siege of Granada. But the *Diario* entry for 26 December indicates that the voyage had an even more ambitious religious motive in Columbus's mind, the financing of a crusade to liberate Jerusalem from the Muslims:

> Y dize que espera en Dios que, a la buelta que él entendía hazer de Castilla, avía de hallar un tonel de oro, que avrían resgatado los que avía de dexar, y que avrían hallado la mina del oro y la espeçería, y aquello en tanta cantidad que los Reyes antes de tres años emprendiesen y adereçasen para ir a conquistar la Casa Sancta, "que así," dize él, "protesté a Vuestras Altezas que toda la ganançia desta mi empresa se gastase en la conquista de Hierusalem, y Vuestras Altezas se rieron y dixeron que les plazía, y que sin esto tenían aquella gana."
>
> (Varela, 101)

And he says that he hopes in God that on the return that he would undertake from Castile he would find a barrel of gold that those who were [to be] left would have acquired by exchange; and that they would have found the gold mine and the spicery and those things in such quantity that the Sovereigns, before three years [are over], will undertake and prepare to go conquer the Holy Sepulchre; for thus (says he) I urged Your Highnesses to spend all the profits of this my enterprise on the conquest of Jerusalem, and Your Highnesses laughed and said that it would please them and that even without this profit they had that desire.

(Dunn & Kelley, 291)[72]

The preceding passage is notable for its blending of the material and spiritual objectives of the voyage: the barrel of gold of the Indies for the conquest of the Holy Sepulchre. Such a blurring of the enterprise's religious and secular purposes is reflected throughout the *Diario* in the articulation of the destination and of the geography experienced throughout the journey. Originally constituted as a commercial enterprise and a political embassy to the Indies of the Grand Khan in the document of commission issued by the Crown in April 1492, the voyage begins to acquire strong religious overtones in the *Diario*. The human and physical landscapes described by Columbus simultaneously belong to an objective, practical, materialistic geography—Çipango, Zaitón, Quinsay; lands of "grandíssima suma de oro" (a very great quantity of gold)[73]—and a spiritual one, which points to the transcendental anagogical significance of the journey experience. Such toponyms as San Salvador, Santa María de la Concepción, Monte Christo, río de Gracia, Cabo Sancto, Valle del Paraíso, and Mar de Nuestra Señora name a topography characterized by its edenic qualities and inhabitants who are

gente de amor y sin cudiçia y convenibles para toda cosa, que certifico a Vuestras Altezas que en el mundo creo que no ay mejor gente ni mejor tierra. Ellos aman a sus próximos como a sí mismos, y tienen una habla la más dulçe del mundo, y mansa y siempre con risa.

(Varela, 98)

a loving people, and without greed, and docile in everything. And I assure Your Highnesses that I believe that in the world there are

no better people or a better land. They love their neighbors as
themselves, and they have the sweetest speech in the world; and
[they are] gentle and always laughing.

(Dunn & Kelley, 281)

The identification of the location of the Terrestrial Paradise in the
vicinity of the discovered lands, announced on 21 February during
the return voyage, seems almost an inevitable finale to the inter-
twining of a figurative paradisiacal geography with the "scientific"
and commercial nautical one throughout much of the *Diario*.[74]

The voyage experience as expressed in the *Diario* is defined by a
chronotope that is constituted through a predominantly objective
and systematic chronology linking a sequence of actual points on
the navigation's trajectory into a practicable geography. Yet the portolan cartography that plots and traces the course to and through
the Indies is by no means perfect.[75] It repeatedly breaks down as the
discourse assumes a subjective and figurative cast, rendering Columbus's verbal map an erratic and at times incoherent navigation
guide. As the Crown was quick to point out to the Admiral in the
letters of September 1493, the account of the first voyage as it was
initially presented at court was deemed incomprehensible and in
need of considerable supplementation.

TIERRA DE GRACIA

> Littera gesta docet:
> quid credas allegoria;
> moralis quid agas;
> quo tendas anagogia.
>> Jean Gerson, *In Decretis*, quoted by
>> Columbus in *Libro de las profecías*

> The literal teaching tells facts:
> The allegory tells what you should believe;
> The moral interpretation tells how you should act;
> The anagogy tells where you are going.
>> (West & Kling, 101)

The regrettable loss of the *diarios* of the second, third, and fourth
voyages makes it difficult to trace the development of the textual
cartography of the Discovery. In the *Diario* and letters of the first and
second voyages, the portolan chronotope of exploration describes

the journey to the Indies. The spiritual chronotope of pilgrimage, however, begins to make itself felt once Jerusalem and Paradise make their appearance on the face of Columbus's verbal map. Las Casas seems to suggest just such a development in his summary-transcription of the *Diario* and the "Relación del tercer viaje." When one reads these texts together, as distinct yet integral parts of the larger journey of discovery, one observes how the portolan textual cartography, which prevails in the accounts of the early voyages, is overwhelmed by a figurative spiritual mapping strategy that situates the mainland of Paria (discovered during the third voyage) on the same ideological meridian as Paradise and Jerusalem as they appear on the *mappaemundi*. What was stated somewhat ostentatiously as a practical goal in the *Diario*—that the gold and spices of the Indies would pay for the crusade to reconquer Jerusalem from the Muslims—is expressed in ever more mystical terms throughout the account of the third voyage.

Early in the "Relación" of this voyage Columbus renames the mainland of Paria as Tierra de Gracia (Land of Grace), proceeds to describe it as "otro mundo," and explicitly identifies it with lands whose discovery was prophesied by the Old Testament prophet Isaiah. It is unclear from the text exactly which of Isaiah's prophecies Columbus is referring to, but the vague allusion is subsequently explained in the letter to doña Juana de la Torre, written upon his return to Spain from the third voyage: "Del nuevo cielo y tierra que dezía Nuestro Padre por Sant Juan en el Apocalipsi, después de dicho por boca de Isaías, me hizo mensajero y me amostró aquella parte" (Varela, 264; Of the new heaven and earth of which Our Father spoke through Saint John in the Apocalypse, after it was spoken through the mouth of Isaiah, he made me messenger and showed me that place). The profound mystical character of this divinely revealed geography is clarified in the biblical passages Columbus alludes to, which identify the new heaven and earth as the New Jerusalem. In the Old Testament, Isaiah's prophecy of the New Jerusalem is defined by an earthly chronotope: the Messiah will rule in this world, initiating a new period of human history. In the apocalyptic vision of Saint John, the New Jerusalem, the Holy City, functions as a symbol for the salvation of humankind made possible by the Second Coming and the end of this world.[76] The Christian prophecy is characterized by an otherworldly chronotope in which time becomes eternity and Paradise is the dwelling place of the faithful. In Revelation, Saint John presents a figurative reading of Isaiah in which the earthly Jerusalem of Judaism is treated as a metaphor for the redeemed soul's abode in the Heavenly City. The significance of Columbus's use of the same phrase to designate his discovery of the mainland must be understood in this figurative sense.[77]

If one situates Columbus's onomastics in the context of his textual cartography of the third voyage this interpretation becomes even more compelling. The mainland of Paria, baptized by Columbus as Tierra de Gracia and later referred to as "nuevo cielo y tierra" (new heaven and earth), is rendered meaningful in the context of a figurative voyage trajectory that began in Spain in the year of the fall of the last Muslim city, Granada, to the Catholic Monarchs and was projected to culminate, not with the discovery of the Indies, but with the reconquest of Jerusalem. In the *Libro de las profecías*, a handbook of prophecies collected by Columbus from various sources (most of them biblical) with the help of his friend Fray Gaspar Gorricio, the discovery of the mainland is interpreted as the decisive point on a prophetic itinerary whose ultimate goal is spiritual.[78]

From this perspective the proposed liberation of Jerusalem and its restitution to Christendom is seen not as an end in itself, but as an essential step in a collective mystical journey whose destination (understood anagogically) is the New Jerusalem, the Heavenly City prophesied in the Bible.[79] Just as the earthly Jerusalem is to be attained by way of the Indies (i.e., through its riches), so must the heavenly Jerusalem be achieved through the restoration of Zion and the evangelization of the rest of the non-Christian world. It is this prophetic journey that Columbus believed he had been divinely inspired to undertake:

> Ya dise que para la hesecuçión de la inpresa de las Indias no me aprovechó rasón ni matemática ni mapamundos; llenamente se cunplió lo que dijo Isaías. Y esto es lo que deseo de escrevir aquí por le redusir a Vuestras Altezas a memoria, y porque se alegren del otro que yo le diré de Jherusalem por las mesmas autoridades, de la cual inpresa, si fee ay, tengan por muy cierto la victoria.
>
> (Varela, 280)

> Already I pointed out that for the execution of the journey to the Indies I was not aided by intelligence, by mathematics or by maps.

It was simply the fulfillment of what Isaiah had prophesied, and
this is what I desire to write in this book, so that the record may
remind Your Highnesses, and so that you may rejoice in the other
things that I am going to tell you about our Jerusalem upon the basis of the same authority. If you have faith, you may be certain that
there will be success also in that other project.

(West & Kling, 111)

The *Diario* had already been explicit on this issue—the gold of the
Indies would liberate the Holy Sepulchre—and this assertion is re-
iterated in the letter of 4 March 1493. The same gold, as Columbus
writes in the account of the fourth voyage, would also gain admittance to Paradise (Varela, 327), perhaps in the form of alms, as Varela has suggested or, more probably, as the direct consequence of and
divine reward for a sacred crusade by Spain to liberate the Holy
Land itself, financed with the riches of the Indies.

In the textual cartography of the third voyage, the Indies is not
only on the figurative way to Jerusalem, it is also in the vicinity of
Paradise. Such a geography makes sense only in the context of a
paradigmatic cartographic discourse in which spatiotemporal coordinates are determined ideologically rather than empirically. Columbus describes the voyage's trajectory from west (Spain) to far
east (the presumed Asiatic mainland) as an ascent up the slope of
a pear-shaped southern hemisphere toward the Terrestrial Paradise, situated at the very top, on the spot closest to heaven:

> Yo no tomo qu'el Paraíso Terrenal sea en forma de montaña áspera,
> como el escrivir d'ello nos amuestra, salvo qu'él sea en el colmo, allí
> donde dixe la figura del peçón de la pera, y que poco a poco an-
> dando hazia allí desde muy lejos se va subiendo a él.
>
> (Varela, 216)

> I do not think that the Terrestrial Paradise is the shape of a rugged
> mountain, like the writings about it show us, but rather that it is at
> the very top, which I described in the figure of the nipple of the
> pear, and that bit by bit traveling toward it from a great distance
> one ascends to it.

This new cosmographical interpretation, offered as a correction to
Ptolemy and others who believed the earth was perfectly round (a
view Columbus found acceptable for the northern hemisphere,
which he describes as the bottom of the pear), shows just how much

the spiritual geography of the *mappaemundi* came to inform the cartographic image Columbus fashioned to represent the Discovery. In the "Relación del tercer viaje" he continues to develop this cosmographical theory into an elaborate topography. Gaining entrance to Paradise itself, he notes, is impossible without divine intervention.[80] Yet the closer one gets to Paradise, the more its influence becomes manifest. The paradisiacal qualities of both the human and natural landscapes intensify as he approaches that part of the earth which is, according to the "Relación," "más propincua y noble al cielo" (closest and most noble to heaven):

> cuando yo llegué a la isla de la Trinidad, adonde la estrella del Norte, en anocheciendo, también se me alçava cinco grados, allí en la tierra de Gracia hallé temperançia suavíssima, y las tierras y árboles muy verdes y tan hermosos como en Abril en la güertas de Valencia, y la gente de allí de muy linda estatura y blancos más que otros que aya visto en las Indias, e los cabellos muy largos e llanos, e gente más astuta e de mayor ingenio, e no cobardes. Entonces era el sol en Virgen, ençima de nuestras cabezas e suyas. Ansí que todo esto proçede por la suavíssima temperançia que allí es, la cual proçede por estar más alto en el mundo.
>
> (Varela, 214)

> when I reached the island of Trinidad, where the north star rose five degrees as night came on, there, and in the land of Gracia, I found the temperature exceedingly mild; the fields and the foliage likewise remarkably fresh and green, and as beautiful as the gardens of Valencia in April. The people there are very graceful in form, less dark than those whom I had before seen in the Indies, and wear their hair long and smooth; they are more shrewd, intelligent, and courageous. The sun was then in Virgo, over our heads and theirs; therefore all this must proceed from the extreme blandness of the temperature, which arises, as I have said, from this country being the most elevated in the world.
>
> (Major, 132–33)

The voyage's trajectory, described by Columbus as an ascent on the slope of the earth toward its highest point in the extreme Orient, can be read figuratively as a spiritual ascension to Paradise or the heavenly Jerusalem. Thus the journey of discovery is simultaneously inscribed in a textual cartography that marks the coordinates of a worldly navigation of exploration and commerce from Spain to the mainland of the Indies (Paria), told in *roteiro*-like fash-

ion in the accounts of the first and second voyages and in the surviving fragments of the *diario* of the third voyage, and in a predominantly mystical "mapping" in the "Relación," which symbolically
renders the journey's itinerary as a spiritual ascension toward the
heavenly Jerusalem passing through a geography characterized by
its otherworldliness. The ultimate goal of this trajectory—marked
by such spiritually charged names as Isla de la Trinidad, Tierra de
Gracia, and Paraíso Terrenal—is the reconquest of the earthly Jerusalem, understood as the anagogical promise of the Heavenly
City. The profound religious symbolism of such names suggests
that the phrase "otro mundo," which has so exercised scholars of
the Discovery, has strong mystical connotations, as it does in the
discourses of pilgrimage. The discovery of the mainland is told in
an otherworldly discourse reminiscent of medieval accounts of
mystical voyages to such extraterrestrial sites as Hell, Purgatory,
and Paradise, which, as Cesare Segre puts it, were the "daily bread"
of the faithful in the Middle Ages.[81]

A similar textual cartography is found in Mandeville's *Travels*,
perhaps the most widely read travel book of the Middle Ages and
one Columbus knew well. Mandeville's *peregrinatione* took him
through Jerusalem to the environs of "Paradise terrestrial." Columbus's figurative destination in the "Relación" was also Paradise, the
ultimate goal of every pilgrim, where spiritual unity with the divin-
ity was the earthly journey's greatest reward. Although neither
traveler entered the sacred space during his journey, each tells the
story of an otherworldly voyage through a geography charged with
spiritual significance.

Mandeville's text combines the pilgrimage genre with that of a
missionary or mercantile expedition to the Orient to constitute what
has been described as a propaganda piece for a new crusade to liberate the Holy Land. As Campbell notes, the origin of Mandeville's
voyage, in both space and time, is the "fallen West," and he eventually proceeds to the gates of the Earthly Paradise in the farthest
east, "back to an unfallen place and time as it takes us to the cardinal
point geographically opposed to England in the extreme West"
(145). Mandeville's description of the approach to Paradise, a place
he did not see, he says, but of which he heard from certain "wise
men beyond," is so elaborate, specific, and intensely sensorial that
it virtually recreates the immediacy of actual experience (although

Mandeville himself was probably no more than an armchair traveler):

> Paradise terrestrial, as wise men say, is the highest place on earth, that is in all the world. . . . And in the most high place of Paradise, even in the middle place, is a well that casteth out the four floods [rivers] that run by divers lands. . . . And men there beyond say, that all the sweet waters of the world, above and beneath, take their beginning in the well of Paradise, and out of that well all waters come and go. . . .
>
> And ye shall understand that no man that is mortal ne may not approach to that Paradise. . . . For the water runneth so rudely and so sharply, because it cometh down so outrageously from the high places above, that it runneth in so great waves, that no ship may not row ne sail against it. And the water roareth so, and maketh so huge noise and so great tempest, that no man may hear other in the ship, though he cried with all the craft that he could in the highest voice that he might. Many great lords have assayed with great will, many times, for to pass those rivers towards Paradise, with full great companies. But they might not speed in their voyage. And many died for weariness of rowing against those strong waves. And many of them became blind, and many deaf, for the noise of the water. And some were perished and lost within the waves. So that no mortal man may approach to that place, without special grace of God.[82]

The trajectory of Mandeville's journey takes him "straight east," through the Holy Land and Jerusalem, beyond the Christian lands and isles and deserts of the legendary kingdom of Prester John, past the "dark region," toward Paradise. Columbus, on the other hand, traveled westward, skirting Paradise on his figurative way to the earthly and heavenly Jerusalems. His description of his passage is remarkably similar to Mandeville's, though his westward voyage is the exact inversion of Mandeville's eastward journey. But unlike Mandeville, Columbus seems to approach Paradise with God's blessing, despite the dangers he encountered:

> Cuando yo llegué a esta punta del Arenal, allí se haze una boca grande de dos leguas de Poniente a Levante la isla de la Trinidad con la tierra de Gracia, y que, para aver de entrar dentro para pasar al Septentrión, avía unos hileros de corriente que atravesavan aquella boca y traían un rugir muy grande, y creí yo que sería un

arreçife de baxos e peñas, por el cual no se podría entrar dentro en ella. Y detrás d'este hilero avía otro y otro, que todos traían un rugir grande como ola de mar que va a romper y dar en peñas. Surgí allí a la dicha punta del Arenal fuera de la dicha boca, y fallé que venía el agua del Oriente fasta el Poniente con tanta furia como haze Guadalquivir en tiempo de avenida, y esto de contino, noche y día, que creí que no podría bolver atrás, por la corriente, ni ir adelante, por los baxos. Y en la noche, ya muy tarde, estando al bordo de la nao oí un rugir terrible que venía de parte del austro hazia la nao, y me paré a mirar y vi levantando la mar de Poniente a Levante, en manera de una loma tan alta como la nao, y todavía venía hazia mí poco a poco yençima d'ella venía un filero de corriente que venía rugiendo con muy grande estrépito, con aquella furia de aquel rugir [ ] que [ ] de los otros hileros que yo dixe que me pareçían ondas de mar que davan en peñas, que oy en día tengo el miedo en el cuerpo que no me trabucasen la nao cuando llegasen debaxo d'ella. Y passó y llegó fasta la boca, adonde allí se detuvo grande espaçio.

Y el otro día siguiente enbié las barcas a sondar, y hallé en el más baxo de la boca que avía seis o siete braças de fondo, y de contino andavan aquellos hileros, unos por entrar y otros por salir. Y plugo a Nuestro Señor de me dar buen tiempo, y atravesé por esa boca adentro; y luego hallé tranquilidad.

(Varela, 208)

When I arrived at this point of the Arenal, a great mouth running from east to west and two leagues long is formed there, between the island of Trinidad and the mainland of Gracia. And in order to enter it to pass over to the north there were some tideways that crossed the mouth and made a great roar, and I thought it was a reef, with shallows and boulders, through which one could not pass. And behind this tideway there was another and yet another, so that they all made a huge roar like a wave that breaks upon boulders. I weighed anchor at the aforementioned point of the Arenal, and I found that the water flowed from the east to the west with as much force as the Guadalquivir River in times of flood, and this it did continuously, night and day, so that I thought I would not be able to turn back, because of the current, or go forward, because of the shallows. Then that night, very late, standing on board, I heard a terrible roar heading toward the ship from the south, and I stood to watch and saw the sea rising from west to east, like a hill as tall as the ship, and still it came slowly toward me and at the very top of it there was a crest of current that came roaring with a great din, with such fury [ ] that [ ] of the other tideways that I said seemed to me like waves of the sea hitting boulders, such that today I still feel the fear in my bones that they would overturn the ship as they passed beneath it. And it passed and arrived at the mouth where it was suspended for quite a while.

And the following day I sent boats out to take depths, and I found that at the mouth's shallowest point there were six or seven fathoms, and those tideways did not cease, some waiting to enter, others to exit. And it pleased Our Lord to give me fair weather, and I crossed into the mouth, and then I found peace.

Next, he entered yet another similar "boca," only narrower. Still traveling westward, he found water even fresher and more delightful. And after navigating a great distance, in that same westerly direction, "hallé unas tierras las más hermosas del mundo y muy pobladas. . . . Llamé a este lugar Jardines" (I found the most beautiful lands in the world and very populated. . . . I called this place the Gardens). And beyond the Gardens was the great bay enclosing the mouth of the Orinoco River.

Here the narrative of the navigation proper is clearly subordinated to an interpretation of the symbolic significance of the enterprise. Even those portions of the text that relate the fleet's physical progress through precise chronology, the description of coastlines, the recording of distances traveled, winds, currents, and so forth, are subsumed by an increasingly figurative discourse. In effect, hermeneutical eddies now arrest the narrative flow. The inception of the voyage, for example, is related on at least three different occasions, from differing perspectives, yet the voyage's completion—the arrival of the fleet at Española, where its provisions were anxiously awaited and where Columbus wrote the account—is barely mentioned.

At this point in the journey, the navigation comes to a standstill on the coast of the Tierra de Gracia, site of the Terrestrial Paradise. The ships drift helplessly eastward on a relentless freshwater current that impedes their progress away from the mainland and toward Española:

Y ansí levanté las anclas y torné atrás para salir al Norte por la boca que arriba dixe, y no pude bolver por la población adonde yo avía estado por causa de las corrientes que me habían desviado d'ella.

Y siempre en todo cabo hallava el agua dulce y clara, y que me llevava al Oriente muy rezio fazia las dos bocas que arriba dixe.

(Varela, 211)

I therefore weighed anchor, and sailed in a backward direction,
with the hope of finding a passage to the north by the strait, which
I have already described; but I could not return along the inhabited
part where I had already been, on account of the currents, which
drove me entirely out of my course. But constantly, at every head-
land, I found the water fresh and clear, and we were carried east-
wards very powerfully towards the two straits already mentioned.

(Major, 125–26)

The description of the inexorable eastward thrust of the currents
countering the fleet's intention to sail in a northerly direction marks
the end of the narrative of exploration and the beginning of the hermeneutical portion of the "Relación," which comprises most of the
second half of the text. From this moment the discourse also drifts
irresistibly eastward toward Paradise, leaving behind the real topography in order to describe a space defined symbolically to constitute a spiritual geography of profound mystical significance.

"Y entonces conjeturé" begins the long interpretive portion of
the text, devoted to explaining the importance of the newly found
mainland and the "tan noble empresa" of discovery. The choice of
the verb "conjecture" sets the remainder of the account in a hermeneutical vein. Columbus's conjecturing begins on a cartographic
note: how to explain the topographic relations among the island of
Trinidad, Tierra de Gracia, and the freshwater gulf that lies between
them, which he has tried to represent to Ferdinand and Isabella on
the map accompanying the "Relación." But what initially appears
to be a hydrographic observation—that the water in the gulf is fresh
and flowing eastward, while outside the gulf the water is salty—is
only the first in a series of empirical observations of natural phenomena that are read by Columbus as signs of mystical significance.
Based on the authority of Scripture, selected theologians, and the
usual pantheon of secular masters (Aristotle, Pliny, Seneca, d'Ailly,
de Lira, and so on), Columbus interprets the fresh water of the gulf
as originating in the fountain of the Terrestrial Paradise, source of
the four great rivers. Moreover, the literal empirical explanation—
that a large river flows into the gulf—though noted by Columbus
earlier in the account, is now rejected on the grounds that he does

not believe that such a wide and deep river has ever before been observed:

> Grandes indiçios son estos del Paraíso Terrenal, porqu'el sitio es conforme a la opinión d'estos sanctos e sacros theólogos. Y asimismo las señales son muy conformes, que yo jamás leí ni oí que tanta cantidad de agua dulçe fuese así adentro e vezina con la salada; y en ello ayuda asimismo la suavíssima temperançia. Y si de allí del Paraíso no sale, pareçe aún mayor maravilla, porque no creo que se sepa en el mundo de río tan grande y tan fondo.
>
> (Varela, 216)

> Great signs are these of the Terrestrial Paradise, for the site conforms to the opinion of the holy and wise theologians whom I have mentioned. And likewise, the [other] signs conform very well, for I have never read or heard of such a large quantity of fresh water being inside and in such close proximity to salt water; the very mild temperateness also corroborates this; and if the water of which I speak does not proceed from Paradise then it is an even greater marvel, because I do not believe such a large and deep river has ever been known to exist in this world.

Columbus's "Relación" has typically been read as though it were simply a summary of the lost *diario* of the third voyage.[83] However, the profound differences between the account of this voyage and that of the first in the *Diario*, or even in its epistolary versions, indicate that the texts were inspired not only by different generic conventions (*relación* and *diario*) but also by fundamentally different discursive practices. While the accounts of the first voyage emphasize the recording properties of writing according to a portolanlike narrative strategy in which the journey unfolds syntagmatically, progressing in linear fashion through the sea- and landscape, the "Relación" presents an exegesis of the Discovery and a paradigm of the Voyage.

Over the course of the four voyages, the prophetic and the miraculous come to play an ever more important role in defining Columbus's experience of space. The secular quest for gold and spices becomes accessory to the sacred quest for redemption and salvation. As Leonardo Olschki reminds us, the empirical instinct in medieval culture was secondary and rudimentary compared to the impulse to consider first and foremost the symbolic or hidden meaning of things,[84] and Columbus's later writing increasingly reflects the medieval tendency to favor ideological geography over empirical geographical experience. The discourse of discovery in the "Relación" privileges mystically charged topics, such as the nature and location of the Terrestrial Paradise and the conquest of Jerusalem, over more literal interpretations based on empirical evidence. Scientific observations, such as the deviation of the magnetic compass, the calculation of lunar eclipses, the nature of equatorial currents and astronomical phenomena, are subordinated to the topoi of the dogmatic spiritual geography that informed much of medieval cartography. His seemingly bizarre rejection of an empirically based explanation in favor of a mystically inflected interpretation of the source of the Orinoco River in the closing paragraphs of the account of the discovery of the mainland was not an exceptional or anomalous moment in the story of the journey. On the contrary, it marks a decisive point in an itinerary whose places symbolized stages in the traveler's knowledge of an Other world.[85] The story of the journey of Discovery ultimately was not about finding a place unknown, but of the revelation of the significance of voyaging to a place foretold.

> Vernán los tardos años del mundo ciertos tiempos en los quales el mar Ocçeano afloxerá los atamentos de las cosas, y se abrirá una grande tierra, y un nuebo marinero como aquél que fué guya de Jasón, que obe nombre Tiphi, descobrirá nuebo mundo, y entonces non será la ysla Tille la postrera de las tierras.
>
> (de Lollis, 2:141)

> In the latter years of the world certain times will arrive in which the Ocean Sea will loosen the bonds of things and a great land will be opened up, and a new navigator, like the one who was Jason's guide, whose name was Typhis, will discover a new world, and then the island of Thule will no longer be the hindermost of lands.[86]

Gender and Discovery

Amerigo Vespucci, the voyager, arrives from the sea. A crusader standing erect, his body in armor, he bears the European weapons of meaning. Behind him are the vessels that will bring back to the European West the spoils of paradise. Before him is the Indian "America," a nude woman reclining in her hammock, an unnamed presence of difference, a body which awakens within a space of exotic fauna and flora. . . . An inaugural scene: after a moment of stupor, on this threshold dotted with colonnades of trees, the conqueror will write the body of the other and trace there his own history. From her he will make a historied body—a blazon—of his labors and phantasms. She will be "Latin" America.[1]

This scene Michel de Certeau has lavishly recreated in words, from a drawing by Jan van der Straet (c. 1575), has become an emblem of the Discovery: the reclining woman, nude in a luxuriant New World landscape, greeting the European man who stands on the shoreline before her, armored and bearing a staff with crucifix in his right hand and an astrolabe in the other (Figure 7). Discreetly hidden under his tunic is a sword. De Certeau's critical assessment of this "inaugural scene" reminds us that it is just one in a long series of graphic and verbal representations of the Discovery as an erotic encounter between a fully clothed European male and a naked Amerindian female, an image that has been firmly established in the Western cultural imagination for quite some time.[2]

In Van der Straet's depiction, the European's hands, as noted, are full. The Indian woman's hands, in contrast, are notably empty, and her right hand is held out toward him in a gesture ambiguously suspended between greeting and invitation. It is indeed difficult to discern with absolute certainty if she is rising in order to embrace him or is in the process of reclining and inviting him to join her in the hammock. In any case, far more than a simple erotic encounter is suggested in this scene, the prelude to an exchange whose character

Figure 7. *America*. Engraving by Theodor Galle after a drawing by Jan van der Straet [Stradanus], c. 1575. From Stradanus, *Nova Reperta* (c. 1580). Courtesy of the Burndy Library, Norwalk, Connecticut.

is hardly ambiguous. "America" offers him her unclothed and re-cumbent body; her empty hands show she has nothing else to offer. He reciprocates, erect and in full armor, with his knowledge and his faith. The economy allegorized in Van der Straet's erotic encounter is, of course, much more than simply sexual. Embedded in this gen-dered exchange are cultural values that privilege the European male's posture in contrast to the Indian female's, which is altogether too receptive, open, and empty, despite her undeniably desirable beauty, which is enhanced by the pastoral gardenlike setting. The explicit mark of her denigration resides in the background. Easily missed at first glance, but strategically situated between the two fig-ures, just above her beckoning arm, is a cannibalistic scene. The idyllic, almost sublime, inflection Van der Straet has given to the encounter taking place in the foreground is undercut by the want implied in her gesture (empty hand beckoning), and the curve of her arm seems to cradle the cannibalistic scene situated just above and beyond it. Three other Indians, naked as she, are roasting a human leg.

The one whom de Certeau calls "an unnamed presence of dif-ference," in fact appears to have had a name from the beginning—her name was Woman. The specific textual marks of that name—India, America (it could just as easily have been Columbia)—are not important. The gendered cultural values they all imply equally, their shared semantic valence, are the real ciphers of her signifi-cance. De Certeau's seminal erotic interpretation of Van der Straet's drawing seems to have missed the most obvious point of all—when the conqueror arrives on "America's" shores, "the body of the other," *her* body, has already been inscribed in the feminine mode. Van der Straet's allegory does not invent but translates the signs of a discourse already in existence. It does not represent an "unnamed presence" waiting to be written, but rather inscribes that presence in a woman's body, as object in an exchange already defined by gen-der difference. To probe the founding terms of that exchange, of that sexual economy, I want to revisit the question of gender in the dis-course of the Discovery by considering the source of this mythical scene of the first encounter in the specific discursive context from which it arose—the textual dialogue between the Crown and Co-lumbus regarding the projection of the economic and political will of Castile and Aragon "plus ultra," that is, ever beyond the ex-panding borders of Spain at the close of the fifteenth century.

In the "Capitulaciones de Santa Fe," the prediscovery contract that set the ideological and practical terms of the enterprise of the Indies, Christopher Columbus's legal rights and obligations on his first westward voyage in the Ocean Sea were carefully spelled out. So was the mercantilistic and imperialistic character of the enterprise. In the "Capitulaciones" Columbus was commissioned by the Catholic Monarchs to *discover, take possession, govern,* and *trade* in whatever islands and mainlands he might come across on his westward voyage. For his trouble, the Admiral was guaranteed criminal and civil authority over whatever territories he discovered, as well as a hefty one-third of all maritime cargo, one-third of all income from the fleet's business, and one-third of the "royal fifth" to be gained from future expeditions not under Columbus's own command. The rest belonged to the Crown.[3]

No mention is made, however, of where those lands might be or what manner of people might inhabit them. No direct allusions are made to the Asiatic destination most historians believe to have been the explicit goal of the voyage.[4] The "Capitulaciones" assumed only that the longed-for islands and mainlands would be governable, in other words populated, and that the inhabitants would have objects of value to trade. Yet the pervasive use of the subjunctive mood in the "Capitulaciones" underscores the hypothetical nature of these assumptions, and so of modern assumptions based on them. In its first textualization in the "Capitulaciones," then, "the Indies" (as the New World is always called in the Columbian texts) appears simply as "islands and mainlands," unnamed and undefined. For all practical purposes the islands and mainlands of the "Capitulaciones" were an empty signifier constituting a semantic void.[5]

As I have done in the opening essays of this volume, I want to situate Columbus's writings in the context of the dialogue between the Admiral and the Crown. The contrapuntal structure of petition and response in the contract itself is reinforced by a phrase near the end of the prologue to the *Diario*. There the inception of the voyage and the act of writing are justified precisely in terms of the mandates contained in the "Capitulaciones":

> Y partí del dicho puerto muy abasteçido de muy muchos manteni-
> mientos y de mucha gente de la mar a tres días del mes de agosto
> del dicho año en un viernes antes de la salida del Sol con media
> hora, y llevé el camino de las Islas de Canaria de Vuestras Altezas
> que son en la dicha mar ocçeana para de allí tomar mi derrota y

navegar tanto que yo llegase a las Indias y dar la embaxada de
Vuestras Altezas a aquellos prínçipes y cumplir lo que así me avían
mandado. Y para esto pensé de escrevir todo este viaje muy puntualmente de día en día todo lo que yo hiziese, viese y passasse.

(Varela, 16–17)

I left the said port, very well provided with supplies and with
many seamen, on the third day of August of the said year, on a Friday, half an hour before sunrise; and I took the route to Your Highnesses' Canary Islands, which are in the said Ocean Sea, in order
from there to take my course and sail so far that I would reach the
Indies and give Your Highnesses' message to those princes and
thus *carry out* that which you had commanded me to do. And for
this purpose I thought of writing on this whole voyage, very dili-
gently, all that I would do and see and experience.

(Dunn & Kelley, 19–21;
emphasis added)

The significant linking here of the voyage and the act of writing with
the "Capitulaciones" is unfortunately obscured by the translation,
though it is the most literal one in print. "Carry out" does not adequately render the connotation of the Spanish verb *cumplir*, which
has to do with completing and responding to a command or request. If we substitute the more accurate "comply" for "carry out,"
we come to understand Columbus's meaning: that for the purpose
of complying with the Crown's mandate, he has decided to write a
detailed account of everything that happens during the voyage. To
comply with the mandate of discovery, as Columbus realized, required not just physical exploration or reconnaissance but also reporting back to the Crown on what was found.

A note on terminology: In this essay, I use the term "discovery"
in a sense commonly accepted in the Spanish of Columbus's time.
In the Columbian texts *descubrir* often means to explore or recon-
noiter a territory in preparation for an incursion of a commercial or
military nature. This sense of the word implies strategic research "in
the field," as it were, for the purpose of gaining an advantage—a
definition ideologically consistent with the nature and diction of the
Columbian enterprise.

Here, then, Columbus acknowledges that his acceptance of the
royal commission entails a responsibility to inform the Crown and,
more specifically, in my reading, to fill the semantic void created by
the reticent treatment in the "Capitulaciones" of the unnamed is-

lands and mainlands that were to be Columbus's destination. Through his discourse, conceived in compliance with the economic and political mandates outlined in the contract, Columbus would respond to questions the "Capitulaciones" implicitly raised, and left unanswered, about the nature of the lands and peoples to be discovered.

Combining the rhetoric of testimony and interpretation, Columbus's writings constitute a powerful act of representation, one whose effect on the development of Western notions of difference is still felt today. The interpretation of Amerindian reality presented in his texts articulates a conceptual model of otherness manifested as a series of metaphors of disparity. When the Columbian texts are read as a unified discourse, instead of as discrete documents, these tropes reveal a coherent hermeneutical strategy of feminization and eroticization that ultimately makes gendered difference the determining characteristic of the sign "Indies."

Saussure defined meaning in language as the product of dissimilarity, suggesting that in the most basic way signs mean in relation to what they do not mean. The *Diario* poignantly exemplifies this postulate. The entry for 16 October, just four days after landfall, includes the following observations on the flora and fauna of the islands: "Y vide muchos árboles muy disformes de los nuestros. . . . Aquí son los peçes tan disformes de los nuestros, qu'es maravilla" (Varela, 36–37; And I saw many trees, very different from ours. . . . Here the fish are so different from ours that it is a marvel, Dunn & Kelley, 89). And on the following day:

> y los árboles todos están tan disformes de los nuestros como el día de la noche, y así las frutas y así las yervas y las piedras y todas las cosas. Verdad es que algunos árboles eran de la naturaleza de otros que ay en Castilla; porende avía muy gran diferençia, y los otros árboles de otras maneras eran tantos que no ay persona que lo pueda dezir ni asemejar a otros de Castilla.
>
> (Varela, 38)

> And all the trees are as different from ours as day from night; and also the fruits and grasses and stones and everything. It is true that some trees are of the same character as others in Castile; nevertheless, there was a very great difference. And the other trees of other kinds were so many that there is no one who can tell it or compare them with others of Castile.
>
> (Dunn & Kelley, 93)

The insistence on difference from the European norm as the definitive semantic characteristic of the sign "Indies" is so pervasive in Columbus's earliest observations as to become monotonous. Moreover, it persists as an important characteristic of the discourse of the Discovery through the narrative of his fourth and final voyage.

Frequently in the *Diario* dissimilarity is explained in terms of the marvelous:

> y aves y paxaritos de tantas maners y tan diversas de las nuestras que es maravilla. Y después ha árboles de mill maneras y todos dan de su manera fruto, y todos güelen qu'es maravilla, que estoy el más penado del mundo de no los cognosçer.
>
> (Varela, 41)

> and birds of so many kinds and sizes, and so different from ours, that it is a marvel. And also there are trees of a thousand kinds and all [with] their own kinds of fruit and all smell so that it is a marvel. I am the most sorrowful man in the world, not being acquainted with them.
>
> (Dunn & Kelley, 105)

The quality of such exclamations is undeniably euphoric. Yet enthusiasm cannot disguise the fact that in the earliest Columbian hermeneutics difference represents the ineffable, that which resists interpretation and assimilation. The qualifier "marvelous" does little to resolve the situation. For Columbus, "marvel" is analogous in the natural realm to "miracle" in the realm of faith—that which cannot be expressed or explained. The exclamation may function as an attempt to disguise the narrator's aphasia in the face of difference, an aphasia that was not the result of some personal shortcoming, but of the essential incapacity of the discourses at his disposal adequately to express such difference.

> Alliende de las sobredichas yslas e hallado otras muchas en las Yndias, de que no curo de dezir en la presente carta. Las quales, con estas otras, son en tanta fertilidad, que aunque yo lo supiese dezir, no hera maravilla ponerse dubda en la crehençia; los aires temperatísimos, los árboles y frutos y yervas son en estrema fermosura y mui diversos de los nuestros, los rríos y puertos son tantos y tan estremos en bondad de los de las partidas de christianos ques maravilla.
>
> ("Carta a los Reyes";
> Rumeu, 2:437)

Besides the above-mentioned islands, I have found many others in the Indies, of which I have not been able to tell in this letter. They, like these others, are so extremely fertile, that even if I were able to express it, it would not be a marvel were it to be disbelieved. The breezes [are] most temperate, the trees and fruits and grasses are extremely beautiful and very different from ours; the rivers and harbors are so abundant and of such extreme excellence when compared to those of the Christian lands that it is a marvel.

Columbian discourse represents "that" as "not this." The "Indies" are defined in terms of what they are not like—Castile, Africa, the familiar landscapes of the Old World. Some eighty years later the Frenchman Jean de Léry, in his *Voyage fait en terre du Bresil, autrement dite Amérique* (1578), expressed his inarticulateness even more candidly: "[The natives'] gestures and countenances are so different from ours, that I confess to my difficulty in representing them in words, or even in pictures."[6]

The dissimilarity of the natural landscape is initially articulated as a semantic void, thinly veiled in a discourse of the ineffable. But when the dissimilarity pertains to the Indians, it is expressed in terms of lack or deficiency. In his well-known book on the question of the "Other," Tzvetan Todorov argued that Columbus was unable or unwilling to perceive fundamental differences in Arawak culture.[7] I would suggest that, on the contrary, not only are differences indeed recognized in the Columbian texts, they are in fact an essential component of the process of interpretation. Difference is not only a dissimilarity perceived in passing but the very basis of representation in Columbian discourse. The first contact with the natives of Guanahaní, on 12 October, is described thus:

y creo que ligeramente se harían cristianos, que me pareçió que ninguna secta tenían. Yo plaziendo a Nuestro Señor levaré de aquí al tiempo de mi partida seis a Vuestras Altezas, para que deprendan fablar.

(Varela, 31)

and I believe that they would become Christians very easily, for it seemed to me that they had no religion. Our Lord pleasing, at the time of my departure I will take six of them to Your Highnesses in order that they may learn to speak.

(Dunn & Kelley, 69)

A similar observation, reaffirming his first impressions, is repeated in the *carta-relación* of January 1494 concerning the second voyage:

> Yo screví, agora a un año, a Vuestras Altezas de todo lo que me pareçía de todos estos pueblos, de su conversaçión con nuestra fee santa, que paresçía mui ligera, entendiéndo nos ellos, y fuésemos entendidos; yo muy más lo afirmo, porque veo que seta alguna no le ynpide.

> (Rumeu, 2:461)

> I wrote Your Highnesses, one year ago, concerning my impressions about all these peoples, of their conversion to our holy faith, which seemed very easy if we understood them and were understood by them; I affirm it all the more [now], because I see that no sect impedes it.

In the letter to Santángel, announcing the discovery, another deficiency is observed: "Andovieron tres iornadas y hallaron infinitas poblaciones pequeñas i gente sin número, mas no cosa de regimiento" (Varela, 140; They [two Spaniards] reconnoitered the country for three days and found an infinite number of small settlements and countless people, but without order or government). The rhetoric is ingenious, though the terms of the argument are hardly credible. Arawak difference in three fundamental areas of human behavior—worship, speech, and government—is expressed as a lack, though probably not because Columbus had any reason to believe they did not have a religion (how could he have determined this from such brief contact?), or some form of government (he later acknowledged they had "kings"), or could not speak (are we to believe that the first encounter was totally mute?). In this context the notion of lacking must be understood as a value judgment—the Indians had no religion or language or government worthy of the name, judged by Columbus's European standards of value.

Value is, in fact, the crux of the matter in Columbian hermeneutics. Difference could be represented as an absence, a lack or deficiency, but it absolutely could *not* be valueless or value-neutral. The mandate in the "Capitulaciones" is expressed in a discourse concerned with issues of power and economic exploitation.[8] Columbus replies in an ideologically complementary discourse of appropriation and domination, but the interpretative character of his response advocates terms distinct from those employed by the Crown. For example, instead of the notoriously elusive gold, spices, and precious gems, stipulated as the preferred merchandise in the "Capitulaciones," the land itself—fertile, productive, and beautiful—is the most valuable treasure in the natural economy of the *Diario*. Passages in praise of the land abound in the Columbian texts; the ones in the *Diario* are particularly poignant because they are products of the original encounter:

> En toda Castilla, no ay tierra que se pueda comparar a ella en hermosura y bondad. Toda esta isla y la de la Tortuga son todas labradas como la campiña de Córdova; tienen sembrado en ellas ajes, que son unos ramillos que plantan, y al pie d'ellos naçen unas raízes como çanahorias, que sirven por pan y rallan y amassan y hazen pan d'ellas, y después tornan a plantar el mismo ramillo en otra parte y torna a dar cuatro y cinco de aquellas raízes que son muy sabrosas: propio gusto de castañas. . . . Y los árboles de allí diz que eran tan viçiosos que las hojas dexavan de ser verdes y eran prietas de verdura. Era cosa de maravilla ver aquellos valles y los ríos y buenas aguas y las tierras para pan, para ganado de toda suerte, de qu'ellos no tienen alguna, para güertas y para todas las cosas del mundo qu'el hombre sepa pedir.
>
> (Varela, 83)

> In all of Castile there is no land that can be compared to it [the island] in beauty and goodness. All of this island and that of Tortuga are cultivated like the plain of Cordova. They have sown yams, which are some little twigs that they plant, and at the foot of the twigs some roots like carrots grow, which serve as bread; and they scrape and knead and make bread of them. And later they plant the same twig elsewhere and it again produces four or five of those roots which are very tasty, having the same flavor as chestnuts. . . . And the trees there, he says, were so vigorous that the leaves ceased to be green, they were so dark in foliage. It was a wonderful thing to see those valleys and rivers and good water; and the lands [good] for bread and for livestock of all kinds—of which they have none—and for vegetable gardens and everything in the world that man can ask for.
>
> (Dunn & Kelley, 233)

The land thus becomes the substitute merchandise, the desirable object to be possessed. In the letter to Santángel, Cuba is described in these terms: "It is a desirable land, and once seen, is never to be

relinquished" (Morison, 185). The text creates in the reader a long-
ing for the land, through a rhetoric of desire that inscribes "the Indies" in a psychosexual discourse of the feminine whose principal
coordinates are initially beauty and fertility and, ultimately, possession and domination.[9]

At issue here are the very questions of political power and economic value expressed in the "Capitulaciones," but an aesthetic dimension has been added to the commercial one. The Columbian
texts exhibit a curiously dichotomized discourse whose parts may,
at first, even appear contradictory. On the one hand, the idealized
and poeticized descriptions of the natural and human landscapes
recall the classical *locus amoenus* and the legends of the Golden Age.
These passages invariably emphasize the physical or spiritual
beauty of the indigenous element. On the other hand, the mercantilistic and imperialistic discursive mode, an explicit response to the
tone and terms of the mandate outlined in the "Capitulaciones,"
conveys a marked disdain for the Indians. While these two modes
may seem at odds with one another, they are, we shall see, complementary parts of a discursive whole.[10]

Although they are radically different in their specific terms, the
poeticized-idealized and mercantilistic-imperialistic discursive modalities often appear contiguously in the text. In the way of punctuation, compositional divisions, style, context, or tenor, very little
differentiates the two modes.[11] In many of the testimonial passages
in the *Diario* the writing appears to flow seamlessly between one
mode and the other, and the effect is awkward and somewhat jar-
ring:

> Esta costa toda y la parte de la isla que yo vi es toda cuasi playa, y
> la isla la más fermosa cosa que yo vi, que si las otras son muy her-
> mosas, esta es más. Es de muchos árboles y muy verdes y muy
> grandes, y esta tierra es más alta que las otras islas falladas, y en
> ella algún altillo, no que se le pueda llamar montaña, mas cosa que
> aformosea lo otro, y pareçe de muchas aguas. Allá, al medio de la
> isla, d'esta parte al Nordeste haze una grande angla, y a muchos ar-
> boledos y muy espessos y muy grandes. Yo quise ir a surgir en ella
> para salir a tierra y ver tanta fermosura, mas era el fondo baxo y no
> podía surgir salvo largo de tierra, y el viento era muy bueno para
> venir a este cabo, adonde yo surgí agora, al cual puse nombre Cabo
> Fermoso, porque así lo es. Y así no surgí en aquella angla, y aun

porque vide este cabo de allá tan verde y tan fermoso, así como todas las otras cosas y tierras d'estas islas que yo no sé adónde me
vaya primero, ni me se cansan los ojos de ver tan fermosas ver-
duras y tan diversas de las nuestras, y aun creo que a en ellas muchas yervas y muchos árboles que valen mucho en España para tin-
turas y para medicinas de espeçería, mas yo no los cognozco, de
que llevo grande pena. Y llegando aquí a este cabo, vino el olor tan
bueno y suave de flores o árboles de la tierra, que era la cosa más
dulçe del mundo. De mañana, antes de que yo de aquí vaya, iré en
tierra a ver qué es; aquí en el cabo no es la poblaçión salvo allá más
dentro, adonde dizen estos hombres que yo traigo qu'está el rey y
que trae mucho oro. Y yo de mañana quiero ir tanto avante que
halle la poblaçión y vea o aya lengua con este rey que, según estos
dan las señas, él señorea todas estas islas comaracanas, y va ves-
tido y trae sobre sí mucho oro, aunque no doy mucha fe a sus de-
zires, así por no los entender yo bien como en cognoscer qu'ellos
son tan pobres de oro que cualquiera poco qu'este rey traiga los pareçe a ellos mucho. Este, a qui yo digo Cabo Fermoso, creo que es
isla apartada de Samoeto y aun a[y] ya otra entremedias pequeña.
Yo no curo así de ver tanto por menudo, porque no lo podría fazer
en çincuenta años, porque quiero ver y descubrir lo más que yo pudiere para bolver a Vuestras Altezas, a Nuestro Señor aplaziendo,
en Abril. Verdad es que fallando adónde aya oro o espeçería en
cantidad, me deterné fasta que yo aya d'ello cuanto pudiere, y por
esto no fago sino andar para ver de topar en ello.

(Varela, 39–40)

All of this coast and the part of the island that I saw is almost all
beach, and the island the most beautiful thing that I have ever
seen. For if the others are very beautiful this one is more so. It is an
island of many very green and very large trees. And this land is
higher than the other islands found, and there are on it some small
heights; not that they can be called mountains, but they are things
that beautify the rest; and it seems to have much water. There in
the middle of the island, from this part northeast, it forms a great
bight and there are many wooded places, very thick and of very
large extent. I tried to go there to anchor in it so as to go ashore
and see so much beauty; but the bottom was shoal and I could not
anchor except far from land, and the wind was very good for going
to this cape where I am anchored now, to which I gave the name
Cabo Hermoso because such it is. And so I did not anchor in that
bight and also because I saw this cape from there, so green and so
beautiful; and likewise are all the other things and lands of these islands, so that I do not know where to go first; nor do my eyes grow

tired of seeing such beautiful verdure and so different from ours. And I even believe that there are among them many plants and many trees which in Spain are valued for dyes and for medicinal spices; but I am not acquainted with them, for which I feel great sorrow. And when I arrived here at this cape, the smell of flowers or trees that came from the land was so good and soft that it was the sweetest thing in the world. In the morning, before I leave this place I will go ashore to see what is here on the cape. The town is not here but further inland where these men that I bring say the king is and that he wears much gold. And in the morning I want to go forward so far that I find the town and see or talk with this king of whom these men give the following details: he is the lord of all these nearby islands and he goes about dressed and wearing much gold on his person. Although I do not give much credit to what they say, from not understanding them well and also from recognizing that they are so poor in gold that any little bit that the king may wear seems much to them. This cape here that I call Cabo Hermoso I believe is on an island separate from Samoet and also that there is still another small one in between. I am not taking pains to see so much in detail because I could not do it in 50 years and because I want to see and explore as much as I can so I can return to Your Highnesses in April, Our Lord pleasing. It is true that, finding where there is gold or spices in quantity, I will stay until I get as much of it as I can. And for this reason I do nothing but go forward to see if I come across it.

(Dunn & Kelley, 101–3)

In its sheer exuberance and proliferation of observations on the aesthetic qualities of the land, this passage is typical of the geographical descriptions found in the Columbian texts. But the idealizing or poeticizing mode of diction, intended to provoke aesthetic appreciation (even rapture) in the reader, abruptly gives way to a quite prosaic consideration of the possible economic value and exploitability of the land and the wealth of its inhabitants. This conceptual and rhetorical shift may strike the reader as contradictory, but apparently it was not so to the narrator. The expressed motivation to go inexorably forward and without delay in search of gold and spices casually follows the admission that a cape, notable only for its beauty, detains Columbus overnight and into the next morning. The tensionless juxtaposition of the two competing purposes is quite striking when one recalls that the report is addressed to the

Crown, which was footing the costs of the expedition and no doubt anxiously awaiting its returns.

The idealization of the land has its counterpart in the human economy, in the appreciation of the Indians' physical beauty and their complementary suitability for evangelization. Protracted and detailed descriptions of their bodies, as in the entry of 13 October, the day after landfall, abound in the *Diario*:

> Luego que amaneció, vinieron a la playa muchos d'estos hombres, todos mançebos, como dicho tengo, y todos de buena estatura, gente fermosa; los cabellos no crespos, salvo corredíos y gruessos como sedas de cavallo, y todos de la frente y cabeça muy ancha, más que otra generación que fasta aquí aya visto; y los ojos muy fermosos y no pequeños; y ellos ninguno prieto, salvo de la color de los canarios. . . . Las piernas muy derechas, todos a una mano, y no barriga, salvo muy bien hecha.
>
> (Varela, 31)

> As soon as it dawned, many of these people [i.e., men] came to the beach—all young, as I have said, and all of good stature; very handsome people, with hair not curly but straight and coarse like horsehair and all of them very wide in the forehead and head, more so than any other race that I have seen so far. And their eyes are very handsome and not small; and none of them are black, but of the color of Canary Islanders. . . . All alike have very straight legs and no belly but are very well formed.[12]

The absence of paintbrush or even camera lens is hardly noticed in the presence of Columbus's abilities in verbal portraiture. In the entry for the following day, he observes with equal interest the tumultuous welcome that greeted the Spaniards and the generosity and willingness of the Indians to provide them with food and water, apparently (he thought) because the Indians believed they had come from the heavens. He relates his search for an apt site for a fort, describes his hosts' lack of military skill, and then adds:

> Vuestras Altezas cuando mandaren puédenlos todos llevar a Castilla o tenellos en la misma isla captivos, porque con cincuenta hombres los ternán todos sojuzgados, y les harán hazer todo lo que quisieren.
>
> (Varela, 33)

whenever Your Highnesses may command, all of them can be
taken to Castile or held captive in this same island; because with 50
men all of them could be held in subjection and can be made to do
whatever one might wish.

(Dunn & Kelley, 75)[13]

He concludes the entry with the following observation, "y se hazen
guerra, la una a la otra, aunque estos son muy símpliçes y muy lin-
dos cuerpos de hombres" (33; and they make war on one another,
even though these men are very simple and very handsome in body,
77). Especially striking in this passage is the notion that somehow
the Indians' martial simplicity is related to their physical beauty. Or,
to put it another way, that their beauty explains and even justifies
their lack of skill in warfare. Such observations reveal how fine the
line is between idealization and denigration in these texts. On the
one hand, bodily beauty is complemented by a fairness of spirit, a
grace of being.[14] But these same charms readily become a degrading
of the Indians when articulated to define Indian-Spanish relations
so as to justify the projection of European power in the subjugation
of the natives.

Desire and disdain cohabit in the Columbian texts, nondisjunc-
tively and noncontradictorily in the same discursive space. In the
letter to Santángel, the following observations are made:

> La gente d'esta isla y de todas las otras que he fallado y havido ni
> aya havido noticia, andan todos desnudos, hombres y mugeres, así
> como sus madres los paren, haunque algunas mugeres se cobijan
> un solo lugar con una foia de yerva o una cosa de algodón que para
> ello fazen. Ellos no tienen fierro ni azero ni armas, ni son para ello;
> no porque no sea gente bien dispuesta y de fermosa estatura, salvo
> que son muy temerosos a maravilla. . . . que muchas vezes me ha
> acaecido embiar a tierra dos o tres hombres a alguna villa para
> haver fabla, i salir a ellos d'ellos sin número, y después que los
> veían llegar fuían a no aguardar padre a hijo. Y esto no porque a
> ninguno se aya hecho mal, antes a todo cabo adonde yo aya estado
> y podido haver fabla, les he dado de todo lo que tenía . . . sin rece-
> bir por ello cosa alguna, mas son así temerosos sin remedio.

(Varela, 141–42)

The inhabitants of this island, and of all the others I have seen or of
which I have received information, all go naked, the women as well
as the men, just as their mothers bore them, with the exception of
some women who cover themselves with a leaf or something made

of cotton which they make for that purpose. They do not have any iron or steel or weapons, nor are they capable of using them; not from any deformity of body, but because they are incredible cowards . . . for it has sometimes occurred that when I have sent two or three men to some village to speak with the natives, they have been greeted by countless Indians and after they saw them arrive they fled so that even the fathers forsook their children. And it is not the result of any harm that we might have done them, for on the contrary, everywhere I have been and have been able to speak to the natives, I have given them everything that I had . . . without receiving anything in return, but they are hopeless cowards.

Here the distinction between physical beauty and moral valor is clearly drawn. The Indians have the former but lack the latter; they are physically well-endowed but morally deficient. Notably, the repeated remarks about nudity typically function to underscore the natives' vulnerability in confronting the Spaniards and not, as one might expect, their physical attractiveness.[15]

In a passage cited earlier, *mancebo* (male adolescent, youth) is used to describe the Indians who come to the beach to greet Columbus and his crew. While the choice of this term could be interpreted as an idealizing tribute to their youthful physical beauty, *mancebo* also has the important connotations of incomplete masculine sexual, intellectual, and moral development (Figure 8). In the first dictionary of the Spanish language, published in 1611, Covarrubias defines *mancebo* as a male-child still under his father's authority. The paternalistic implications evoked by this word choice are unmistakable in a passage from a letter of the second voyage, dated 20 April 1494:

Todos fechos son como de niños . . . estos fazen lo que been fazer porque, si alguno furta o faze otro mal, es de la misma manera que entre los niños se haze; ellos son sotiles que luego hazen lo que veen hazer, mas es çierto, y para su govierno y plazer, ningún ayuntamiento hazen al oro ni de otra cosa alguna; salvo por ynvidia, de que son ocupados, cogen oro u otra cosa para que se les dé lo que desean; la cual ynbidia es propia como de niños.

(Rumeu, 2:475–76)

All their deeds are like children's . . . these [people] do what they see others do; if one of them steals or does some other ill deed, it is in the same fashion as among children; they are smart in that they do what they see done, but it is also true that for their government

Figure 8. *Ynsula hyspana*. Adolescent-like Indians greeting the Spaniards. Woodcut print from *De insulis epistola Cristoferi Colom* (Basel, 1493). Courtesy of the John Carter Brown Library, Brown University.

and pleasure they do not collect gold or anything else, except out of envy, which preoccupies them; they gather gold or other things so that one will give them what they desire—which envy is like that proper to children.

Arawak inferiority is defined in relation to Spanish superiority, which initially manifests itself as a benevolent custodianship:

> Yo defendí que no se les diesen cosas tan siviles como pedazos de escudillas rotas y pedazos de vidrio roto y cabos de agugetas; haunque cuando ellos esto podían llegar, los parescía haver la mejor ioya del mundo: que se acertó haver un marinero por una agugeta, de oro de peso de dos castellanos y medio. . . . Fasta los pedazos de los arcos rotos de la pipas tomavan y davan lo que tenían como bestias.
>
> (Varela, 142)

> I forbade that they be given such vile things as pieces of broken dishes, glass or latchets, although when they could obtain one, they considered it the best jewel in the world. A sailor managed to get gold worth two and a half castellanos for a latchet. . . . Even for the broken stems of pipes, they gave anything they possessed, like animals.

The explicit comparison of the Indians to beasts—in order to explain the qualitative differences in intellectual aptitude between them and the Europeans—turns the Arawaks' generosity, initially an aspect of Columbus's spiritual idealization of the Indians, into an inability to discriminate between the priceless and the worthless, an intellectual deficiency typical of animals.[16] This inequality of exchange, Stephen Greenblatt has observed, became a commonplace in the European literature of exploration and conquest, to describe Indian intellectual inferiority:

> The European dream . . . is of grossly unequal gift exchange: I give you a glass bead and you give me a pearl worth half your tribe. The concept of relative economic value—the notion that a glass bead or hawk's bell would be a precious rarity in the New World—is alien to most Europeans; they think that the savages simply do not understand the natural worth of things and hence can be tricked into exchanging treasure for trifles, full signs for empty signs.[17]

The comparison of the Indians to beasts is not, however, to be read as a denial of their humanity. Quite to the contrary, Columbus consistently affirms that the newly found peoples can and should be converted to Christianity. But, while the Indians' humanness per se is never doubted, they are judged an inferior class of human being, pusillanimous, martially inept, and lacking in discrimination. Even though the Caribs are described as aggressive in the letter to Santángel, their perceived inferiority in relation to Europeans is evident:

> Así que mostruos ne he hallado ni noticia, salvo de una isla que es Carib, la segunda a la entrada de las Indias, que es poblada de una iente que tienen en todas las islas por muy ferozes, los cualles comen carne umana. Estos tienen muchas canuas, con las cuales corren todas las islas de India, roban y toman cuanto pueden. Ellos no son más disformes que los otros, salvo que tienen en costumbre de traer los cabellos largos como mugeres. . . . Son ferozes entre estos otros pueblos que son en demasiado grado covardes, mas yo no los tengo en nada más que a los otros.
>
> (Varela, 144–45)

> Thus, as I have said, I found not a trace of monsters, nor did I hear of any except for a certain island called Carib, the second island as one enters the Indies, which is inhabited by a people considered very fierce throughout these islands, and they eat human flesh. They have many canoes with which they travel to all these islands of India, stealing and taking whatever they can. They are no more different than the others except that they wear their hair long like women. . . . They are considered fierce among the other peoples who are exceedingly cowardly, but I think no more of them than of the rest.[18]

Beyond the patent contempt expressed in this passage, the allusion to monsters again strikes the fundamental chord of the Columbian representation of New World reality—difference. But deficiency and dissimilarity are inextricably linked in the interpretation of the significance of that reality.

The triad—monsters, Caribs, women—forms a complex metaphor for inferiority whose ideological source can be traced to Aristotelian notions of difference. Aristotle maintained that the male principle governed the workings of the universe. Deviation from the male principle thus constituted a degeneration. Femaleness was a step toward imperfection, which in its most extreme manifestations yielded monstrosity. The triumph of female matter over the male principle, although necessary for the survival of the species, and therefore not monstrous in itself, opened the door, as it were, to imperfection and consequently to the possibility of monstrosity. In the *Politics* this ontology of difference acquires a pragmatic socio-political dimension. Aristotle's concept of natural slavery, articulated in book 1, is the centerpiece of a theory of domination and subjugation that pretended to explain the innate inferiority of certain types of human beings in order to justify the exercise of power by elite males in the subjugation of others. According to Aristotle, the natural slave is a physically gifted but intellectually and morally deficient being. From birth all creatures are marked for either subjugation or domination, Aristotle argues, and the rule of those deemed superior over those deemed inferior is both natural and expedient. In this scheme, of course, the female is inferior to the male:

> Again, the male is by nature superior, and the female inferior; and the one rules and the other is ruled; this principle of necessity extends to all mankind. Where then there is such a difference as that between the soul and body, or between men and animals (as in the case of those whose business is to use their body, and who can do nothing better), the lower sort are by nature slaves, and it is better for them as for all inferiors that they should be under the rule of a master.[19]

In this context, Columbus's use of "monster" denotes someone who does not conform either in appearance or behavior to the European norm, someone who belongs to the Aristotelian categories of natural servants or slaves—animals, women, and intellectually and morally deficient men. The Caribs' anthropophagy and their long feminine hair—symbols of difference and inferiority—strike Columbus as monstrous. In Columbus's portrait of the Indians, as in Aristotle's description of the natural slave, inferiority is expressed as a *lacking*, especially in the areas of intellectual and moral capacity, while superiority is conceived as possession of a full complement of the attributes that constitute humanness in its highest form. In the Columbian texts, as in Aristotle's *Politics*, domination is presented as a philanthropical and paternalistic act: the "haves" (the fully human elite males or citizens) supplement the deficiency of the "have nots," or natural slaves, through paternalistic intervention. By dominating the natural slaves, the elite allows them to lead better lives. Superiority, then, means to possess or have, but especially to be able to supplement a deficiency in others, to complete, to fill an empty space. Inferiority is one of the marks of difference in Columbian writing. The other, as we have seen, is ideality. Columbian discourse oscillates continually between these two poles, between disdain and desire:

> he fecho . . . grande amistad con el Rey de aquella tierra, en tanto grado que se preciava de me lllamar y tener por hermano. E haunque le mudase la voluntad a hoffender esta gente, él ni los suios no saben qué sean armas, y andan desnudos como ya he dicho. Son los más temerosos que ay en el mundo, así que solamente la gente que allá queda es para destroir toda aquella tierra.
>
> (Varela, 144)

> I have become . . . great friends with the king of that land, to such a degree that he took pride in calling me brother. And even if he should decide to hurt these people [the Spaniards left at La Navidad], neither he nor his subjects know what weapons are, and they go naked, as I have said. They are the most timorous in the world, so that the people who remain there alone are enough to destroy the entire country.

> Esta gente, como ya dixe, son todos de muy linda estatura, altos de cuerpos e de muy lindos gestos, los cabellos muy largos e llanos y traen las cabeças atadas con unos pañuelos labrados, como ya dixe, hermosos, que pareçen de lexos de seda y almaizares.
>
> (Varela, 210)

> These people, as I have said, are all of graceful stature, tall of body and beautiful of countenance; their hair [is] very long and straight, and they wear their heads wrapped in beautifully wrought scarves, as I have said, that from a distance appear to be like turbans made of silk.

At issue in both these passages is the interpretation of the relationship of European domination over the Indians and the establishment of the Spaniards' right of possession. The idealized feminizing descriptions of the Indians, such as in the second passage, ultimately are as much at the service of the interpretation of the power imbalance as the obviously denigrating passages.

In Columbian hermeneutics the dichotomy between Spaniard

and Indian is ideologized in terms of a masculine-feminine contrast and articulated through the rhetorical feminization of the term "Indian." Among the numerous remarks in the *Diario* that ascribe effeminate characteristics to the Indians are passages concerning the Arawaks' physical attributes, their cowardice, and their apparently spontaneous and natural subservience to the Spaniards.

> y alguno de los de mi compañía salieron en tierra tras ellos, y todos fugeron como gallinas.
>
> (Varela, 34)

> and some of the men of my company went ashore after them, and they all fled like hens.

> se folgavan mucho de nos hazer plazer.
>
> (Varela, 36)

> they delighted in giving us pleasure.

> Esta gente es muy mansa y muy temerosa, desnuda como tengo dicho, sin armas y sin ley.
>
> (Varela, 51)

> These people are very gentle and very timid, naked, as I said before, without weapons and without law.

> certifica el Almirante a los Reyes que diez hombres hagan huir a diez mill, tan cobardes y medrosos son, que ni traen armas, salvo unas varas y en el cabo d'ellas un palillo agudo tostado.
>
> (Varela, 71)

> the Admiral assures the Sovereigns that ten men can make ten thousand [Indians] flee, so cowardly and fearful are they that they do not even carry weapons, except for wooden javelins with a fired sharp stick at the tip.[20]

In these and other passages, the Indians are defined through a series of gender-specific oppositions that are hierarchized in Western culture: courage/cowardice, activity/passivity, strength/weakness, intellect/body. In activating these cultural dichotomies, Columbian writing ultimately interprets the difference between Europeans and Indians as a gender difference, not in the sexual or biological sense, but as difference ideologized and inscribed onto a cultural economy

Figure 9.   Long-haired Indians. Woodcut print from *La lettera dellisole che ha trovato nuovamente il Re dispagna* (Florence, 1493). Courtesy of the Alderman Library, University of Virginia.

where gender becomes fundamentally a question of value, power, and dominance (see Figure 9).

In the "Relación" to the Crown recounting his third voyage, Columbus makes a striking and seemingly aberrant observation. He refers to the newly discovered lands as "otro mundo" (other world). Moreover, he affirms that the globe is not round at all, as most of the authorities on the subject believed; rather it is shaped more like a pear, or a woman's breast. As he sailed to this "other world," he claims, he was actually moving upward on the slope of the breast, toward the location of the Earthly Paradise. The Garden, he declares, is situated on the nipple; very appropriately so, he adds, since it is the spot closest to heaven. This startling interpretation of the shape and location of Paradise, significantly anchored on the term "other world," illustrates the culmination of the process of feminization—in this case, even eroticization—of the sign "Indies" that began in the *Diario*. The metaphor of the paradisiacal breast is no aberration, but an emblem or avatar, the product of a hermeneutical process that began as early as 12 October 1492.[21]

Paradise, Columbus warns, is not accessible to men except through divine intervention. As in classical and medieval literature, the Garden is symbolic of the ideal, of yearning and nonpossession, of desire and inaccessibility.[22] But through the eroticization in the "Relación" Paradise enters abruptly—as a fruit-breast—into the discursive economies of appropriation and domination: it becomes acquirable. Through metaphor, Columbus "delivers" the Indies-cum-Paradise to Ferdinand and Isabella, according to the terms stipulated in the "Capitulaciones." Divine injunctions against entering Eden notwithstanding, it was now up to the Catholic Monarchs to figure out how to move God to open up the gates. No doubt, Columbus's urging that the Crown use the gold of the Indies to mount a crusade to liberate the Holy Land was motivated by his desire to gain admittance to Paradise, if not in this life then in the next.

Throughout the Middle Ages and into the Renaissance, the correspondence of sexual desire and the paradise image as inaccessible ideal is made explicit; the theme appears in the works of Dante, Ariosto, Spenser, and Shakespeare, among others. But Columbus's articulation of this topic reflects his familiarity not with Dante but with popular treatments of the paradise theme in the context of mercantile and conquest literature. Closer to Columbus's own ambitions and dearer to what we know of his reading tastes was the account of Marco Polo's travels in the Far East, a keystone text for Columbus during the period in which he formulated the nature and goals of the enterprise of the Indies.[23] In the mercantilistic discourse of the *Travels*, Polo establishes the link between commerce, desire, and paradise in describing the ancient Chinese city of Kin-sai, or Qinsay (Hangzhou): "At the end of three days you reach the noble and magnificent city of Kin-sai, a name that signifies 'the celestial city,' and which it merits from its preeminence to all others in the world, in point of grandeur and beauty, as well as from its abundant delights, which might lead an inhabitant to imagine himself in paradise." The erotic element is made more explicit a few pages later, in Polo's description of one of Kin-sai's primary delights—its prostitutes: "Thus intoxicated with sensual pleasures, when they [the merchants] return to their homes they report that they have been in Kin-sai, or the celestial city, and pant for the time, when they may be enabled to revisit paradise." Notably, Kin-sai is precisely the city mentioned by Columbus as his destination in the *Diario* and in a letter of the second voyage, where he hoped to find the Grand Khan.[24]

For Columbus, the metaphorical linking of eroticized gender difference, the idealization of territory, and the interpretation of otherness had an important contemporary antecedent in the popular ballads associated with the Christian reconquest struggles against the Moors. In the historical ballads of the *romanceros*, military conflict is frequently related to erotic situations or topics, and the Other (the enemy) may appear as the object of the subject's desire or scorn. For example, the well-known ballad "Abenámar, Abenámar" articulates the Christian siege of the Moorish city of Granada as a seduction. The Christian besieger is presented as a suitor, the city is personified as a reluctant woman, and the territorial appropriation represented by the siege itself is eroticized through a rhetoric of love and betrothal.

In the Columbian texts, the feminization and eroticization of the sign "Indies" is articulated in two seemingly contradictory operations—idealization and denigration. Yet in a cultural economy where the masculine is valued above the feminine, eroticization of the subordinate feminine implies both desire and disdain. As a rhetorical operation, eroticization permits the idealization and denigration of the feminized object to inhabit the same discursive space without disjunction or contradiction.[25] The surface contradiction—the oscillation between the romantic and vilified visions of the Indies—now reveals itself as a complementarity, a pair of attitudes allied to the ideology of discovery proposed by the "Capitulaciones."

In the letter of the fourth voyage, Columbus's denigration of the Indies culminates in an apocalyptic discourse grounded in Christian providentialism. Nature and the Indians turn against Columbus with an ire that threatens the very survival of the expedition. The ships are battered, the crew is tired and sick, and the Indians have suddenly become hostile, when a delirious Columbus hears a voice in the darkness assuring him that he is God's chosen one and urging him to persevere. The Indies have finally turned Medusa-like, a devourer of men, an untameable shrew. Only through divine intervention are Columbus and his crew saved from her wrath.[26]

The feminine paradigm, in its negative Aristotelian dimension, became a central component in the construction of New World otherness by the Spanish humanists of the sixteenth century, who continued the process of defining the Amerindian in terms of Spanish hegemony.[27] In contrast to these later texts, Columbian discourse is more medieval in its Christian-chivalric idealization of the feminine, but also considerably more subtle and complex. Sixteenth-century interpretations turned a dialectic formulation into a monolectic one by eliminating the idealizing element of the Columbian paradigm (as Vitoria and Sepúlveda did) or by suppressing the negative or disdainful dimension (Las Casas's strategy).

In a discussion of phallocentrism and difference in *The Newly Born Woman*, Hélène Cixous has argued that Western culture defines otherness in relation to sameness, thereby constituting a hierarchized dichotomy where identity is the privileged status. Identity, Cixous explains, can be the product of an inherent sameness or of a process of assimilation or appropriation. It can be triggered by a desire to make something one's own, to possess something considered to be unequal, something understood not just as different but as less than self.[28] Woman, therefore, enters into the cultural economy not only as the opposite of man, but as less than man. She acquires her value as use-value, as merchandise for exchange among men, as Luce Irigaray puts it.[29] A passage in the *Diario* exemplifies this commodification of women. The phrasing is chillingly blunt and to the point:

> Y después enbié a una casa que es de la parte del río del Poniente, y truxeron siete cabeças de mugeres, entre chicas e grandes y tres niños. Esto hize por que mejor se comportan los hombres en España haviendo mugeres de su tierra que sin ellas.
>
> (Varela, 56)

> And later I sent [men] to a house that is to the west of the river, and they brought seven head of women, counting young ones and adults, and three boys. This I did because men behave better in Spain having women from their country than without them.[30]

In Spanish as in English, then and now, "cabeças"/head is not applied to people, but to livestock. Nevertheless, Columbus applies it
to the Indian females, while the "niños" are counted separately. The
livestock imagery is unfortunately appropriate: the seven women
were rounded up and brought on board to mollify the Indian men
who had earlier been taken captive. These women were not the
wives of the men, just samples, as it were, taken from the same island. One suspects they were also expected to satisfy the Spanish
crew during the long return voyage, but the text is silent on that
matter.

In Columbian writing, Antonello Gerbi has argued, contrast
"gives way to a vague but significant awareness of affinities and
similarities." According to Gerbi, similitude is the sign of assimila-
bility. Although his case for the role of similitude in these texts
seems much overstated—"Haiti is the *isla Española*, the 'Spanish Island.' It is Spain, it belongs to Spain and resembles Spain in every
way"—it is nevertheless an important observation. Columbian discourse not only attempts to define the "Indies" but, above all,
strives to absorb it. Affinity and resemblance ultimately are at the
service of the articulation of New World inferiority. Nature in the
Indies resembles an idealized and poeticized Spanish landscape,
but, as Gerbi himself notes, it is a landscape especially suited for
Spanish domination.[31] Thus resemblance effected through the feminization and eroticization of the sign "Indies" becomes yet another
marker of difference and consequently, yet again, of inferiority.

Columbus's supposed inability to perceive difference can instead
be viewed as a desire to appropriate, to assimilate otherness, to
obliterate the autonomy that otherness implies within a relationship of equality. The will to appropriate expressed in Columbian
discourse is far more complex than that articulated in economic and
political terms by the Crown. The strength of Columbian discourse
is derived from its interpretative nature—from its successful inscription of New World reality into the Western cultural economy.
If the contract between Columbus and Isabella and Ferdinand mandated political and economic domination of whatever lands might
be discovered, Columbus's writings responded by interpreting the
nature of the newly found territories and their inhabitants in relation to European norms. They articulate the terms of the relation-

ship self-servingly, rendering possession and domination by the Europeans the only correct and most expedient actions.

I have suggested that Columbian discourse ultimately responds, in Cixous's words, to a "political economy of the masculine and feminine." That is, these texts interpret the central issues of power, dominance, and appropriation in terms of the sexual dichotomy.[32] Columbus does not merely describe difference, which is a value-neutral operation; he interprets difference in dialogue and compliance with the political and economic terms set forth in the "Capitulaciones de Santa Fe" and other pre-Discovery documents. The Discovery thus is inscribed in a gendered discourse defined by a contradiction: desire for the Other cohabits with a profound sense of alienation from difference. As in Van der Straet's allegory of the first encounter between Europeans and Amerindians, just beyond the inviting body of the feminine Other lies the body of the self dismembered—a warning of the dangers of contact. Yearning for the ideal continually alternates with denigration of that which is deemed barbarous, in other words, alien and inferior. Columbus's "Indies"—a feminized and ultimately eroticized sign, desired and reviled—was inscribed into the Columbian exchange as a feminine value, intended for consumption in a cultural economy where discovery means gaining an advantage by uncovering a weakness, and femininity is synonymous with exploitability.

Appendix

Carta a los Reyes de 4 marzo 1493

†

(Fol. 1 r.) Christianísimos e mui altos e mui poderosos prínçipes. Aquel eterno Dios que a dado tantas victorias a Vuestras Altezas, agora les dio la más alta que hasta oi a dado a prínçipes. Yo bengo de las Yndias con el armada que Vuestras Altezas me dieron, a donde yo pasé en treinta y tres días, después que yo partí de vuestros rreinos; a los catorze, destos treinta y tres, fueron calmerías, en que anduve mui poco camino. Hallé gente sin número y mui muchas yslas, de las quales tomé posesión en nombre de Vuestras Altezas, con pregón rreal e vandera rreal de Vuestras Altezas estendida y no fue contra dicho. A la primera, puse nombre la ysla Sant Salvador, a memoria de Su Alta Magestad; a la segunda de Santa María de Conçibiçión; a la terçera Fernandina; a la quarta La Ysavela; a la quinta la Juana, y a las otras, casi nombre nuevo. Después que yo llegué a La Juana seguí la costa della al poniente y la hallé tan grande que yo pensé que no sería ysla, salvo tierra firme, y que sería la provinçia del Catayo, ni podría aver dello notiçia porque en todo cavo, donde yo llegava, huía la gente y no podía aver habla; y porque no podía aver fallado poblaçón notable, creía que andando por costa no podría herrar de hallar alguna villa o gran çiudad, así como quentan aquéllos que an estado por tierra en la dicha provinçia; y después que seguí mucho esta tierra, hallé que yo dexava al poniente y me llevava al setrentrión y hallé el viento que de allá venía, con el qual quise porfiar fasta que pasase y viniese otro, porque ya era el ynbierno encarnado, y no tenía el propósito salvo de huir del austro, y así tomé la buelta atrás; en este medio ya entendía algo de la fabla y

señas de unos yndios, que yo avía tomado en la ysla de
Sant Salvador, y entendía que todavía hera esta ysla; y ansí
vine en un mui buen puerto, del qual enbié dos hombres
la tierra adentro, tres jornadas, con uno de los mismos
yndios que yo traía, el qual avía tomado amistad conmigo,
por que viesen y supiesen si avía çiudades o grandes poblazones y qué tierra hera y qué avía en ella. Hallaron muchas poblazones y gente sin súmero, mas no cosa de gran
rregimiento. Y ansí se bolvieron, y yo partí y tomé en el
dicho puerto çiertos yndios por que tanbién yo pudiese
dellos entender o comprehender de las dichas tierras. Y así
seguí la costa de la mar desta isla al oriente çiento y siete
leguas hasta adonde hazía fin; y antes que yo della partiese, yo vide otra isla al oriente, distante desta diez y ocho
leguas, a la qual luego lamé La Española, y me fue luego
a ella y seguí su costa de la parte del setrentrión así como
de La Juana, siempre rrecta lignea al oriente çiento y
ochenta y ocho leguas bien grandes; y seguí em mui muchos puertos en los quales, y en todos los otros de las otras
yslas, puse una grandísima cruz, en lugar más ydóneo, y
obe en muchos lugares lenguas abasta; que yo andove ansí
fasta diez y seis días de henero, que yo determiné de bolver a Vuestras Altezas, así por aver ya fallado lo más de lo
que yo deseava, como porque ya no tenía salvo una caravela, que la nao que yo llevé avía dexado con la gente en
la villa de La Navidad, de Vuestras Altezas, fortaleçiéndose
en ella; como después avía una otra caravela, uno de Palos,
a quien yo avía dado cargo della, esperando buen serviçio,
se me avía ydo con ella, con pensamiento de tomar mucho

(Fol. 1 v.) (*roto*) . . . de una isla, de la qual avía dado nuevas un
yndio, que con él yo (*roto*) . . . después hazer lo que vien
viniese. (*roto*) . . . y es la más dulçe para navegar que ay
en el mundo y con menos pe[ligro] para naos y navíos de
toda suerte; más para descubrir, las caravelas [peq]ueñas
son mejores, porque andando junto con tierra y con rríos,
a menester para descubrir mucho, que demanden poco
fondo y se ayude de rremos; ni ay jamás tormenta, que

beo en todo cavo adonde e estado la yerva y los árboles hasia dentro de la mar.

Alliende de las sobredichas yslas e hallado otras muchas en las Yndias, de que no curo de dezir en la presente carta. Las quales, con estas otras, son en tanta fertilidad, que aunque yo lo supiese dezir, no hera maravilla ponerse dubda en la crehençia; los aires temperatísimos, los árboles y frutos y yervas son en estrema fermosura y mui diversos de los nuestros, los rríos y puertos son tantos y tan estremos en bondad de los de las partidas de christianos ques maravilla; todas estas yslas son popularísimas de la mejor gente, sin mal ni engaño, que aya debaxo del çielo. Todos, ansí mugeres como hombres, andan desnudos como sus madres los parió, aunque algunas mugeres traen alguna cosita de algodón o una foja de yerva con que se cubijan; no tienen fierro ni armas, salvo unas çimas de cañas en que ponen al cavo un palillo delgado agudo; todo lo que labran es con piedras; y no e podido entender que alguno tenga bienes propios, porque algunos días que yo estuve con este rrey en la villa de La Navidad, vía que todo el pueblo, y en espeçial las mugeres, le traían los agís, ques su vianda que comen, y él los mandava destribuir, mui singular mantenimiento.

En ninguna parte destas yslas e conoçido en la gente dellas seta ni ydolatría ni mucha diversidad en la lengua de unos a otros, salvo que todos se entienden; conoçí que conoçen que en el çielo están todas las fuerças, y generalmente en quantas tierras yo aya andado, creieron y creen que yo, con estos navíos y gente, venía del çielo; y con este acatamiento me rreçibían, y oy, en el día, están en el mesmo propósito ni se an quitado dello, por mucha conversaçión que ayan tenido con ellos; y luego en llegando a qualquiera poblazón, los hombres y mugeres y niños andan dando bozes por las casas: "Benid, benid a ver la gente del çielo". Quanto tienen y tenían davan por qualquiera cosa que por ella se le diese, hasta tomar un pedazo de vidrio o de escudilla rrota o cosa semejante, quiera fuese oro quier fuese otra cosa de qualquier valor;

los cavos de las agujetas de cuero ovo un marinero más
de dos castellanos y medio; y destas cosas ay diez mill de
contar.

Estas islas son todas mui llanas y tierra mui baja, salvo La
Juana y La Española; éstas dos son tierra mui alta, y en
ellas ay sierras y montañas altísimas, sin conparaçión de
la ysla de Tenerifee; son las montañas todas de mill he-
churas y todas fermosísimas y fertilísimas y andables y
llenas de árboles; paresçe que llegan al çielo; e la una y la
otra destas dichas yslas son

(Fol. 2 r.)   son mui grandes, que, como dicho tengo, yo andove por
la lígnea rreta . . . *(roto)* y siete leguas por La Juana, y me
quedavan dos provinçias por a . . . *(mancha y roto)* parte de
nurueste en que según pude comprehender destos yndios
que . . . *(roto)* no puede aver menos de çinquenta o sesenta
leguas, ansí ques la . . . *(mancha y roto)* gumento es mui
maior que Yngalaterra y Escoçia juntas; esta otra . . . *(mancha)* la es maior en çierto que toda La Española que, como
dixe arriba, anduve por la lígnea rrecta, de poniente a
oriente, çiento y ochenta y ocho grandes leguas que en ella
ay en aquella quadra. La Juana es de muchos rríos, y en
ella ay grandes montañas y grandísimos valles y vegas y
campos, y toda llena de árboles y palmas grandísimas y
de mill maneras a maravilla. La Spañola en todo tiene ven-
taja, los árboles no son tan altos ni me la mesma calidad,
salvo mui frutíferos y spaçiosos; y deleytables tierras para
todas cosas y para sembrar y plantar y criança de ganados,
de que en ninguna isla e visto de ningún speçie. Tiene esta
isla los aires a maravilla templanos, y las vegas y campiñas
a maravilla y sin comparaçión de las de Castilla, y eso
mismo los rríos en grandes y buenas aguas y los más traen
oro; los puertos de la mar son tantos y tam buenos que no
lo creerán salvo por vista. En éstas ni en las otras yslas no
me e detenido por muchos rrespectos, como ya ençima
dixe, en speçial porque açierta de ser ynbierno quando yo
corría estas costas, las quales no davan lugar para que yo
pudiese yr al austro porque estava a la parte del setentrión

[*sic*] dellas, y los (*sic*) siempre fueron casi este tiempo le-
vantes, que eran contrarios a seguir mi navegaçión; después yo no entendía aquella gente ni ellos a mí, salvo
quanto el alvedrío enseñava, bien quellos llevavan pena y
yo mucho más, porque yo deseava aver buena ynforma-
çión de todo; y el descanso que yo para esto tomé fue los
yndios que yo tenía, quellos deprendían nuestra lengua y
nos la suia, y después, al tanto del otro viaje, se sabrá; así
que no avía rrazón de me detener a perder tiempo en ningún puerto, en quanto yo tuviese lugar de navegar; y también, como dicho tengo, estos navíos, que yo traya, heran
mui grandes y pesados para semejante fecho, en espeçial
la nao que yo traía; de que vien temeroso estava yo antes
que de Castilla partiese; bien quisiera llevar pequeñas caravelas, mas como era éste el primer viaje y la gente que
llevava eran temerosos de hallar la mar brava y dubdosos
del viaje, y avía y a avido tantas contrariedades, y se
atrevía quienquiera a contradezir este camino y poner en
ello mill peligros sin alguna rrazón que a ello pudiesen
darme, hizieron negar mi voluntad; y hazer todo lo que
aquéllos que conmigo avían de ir querían, y por fazer una
vez el biaje y hallar la tierra; más Nuestro Señor, ques
lumbre y fuerça de todos aquellos que andan a buen fin y
les da victoria de cosas que pareçen ynposibles, quiso hor-
denar que yo hallase y oviese de hallar oro y minas dél y
espeçería y gente sin número

(Fol. 2 v.) (*roto y mancha*) número dispuestos para ser christianos y
otros para que los christianos (*roto y mancha*) . . . ellos y
medio lugar con maravilla besible adonde yo hizie- (*roto y*
mancha) . . . leza, la qual agora ésta deve estar acavada del
todo y hordeno que . . . (*mancha*) . . . dexase en ella, en
posesión de la villa de La Navidad, la gente que yo traía
en la nao y algunas de las caravelas, probeídos de man-
tenimientos para más de un año y mui mucha artillería y
mui sin peligro de nadie, antes con mucha amistad del
rrey de ay, el qual se preçiava de me llamar y tener por
hermano; el qual todo amostrava de aver en la maior dicha
del mundo, como dixe, y así el rrei como los otros, de ma-

nera que la gente que allá dexé es para sojudgar toda la
ysla sin peligro; esta ysla es en lugar, como dicho tengo,
aseñalado por manos de Nuestro Señor, por donde espero
que Su Magestad de dar a Vuestras Altezas tanto oro como
abrán menester, espeçería de una pimienta, quantas naos
Vuestras Altezas mandare[n] cargar y almastiga quanta
mandare[n] cargar; de la qual no se halla hasta oy salvo en
la ysla de Gio, en Greçia, y la venden el Señorío como
quieren que creo que saquen más de quarenta y çinco mill
ducados della, cada año, y la linanoe quanto mandaren
cargar, y algodón quanto mandaren cargar, y esclavos tantos que no ay número, y serán de los ydólatras, y creo aver
hallado rruibarvo y canela; esto todo hallé agora que fue
así de corrida, más espero en Dios que a la buelta abrá hallado la gente que yo allá dexé otras mill cosas de gran sus-
tançia porque ansí les dexé uncargado; y les dexé barca y
aparejos para ello y para fazer barcas y fustas, y maestros
de todas artes de la mar; y sobre todo tengo por de Vuestras
Altezas las sobredichas yslas todas y que puede[n] dis-
poner dellas, así como puede[n] y más cumplidamente de
los Reynos de Castilla, y en espeçial desta Española.

Concluio aquí: que mediante la graçia divinal, de aquél
ques comienço de todas cosas virtuosas y buenas y que da
favor y victoria a todos aquéllos que van en su camino, que
de oy en siete años yo podré pagar a Vuestras Altezas çinco
mill de cavallo y çinquenta mill de pie en la guerra e conquista de Ih[e]rusalem, sobre el qual propósito se tomó
esta empresa; y dende a çinco años otros çinco mill de cavallo y çinquenta mill de pie, que serían diez mill de cavallo
y çient mill de pie; y esto con mui poca costa que faga[n]
agora Vuestras Altezas en este comienço para que se tengan
todas las Yndias y lo que en ellas ay en la mano, como después diré, por palabra, a Vuestras Altezas; y para esto tengo
rrazón y no hablo ynçierto y no se deve dormir en ello,
como se a fecho en la esecuçión desta enpresa, de que Dios
perdone a quien a sido causa dello.

Mui poderosos prínçipes: de toda la Christiandad deve[n]
hazer mui grandísimas fiestas, y en espeçial la Yglesia de

Dios, por aver fallado tanta multidumbre de pueblos tan
allegados, para con poco travajo se tornen a nuestra Sancta
Fee, y de tantas tierras llenas de tantos bienes, a nos mui
neçesarios, en que abrán todos christianos rrefrigerio y
ganançia; de que todo estava yncógnito ni se contava dello

(Fol. 3 r.) dello salvo en manera de fábulas; grandes alegrías y fiestas
en las yglesias . . . *(roto)* chas alabanças a la Sancta Trinidad
deve[n] en espeçial mandar hazer Vuestras Altezas . . .
(roto) sus rreinos y señoríos, por el gran amor que les a
mostrado, más que a otro prínçipe.

Agora, serenísimos prínçipes, acuerde[n] Vuestras Altezas
que yo dexé muger y hijos y vine de mi tierra a les servir,
adonde gasté lo que yo tenía, y gasté siete años de tiempo
y rreçibí mill oprovios con disfama y çofrí muchas neçesi-
dades; no quise entender con otros prínçipes que me rro-
garon, puesto que Vuestras Altezas aya[n] dado rrecaudo a
este viaje, que a sido más por ynportunidad mía que no por
otra cosa; y que no solamente se me a hecho merçed, más
aún no se a cumplido lo que se me avía prometido. Yo no
demando merçed a Vuestras Altezas para athesorar, porque
yo no tengo condiçión salvo de servir a Dios y a Vuestras
Altezas y traer este negoçio de las Yndias a perfectión, como
el tiempo hará dello testimonio; y por tanto les suplico que
la honrra me sea dada según el serviçio.

Tanbién la Iglesia de Dios deve de entender en esto: a pro-
beer de perlados y devotos y savios rreligiosos; y porque
la cosa es tan grande y de tal calidad, ques rrazón que provea
el Sancto Padre de perlados que sean mui fuera de cobdiçia
de bienes temporales y mui propio[s] al serviçio de Dios y
de Vuestras Altezas; y, por tanto, a ella suplico que en la
carta que escriva[n] desta victoria, que le demanden un
cardenalgo para mi hijo y que puesto que no sea en hedad
ydónea se le dé, que poca diferençia ay en el tiempo dél y
del hijo del ofiçio de Médizis de Florençia a quien se dio el
capelo, sin que aya servido ni tenga propósito de tanta
honrra de la Christiandad, y que me faga[n] merçed de la
carta desto porque yo lo embíe a procurar.

Otrosí, serenísimos prínçipes, porquel pecado del desa-
gradeçimiento fue el primero punido, yo conozco que por
yo no tenerlo soi a todo *tiem*po de procurar con V*uestras*
Al*tezas* este negoçio, que sin dubda que sino fuera Villacorta el qual a todo *tiem*po que era menester rrequería y tra-
vajava porque yo ya estava aborrido del todo y todos ya
cansados, los que avían entendido y entendían en ello. Por
tanto sup*l*ico a V*uestras* Al*tezas* que me hagan merçed de le
hazer contador maior de las Yndias, que yo quedo por fia-
dor que lo hará él bien.

Por ende es rrazón que V*uestras* Al*tezas* sepa*n* que la prima
isla de las Yndias, más llegadas a España, es toda poblada
de mugeres, sin nungún hombre; y su trato no es femenil,
salvo usar armas y otros exerçiçios de hombre; traen arcos
y frechas y se adornan de las minas de alambre, del qual
metal tienen en mui grande cantidad; a esta ysla llaman
Matenino; a la segunda Caribo (*blanco*) leguas desta distante; aquí están aquellos pueblos, de que están todos los
rrestantes de las otras islas de Yndia[s] temerosos; éstos comen carne umana, son grandes frecheros, tienen muchas
canoas, casi tan grandes como fustas de rremo, con las
quales corren todas las islas de Yndia[s], y son tan temidos
que no an par ni evento; ellos andan desnudos como los
otros, salvo que traen los cavellos

(Fol. 3 v.)   (*roto:* cavel-) los mui cumplidos como mugeres creo q*u*e la
cobardía tan gra*n*de (*roto*) . . . pueblos de las otras yslas,
ques sin rremedio, hagan dezir questos de Caribe sean
osados; más yo los tengo en la estima de los otros, y
quando V*uestras* Al*tezas* mandare[n] que yo les e*n*bíe esclavos, espero yo de los traer o enbiar destos la maior
parte; éstos son aquéllos que tratan con las mugeres de
Matenino, los quales si paren hembra, tienenla consigo y
si muchacho, críanle hasta que pueda comer por sí, y después e*n*bíanlo a Cardo. Entremedia destas yslas de Cardo
y de La Española está otra isla que llaman Bori*n*que, y todo
es en poca distançia de la otra parte de la isla Juana, aquéllos llaman de Cuba; de la parte más oçidental, en una de

las dos probinçias que yo dexé de andar, la qual se llama Faba, naçen todos con cola. Detrás desta ysla Juana, aún a vista, ay otra q*ue* me asiguravan estos yndios que otra ay maior quella, a que llaman Jamaica; adonde toda la gente della son si cabellos, en ésta ay oro sin medida, e agora traygo yndios conmigo que an estado e*n* las unas y e*n* las otras y saven la lengua y las costumbres. No más, salvo que la Santísima Trinidad guarde y prospere el rreal estado de V*uestras* A*ltezas*, a su santo serviçio. Fecha en la mar de España, a quatro días de março de mill y quatroçientos y noventa y tres años. E*n* la mar.

Letter to the Sovereigns
of 4 March 1493

✝

Most Christian and lofty and powerful sovereigns:

That eternal God who has given Your Highnesses so many victories now gave you the greatest one that to this day He has ever given any prince. I come from the Indies with the armada Your Highnesses gave me, to which [place] I traveled in thirty-three days after departing from your kingdoms; after fourteen of the thirty-three there were light winds in which I covered very little ground. I found innumerable people and very many islands, of which I took possession in Your Highnesses' name, by royal crier and with Your Highnesses' royal banner unfurled, and it was not contradicted.[1] To the first [island] I gave the name of San Salvador, in memory of His Supreme Majesty [Jesus Christ], to the second Santa María de la Concepción, to the third Fernandina, to the fourth Isabela, to the fifth Juana, and to the others almost a new name.[2] After I arrived at Juana I followed its coast to the west and found it to be so large that I thought it was probably not an island, but rather a mainland, and most likely the province of Cathay; but I could not verify this because everywhere I arrived the people fled and I could not speak with them. And because I was unable to find a notable settlement, I thought that by hugging the coast I could not fail to find some town or great city, like those who have gone to that province overland tell it.[3] And after following this land for a long while, I found that I was veering away from the west and it was leading me to the north and I found the wind that came from that direction, with which I tried to contend until it passed and a different one arrived, because it was already winter and I had no other intention but to avoid the south [wind], and so I turned back.[4] In the meantime I already understood something of the speech and signs of certain Indians I had taken on the island of San Salvador, and I understood [from them] that this was still an island. And thus I came to a very good harbor, from which I sent two men inland, three days' journey, with one of the Indians I brought, who had become friendly with me, so that they could see and determine if there were any cities or large settlements, and which land it was, and what there was in it. They found many settlements and innumerable people, but no government of any importance. And so they returned, and I departed and took certain Indians at the said harbor so that I could also hear or learn from them about said lands. And thus I followed the seacoast of this island toward the east one hundred and seven leagues to where it ended. And before leaving it, I saw another island to the east, eighteen leagues out from this one, which I later named Española. And then I went to it and followed its coast on the north side, just like in the case of La Juana, due east for one hundred and eighty-eight very long leagues. And I continued to enter very many harbors, in each of which I placed a very large cross in the most appropriate spot, as I had done in all the other [harbors] of the other islands, and in many places I found promontories sufficient [for this purpose]. So I went on in this fashion until the sixteenth of January, when I determined to return to Your Highnesses, as much because I had already found most of what I sought as because I had only one caravel left, because the *nao*[5] that I brought I had left in Your Highnesses' village of La Navidad, with the men who were using it for fortification. There was another caravel, but a man from Palos whom I had put in charge of her, expecting good service, made off with her, with the intention of taking much[6] [damaged] . . . of [from?] an island about which an Indian had given news, that with him I [damaged] . . . after doing whatever. [damaged] . . . and it is the sweetest [thing] to navigate and with the least danger for ships[7] of all sorts. However, for discovering, small caravels are better suited, because going close to land or rivers, in order to discover much, [vessels] must require but little depth and be capable of being assisted with oars. Neither is there ever stormy weather, since in every place I have been I see the grass and trees growing into the sea.

Besides the above-mentioned islands, I have found many others in the Indies, of which I have not been able to tell in this letter. They, like these others, are so extremely fertile, that even if I were able to express it, it would not be a marvel were it to be disbelieved. The breezes [are] most temperate, the trees and fruits and grasses are extremely beautiful and very different from ours; the rivers and harbors are so abundant and of such extreme excellence when compared to those of Christian lands that it is a marvel. All these islands are densely populated with the best people under the sun; they have neither ill-will nor treachery. All of them, women and men alike, go about naked like their mothers bore them, although some of the women wear a small piece of cotton or a patch of grass with which they cover themselves. They have neither iron nor weapons, except for canes on the end of which they place a thin sharp stick. Everything they make is done with stones [stone tools]. And I have not learned that any one of them has private property, because while I was spending a few days with this king in the village of La Navidad, I saw that all of the people, and the women in particular, would bring him *agís*, which is the food they eat, and he would order them to be distributed; a very singular sustenance.[8]

Nowhere in these islands have I known the inhabitants to have a religion, or idolatry, or much diversity of language among them, but rather they all understand each other. I learned that they know that all powers reside in heaven. And, generally, in whatever lands I traveled, they believed and believe that I, together with these ships and people, came from heaven, and they greeted me with such veneration. And today, this very day, they are of the same mind, nor have they strayed from it, despite all the contact they [the Spaniards at La Navidad] may have had with them. And then, upon arriving at whatever settlement, the men, women, and children go from house to house calling out, "Come, come and see the people from heaven!"[9] Everything they have or had they gave for whatever one gave them in exchange, even taking a piece of glass or broken crockery or some such thing, for gold or some other thing of whatever value. One sailor got more than two and a half castellanos [in gold] for the ends of leather latchets. There are ten thousand like occurrences to tell.

The islands are all very flat and low-lying, except for La Juana and La Española. These two are very high lands, and there are mountain chains and very high peaks, much higher than those of the island of Tenerife. The mountains are of a thousand different shapes and all [are] most beautiful, and fertile and walkable and full of trees; it seems they touch the sky. And both the one and the other of the said islands are very large, such that, as I have said, I traveled in a straight line . . . [the next three lines are damaged; not enough context to translate][10] . . . is much larger than England and Scotland together; this other one [stained] is certainly larger than the whole of La Española such that, as I said above, I traveled in a straight line, from west to east, one hundred and eighty-eight large leagues which comprise that side [of the island].[11] La Juana has many rivers, and great mountains, and very large valleys and meadows and fields, and it is all full of trees and huge palms of a thousand varieties, such as to make one marvel. La Spañola[12] has the advantage in every respect; the trees are not so tall or of the same kind, but rather very fruitful and broad; and [they are] delectable lands for all things, and for sowing and planting and raising livestock, of which I have not seen any kind on any of these islands. This island has marvelously temperate breezes, and marvelous meadows and fields incomparable to those of Castile; and the same can be said of the rivers of great and good waters, most of which are gold-bearing. There are so many and such good sea harbors that it has to be seen to be believed. I have not tarried in these islands or the others for many reasons, as I said above, but especially because it was winter when I sailed these coasts, which did not allow me to go south because I was on their north side and the [winds] were almost always easterly, which were contrary to continuing my navigation. Then I did not understand those people nor they me, except for what common sense dictated, although they were saddened and I much more so, because I wanted to have good information concerning everything. And what I did to remedy this was the Indians I had with me, for they learned our language and we theirs, and the next voyage will tell. So, there was no reason for me to tarry at any harbor wasting time when the opportunity came to set sail. Moreover, as I have said, these vessels I brought with me were too large and heavy for such a purpose, especially the *nao* I brought over, about which I was quite troubled before leaving Castile. I would much have preferred taking small caravels, but since this was the first voyage and the people I brought were afraid of running into high seas and uncertain about the voyage, and there was and has been so much opposition, and anybody dared to contradict this route and ascribe to it a thousand dangers without being able to give me any reasons, they caused me to act against my own judgment and do everything that those who were to go with me wanted, in order to get the voyage finally under way and find the land. But Our Lord, who is the light and strength of all those who seek to do good and makes them victorious in deeds that seem impossible, wished to ordain that I should find and was to find gold and mines and spicery and innumerable peoples . . . [the next four lines are damaged; not enough context to translate] I left in it [La Española], in possession of the village of La Navidad, the people I brought on the *nao* and some from the caravels, stocked with provisions to last over a year, [with] much artillery and quite without danger from anyone, but rather with much friendship from the king of that place, who prided himself in calling me and having me for a brother; who [also] appeared to accept everything as the greatest boon in the world, as I said. And the others [feel] just like the king, so that the people I left there suffice to subjugate the entire island without danger. This island is in a place, as I have said, signaled by the hand of Our Lord, where I hope His Majesty will give Your Highnesses as much gold as you need, spicery of a certain pepper [to fill] as many ships as Your Highnesses may order to be loaded, and as much mastic as you may order to load, which today can only be found on the island of Chios, in Greece, and the government[13] sells it as they see fit, and I believe they get more than 45,000 ducats for it each year. And as much lignum aloe as you may order to be loaded, and as much cotton as you may order to be loaded, and so many slaves that they are innumerable; and they will come from the idolaters. And I believe there is rhubarb and cinnamon. All this I found on this hasty trip, but I have faith in God that upon my return the people I left there will have found a thousand other things of importance, because that is the charge I left them with. And I left them a boat and its equipment and [the tools] to make boats and *fustas*,[14] and masters in all the nautical arts. And above all I consider all the abovementioned islands as belonging to Your Highnesses and you may command them as you do the kingdoms of Castile, and even more completely, especially this one of Española.

I conclude here: that through the divine grace of He who is the origin of all good and virtuous things, who favors and gives victory to all those who walk in His path, that in seven years from today I will be able to pay Your Highnesses for five thousand cavalry and fifty thousand foot soldiers for the war and conquest of Jerusalem, for which purpose this enterprise was undertaken. And in another five years another five thousand cavalry and fifty thousand foot soldiers, which will total ten thousand cavalry and one hundred thousand foot soldiers; and all of this with very little investment now on Your Highnesses' part in this beginning of the taking of the Indies and all that they contain, as I will tell Your Highnesses in person later. And I have reason for this [claim] and do not speak uncertainly, and one should not delay in it, as was the case with the execution of this enterprise, may God forgive whoever has been the cause of it.

Most powerful sovereigns: all of Christendom should hold great celebrations, and especially God's Church, for the finding of such a multitude of such friendly peoples, which with very little effort will be converted to our Holy Faith, and so many lands filled with so many goods very necessary to us in which all Christians will have comfort and profits, all of which was unknown nor did anyone speak of it except in fables. Great rejoicing and celebrations in the churches [damaged] . . . Your Highnesses should order that [many] praises should be given to the Holy Trinity [damaged] your kingdoms and domains, because of the great love [the Holy Trinity?] has shown you, more than to any other prince.

Now, most serene sovereigns, remember that I left my wife and children behind and came from my homeland to serve you, in which [service] I spent what I had. And I spent seven years of my time and put up with a thousand indignities and disgrace and I suffered much hardship. I did not wish to deal with other princes who solicited me, although Your Highnesses' giving of your protection to this voyage has been due more to my importuning [you] than to anything else. And not only has no favor been shown to me, but moreover nothing of what was promised me has been fulfilled. I do not ask favors of Your Highnesses in order to amass treasure, for I have no purpose other than to serve God and Your Highnesses and to bring this business of the Indies to perfection, as time will be my witness. And therefore I beseech you that honor be bestowed upon me according to [the quality of] my service.

The Church of God should also work for this: providing prelates and devout and wise religious; and because the matter is so great and of such a character, there is reason for the Holy Father to provide prelates who are very free of greed for temporal possessions and very true to the service of God and of Your Highnesses. And therefore I beseech you to ask the Church, in the letter you write regarding this victory, for a cardinalate for my son, and that it be granted him although he may not yet be of sufficient age, for there is little difference in his age and that of the son of the Medicis of Florence, to whom a cardinal's hat was granted without him having served or had a purpose so honorable to Christianity, and that you give me the letter pertaining to this matter so that I [myself] may solicit it.

Furthermore, most serene sovereigns, because the sin of ungratefulness was the first one to be punished, I realize that since I am not guilty of it I must at all times try to gain from Your Highnesses the following [favor], because, without a doubt, were it not for Villacorta,[15] who every time it was necessary persuaded and worked on [the enterprise's] behalf, because I was already sick of it and everyone who had been and was involved in the matter was tired [and the enterprise would not have succeeded]. Therefore, I beseech Your Highnesses that you do me the favor of making him paymaster of the Indies, for I vouch that he will do it well.

Wherefore Your Highnesses should know that the first island of the Indies, closest to Spain, is populated entirely by women, without a single man, and their comportment is not feminine, but rather they use weapons and other masculine practices. They carry bows and arrows and take their adornments from the copper mines, which metal they have in very large quantity. They call this island Matenino, the second Caribo, [blank] leagues out from this one. Here are found those people which all of the other islands of the Indies fear; they eat human flesh, are great bowmen, have many canoes almost as big as oar-powered *fustas*, in which they travel all over the islands of the Indies, and they are so feared that they have no equal. They go about naked like the others, except that they wear their hair very full, like women. I think the great cowardice . . . [damaged] peoples of the other islands, for which there is no remedy, makes them say that these of Caribe are brave, but I think the same of them as of the rest. And when Your Highnesses give the order for me to send slaves, I hope to bring or send [you] these for the most part; these are the ones who have intercourse with the women of Matenino, who if they bear a female child they keep her with them, and if it is a male child, they raise him until he can feed himself and then they send him to Cardo. Between the islands of Cardo and Española there is another island they call Borinque,[16] and all of it is a short distance from the other region of the island of Juana which they call Cuba. In the westernmost part [of Cuba], in one of the two provinces I did not cover, which is called Faba, everyone is born with a tail. Beyond this island of Juana, still within sight, there is another that these Indians assured me was larger than Juana, which they call Jamaica, where all the people are bald. On this one there is gold in immeasurable quantities; and now I have Indians with me who have been on these [islands] as well as the others and they know the language and customs. Nothing further, except that may the Holy Trinity guard and make Your Highnesses' royal estate prosper in Its service. Written in the sea of Spain,[17] on the fourth day of March of the year fourteen ninety-three. At sea.

Notes

INTRODUCTION

1. Fernando de Rojas, *Celestina*, ed. Dorothy Sherman Severin, trans. James Mabbe (Warminster: Aris and Phillips, 1987): 18–19.

2. The Crown expressed its confusion in two letters, dated the same day, one from Isabella, the other from both of the sovereigns, to Columbus. Both letters requested clarification and more information, as I discuss in "Voyage to Paradise," later in this volume.

3. For examples of such studies, see the entries in the bibliography for Hayden White, Nancy Struever, Hans Kellner, Enrique Pupo-Walker, and Dominick LaCapra.

4. In his recent book on Latin American narrative, Roberto González Echevarría takes a similar approach to the development of the modern novel; see his *Myth and Archive: A Theory of Latin American Narrative* (Cambridge: Cambridge University Press, 1990).

5. The complete text of this letter and my English translation appear in the Appendix. The letter was recently published for the first time by Antonio Rumeu de Armas, in *Libro Copiador de Cristóbal Colón: Correspondencia inédita con los Reyes Católicos sobre los viajes a América*, 2 vols. (Madrid: Testimonio, 1989), and is reprinted here by permission of the Spanish Ministry of Culture. I am indebted to David Henige for bringing it to my attention.

6. The date given in the postscript is 14 March but, as Rumeu's recent publication of the letter of 4 March indicates, the postscript was in error.

7. According to Ferdinand Columbus, his father kept a journal, or *diario*, for each of the four voyages to the Indies. None of these day-by-day accounts have survived. The *Diario* is Las Casas's edition of Columbus's *diario* of the first voyage.

8. On this point see Barbara Herrnstein Smith, *Contingencies of Value: Alternative Perspectives for Critical Theory* (Cambridge: Harvard University Press, 1988).

READING COLUMBUS

1. He strapped another barrel with like contents to the ship's stern (Varela, 127). Ferdinand Columbus, in his account of the first voyage, quotes his father's words regarding this first letter announcing the Discovery:

escribí en un pergamino, con la brevedad que el tiempo exigía, cómo yo dejaba descubiertas aquellas tierras que les había prometido; en cuántos días y por qué camino lo había logrado; la bondad del país y la condición de sus habitantes, y cómo quedaban los vasallos de Vuestras Altezas en posesión de todo lo que se había descubierto. Cuya escritura, cerrada y sellada, dirigí a Vuestras Altezas con el porte, es a saber, promesa de mil ducados a aquél que la presentara sin abrir. A fin de que si hombres extranjeros la encontrasen, no se valiesen del aviso que dentro había, con la avidez del porte. Muy luego hice que me llevaran un gran barril, y habiendo envuelto la escritura en una tela encerada, y metido ésta en torta u hogaza de cera, la puse en el barril. Y bien sujeto con sus aros, lo eché al mar, creyendo todos que sería alguna devoción. Y porque pensé que podría suceder que no llegase a salvamento, y los navíos aun caminaban para acercarse a Castilla, hice otro atado semejante al primero, y lo puse en lo alto de la popa para que, si se hundía el navío, quedase el barril sobre las olas a merced de la tormenta.

> (Fernando Colón, *Vida del Almirante Don Cristóbal Colón* [Mexico: Fondo de Cultura Económica, 1947], 123, chap. 37)

I wrote on a parchment, as briefly as the state of things required, how I had discovered those lands as I had promised to do; the length of the voyage and the route thither; the goodness of the country and the customs of its inhabitants; and how I had left Your Highnesses' vassals in possession of all I had discovered. This writing, folded and sealed, I addressed to Your Highnesses with a written promise of 1,000 ducats to whoever should deliver it sealed to you; this I did so that if it should fall into the hands of foreigners, they would be restrained by the reward from divulging the information it contained to others. I straightway [sic] had a great wooden barrel brought to me, and having wrapped the writing in a waxed cloth and put it in a cake or loaf of wax, I dropped it into the barrel, which I made secure with hoops and cast into the sea; and all thought this was an act of devotion. I still feared the barrel might not reach safety, but as the ships meanwhile were drawing closer to Castile I lashed a similar cask at the head of the stern, so that if the ship sank, it might float on the waves at the mercy of the storm.

> (Fernando Colón, *The Life of the Admiral Christopher Columbus by His Son Ferdinand*, ed. and trans. Benjamin Keen [Westport, Conn.: Greenwood Press, 1978], 92)

2. According to the *Diario*, Columbus would have been off the coast of the Azores on 15 February 1493, not the Canaries, as the 15 February letter claims. The patent discrepancy supports the argument that the text could not have been written by Columbus or, at least, must have been altered after leaving his hands.

3. Ferdinand Columbus's *Vida del Almirante* and Bartolomé de Las Casas's *Historia de las Indias*.

4. For the background on this copy, see Rumeu, 1:19–20. Rumeu considers the manuscript an authentic sixteenth-century transcription, perhaps two or three copies or more removed from the original and containing a few insignificant errors. For another evaluation of the authenticity of the *Libro Copiador*, see P. E. Taviani, C. Varela, J. Gil, and M. Conti, eds., *Relazione e lettere sul secundo, terzo, e quarto viaggio* (Nuova Raccolta Colombiana), 2 vols. (Rome, Istituto Poligrafico e Zecca dello Stato, 1992), 1:163–

82. The authenticity of the manuscript is likely to be a topic of debate in years to come, however, as more specialists have the opportunity to evaluate it.

5. Demetrio Ramos Pérez, *La primera noticia de América* (Valladolid: Seminario Americanista de la Universidad de Valladolid, 1986). The value of this study, which has not yet received the attention it deserves, is enhanced by Ramos's inclusion of a transcription and facsimile of the archival copy of the letter of 15 February addressed to Santángel.

6. The extent and consequences of Las Casas's editing is the subject of "All these are the Admiral's exact words," later in this volume.

7. See Ramos, *La primera noticia de América*, 74–86. He further argues that there was no letter addressed to Sánchez, but rather that the translator of the Latin version, the only one that names Sánchez as an addressee, confused him with Santángel.

8. I disagree with Morison's translation of *cielo* in this context as "sky," rather than "heaven"; both the 4 March and 15 February letters imply that the Indians took the Spaniards for divine beings, venerating them and making offerings to them as such.

9. The letter was published in Rome, Florence, Barcelona, Basel, Paris, and Amsterdam.

10. See Ramos, *La primera noticia de América*, 62–67.

11. On the evolving importance of Jerusalem within the Columbian articulation of Discovery, see "Voyage to Paradise," later in this volume.

"THIS PRESENT YEAR OF 1492"

1. Las Casas in fact did much more to his source than simply summarize it. I discuss his editorial role in the *Diario* more fully in the next essay.

2. For example, Henri Vignaud, *Histoire critique de la grande entreprise de Christophe Colomb*, 2 vols. (Paris: H. Welter, 1911) and *Le vrai Christophe Colomb et la légende* (Paris: Picard, 1921), or Emiliano Jos, "La génesis colombiana del descubrimiento," *Revista de Historia de América* 14 (June 1942):1–48.

3. Here I am paraphrasing Hayden White's contrast between "communicative" and "performative" discourses. I have substituted "informative" for White's "communicative," since the latter term could be misleading. All discourses are communicative; the fundamental differences are to be found, it seems to me, in the *manner* in which they communicate. See White, *The Content of the Form: Narrative Discourse and Historical Representation* (Baltimore: Johns Hopkins University Press, 1987), 39.

4. Sebastián Horozco de Covarrubias, *Tesoro de la lengua castellana o española* (1611; rpt. Madrid: Ediciones Turner, 1984), s.v. *antiguo* and *simple*.

5. A third (unlikely) possibility is that the text was wholly fabricated by Las Casas. Even if that were the case, however, it would not alter the implicit textual pragmatics or, therefore, the basic terms of my argument.

6. On the *ars dictaminis*, see Ernst Robert Curtius, *European Literature and the Latin Middle Ages* (Princeton: Princeton University Press, 1953); James J.

Murphy, *Rhetoric in the Middle Ages: A History of Rhetorical Theory from Saint Augustine to the Renaissance* (Berkeley: University of California Press, 1974); Charles B. Faulhaber, "The Letter-Writer's Rhetoric: The *Summa dictaminis* of Guido Faba," in *Medieval Eloquence: Studies in the Theory and Practice of Medieval Rhetoric*, ed. James J. Murphy (Berkeley: University of California Press, 1978), 85–111.

7. On the rights and privileges conferred upon Columbus by Ferdinand and Isabella, see Samuel Eliot Morison, *Admiral of the Ocean Sea* (Boston: Little, Brown), 360–67.

8. The phrasing is somewhat confusing as to whether the "libro" and the "pintura" are part of the same whole or two separate entities. The word *pintura* appears on one other occasion in the *Diario*, in the composite "pinturas de mapamundos." Presumably, then, "por pintura" would refer to its common nautical acceptation—cartographic illustration—but perhaps not exclusively; one of the books that influenced Columbus, John Mandeville's *Travels*, was generously illustrated with noncartographic images of the lands, peoples, and other creatures described in the account of the journey.

9. See Curtius, *European Literature and the Latin Middle Ages*, 88.

10. My arguments from this point on are a critical response to ideas I expressed earlier in "El prólogo al *Diario* de Cristóbal Colón," *Insula* no. 522 (June 1990):16–17.

11. The other prediscovery documents issued by the Crown in preparation for the expedition were: "Carta real de provisión ordenando a los marineros de Palos aportar dos carabelas . . . ," "Carta real de provisión a los Concejos y Justicias 'de la costa de la mar del Andalusía' . . . ," "Carta real de provisión mandando suspender el conocimiento de causas criminales . . . ," "Sobrecarta dando comisión al contino Juan de Peñalosa para que se trasladase con plenos poderes a la villa de Palos . . . ," and "Sobrecarta dando comisión al contino Juan de Peñalosa para el exacto cumplimiento de la cédula de 30 de abril, ordenando a las autoridades de la mar de Andalucía prestar la máxima colaboración a Cristóbal Colón . . ." The first three documents are dated 30 April 1492, the other two are from 20 June 1492. For the text of these documents see Rumeu de Armas, *Nueva luz sobre las Capitulaciones de Santa Fe . . .* (Madrid: Consejo Superior de Investigaciones Científicas, 1985), 239–46. For English translations of the prediscovery documents issued by the Crown, see Morison, 27–36.

12. I originally proposed the possibility of reading Columbian writing in the context of Columbus's dialogue with the Crown in a paper delivered in April 1988 at the Kentucky Foreign Language Conference. In that talk I focused on the ways in which Columbian discourse can be understood to complement that of the "Capitulaciones de Santa Fe." The main points of that argument are developed and refined in the final essay of this book, "Gender and Discovery." The rewards of rereading Columbian writing pragmatically, in the context of that dialogue, are far from exhausted, however, as the contrastive strategy employed in the present essay demonstrates.

13. Rumeu, *Nueva luz.* The complete text of the "Capitulaciones" ap-

pears on pages 52–53 of that volume. For an English translation of the document, see *1492–1992: Re/Discovering Colonial Writing*, eds. René Jara and Nicholas Spadaccini (Minneapolis: Prisma Institute, 1989), 383–86, and Morison, 27–29.

14. For the text of this pardon, see Rumeu, *Nueva luz*, 243–44.

15. For the complete text of the "Carta de Merced," see Rumeu, *Nueva luz*, 239–41. It has been translated by Morison (29–30).

16. The Spanish Crown's sovereignty over the newly found territories was confirmed by Pope Alexander VI in a papal bull, "Inter caetera," dated 3 May 1493.

17. One version of the "passport" Columbus presumably carried suggests in rather vague terms that he was on some sort of diplomatic mission of a religious character: "Mittimus in presenciarum nobilem virum Christoforum Colon cum tribus caravelis armatis per maria oceania ad partes Indie pro aliquibus causis et negotiis servicium Dei ac fidem ortodoxe concernentibus" (Jane, 1: lxx). However, the "passport" does not mention an evangelical intention to the mission. The likeliest purpose of this diplomatic document would have been to help shield the emissary from any hostile actions by foreign governments. Another version of the passport, quoted and translated by Morison, does not mention any religious purpose whatever: "Mittimus in presentiarum nobilem virum Xpóforum Colon, cum tribus carauelis armatis per maria oceana ad partes Indie pro aliquibus causis et negotiis." "By these presents we send the nobleman Christopher Columbus with three equipped caravels over the ocean seas toward the regions of India for certain reasons and purposes" (31). This completely ambiguous phrasing is characteristic of the other prediscovery documents issued by the Crown.

18. Juan Manzano Manzano is the most notable and recent exception; see his *Colón y su secreto: El predescubrimiento* (Madrid: Ediciones Cultura Hispánica, 1982).

19. Perhaps some of the imaginary or legendary islands typically depicted in the western Atlantic on portolan charts of the period. For a discussion of Columbian cartography, see J. B. Harley, *Maps and the Columbian Encounter* (Milwaukee: Golda Meir Library of the University of Wisconsin, 1990). I discuss the textual consequences of this cartography in "Voyage to Paradise," later in this volume.

20. The phrase that appears in the "passport," "ad partes Indie" (toward the regions of India), could refer to almost any place in the Far East as it was understood in the oriental geography of Columbus's time. Only Columbus's explicit identification of his destination as the kingdom of the Grand Khan resolves the ambiguity found in the royal documents.

21. In contrast, the positions taken by Vignaud, Rómulo D. Carbia and, more recently, Alejo Carpentier (in his historical essay-cum-novel *El arpa y la sombra*) attribute many of the inaccuracies in the Columbian texts to deliberate falsification by Las Casas and/or Columbus himself; see Carbia, "La historia del descubrimiento y los fraudes del Padre Las Casas," *Nosotros* 72 (1931):139–54.

22. Two of Spain's best-known early poets were so employed: Gonzalo de Berceo (1197–1264) served as notary in his monastery, and Juan de Mena (1411–1456) was secretary for Latin letters to King John II of Castile.

23. For a description of metonymy and its functions, see J. Dubois et al., *A General Rhetoric*, trans. Paul B. Burrell and Edgar M. Slotkin (Baltimore: Johns Hopkins University Press, 1981), 120–22.

24. This spatiotemporal paradigm has a figural counterpart in the Ebstorf map, where the body of Christ (representing the Christian community) encompasses the disparate parts of the world, thus rendering them a coherent whole. I discuss the Ebstorf map in relation to Columbian writing in "Voyage to Paradise," later in this volume.

25. Columbus employed the term *negocio* to refer to both the commercial and the spiritual dimensions of his project, as Milhou notes in *Colón y su mentalidad mesiánica* (Valladolid: Seminario Americanista de la Universidad de Valladolid, 1983), 289:

> El "negocio" o la "negociación" de las Indias tiene, como la palabra "empresa," unas connotaciones dobles: una mercantil, la del mundo de los "negocios" en que se crió Colón, pero también otra religiosa, la del *negotium crucis* de los cruzados al cual equiparaba su "negocio" ultramarino.

> The "business" or the "negotiation" of the Indies has, like the word "enterprise," dual connotations: one mercantile, pertaining to the "business" world in which Columbus was raised, but also a religious one, the *negotium crucis* of the crusaders to which he compared his ultramarine "business."

"ALL THESE ARE THE ADMIRAL'S EXACT WORDS"

1. "There is some reason to believe, however, that the original Journal was still in existence at the end of the last century; it may even be in existence today." Such was Samuel Eliot Morison's opinion in 1939. See his curious anecdote, offered as supporting evidence, in "Texts and Translations of the Journal of Columbus' First Voyage," *Hispanic American Historical Review* 19 (1939):236–37.

2. Las Casas refers to his source as the "libro de su primera navegaçión y descubrimiento d'estas Indias" (Varela, 30; book of his first navigation and discovery of these Indies). There is no internal evidence in his summary that suggests when he did the transcription. Scholarly opinion ranges from shortly after Las Casas's arrival in Española (Haiti) in 1502, to 1552, the date of his visit to the material collected by Ferdinand Columbus in Seville. The weight of opinion seems to favor the later date, and in the absence of compelling arguments to the contrary I accept it here.

3. The bibliography on Las Casas's life and works is immense. Texts essential to an understanding of the man and his writings include: Marcel Bataillon, *Etudes sur Bartolomé de Las Casas* (Paris: Centre de Recherches de l'Institut d'Etudes Hispaniques, 1965); Lewis Hanke, *All Mankind Is One: A Study of the Disputation Between Bartolomé de Las Casas and Juan Ginés de Se-*

púlveda on the Intellectual and Religious Capacity of the American Indians (De Kalb: Northern Illinois University Press, 1974); Juan Friede and Benjamin Keen, *Bartolomé de Las Casas in History* (De Kalb: Northern Illinois University Press, 1971); and Marianne Mahn-Lot, *Bartolomé de Las Casas et le droit des Indiens* (Paris: Payot, 1982). For an influential dissenting opinion, see Ramón Menéndez Pidal, *El padre Las Casas: Su doble personalidad* (Madrid: 1963).

4. Las Casas, "Memorial de los remedios," in *Obras escogidas*, ed. Juan Pérez de Tudela y Bueso (Madrid: Biblioteca de Autores Españoles), 121.

5. Columbus refers to his enterprise as a *descubrimiento*, a term I discuss at length in "Voyage to Paradise," later in this volume. In the *Diario* the term *conquista* appears only in reference to the Holy Land, when Columbus urges the Catholic Monarchs to finance the "conquest" of Jerusalem with the wealth that would be obtained from the enterprise of the Indies. *Conquista* also appears once in reference to the first voyage, but as a paraphrase of a statement made by the King of Portugal, who interviewed Columbus immediately after his return to Europe.

6. New Law #38, for example, placed the "discoveries" under the authority of the Audiencia, the juridical arm of colonial government, and required every "discoverer" to be accompanied by religious; see Bataillon and Saint Lu, *El Padre Las Casas*, 29.

7. See Rómulo D. Carbia, "La historia del descubrimiento y los fraudes del Padre Las Casas," *Nosotros* 72 (1931):139–54; Henri Vignaud, *Le vrai Christophe Colomb et la légende* (Paris: Picard, 1921) and *Histoire critique de la grande entreprise de Christophe Colomb* (Paris: H. Welter, 1911).

8. Morison, "Texts and Translations of the Journal of Columbus' First Voyage," 239. For a dissenting opinion see David Henige, *In Search of Columbus: The Sources for the First Voyage* (Tucson: University of Arizona Press, 1991).

9. Robert H. Fuson, "The *Diario de Colón*: A Legacy of Poor Transcription, Translation, and Interpretation," in *In the Wake of Columbus*, ed. Louis de Vorsey, Jr., and John Parker (Detroit: Wayne State University Press, 1985), 51–75; Varela, ix–xxiii.

10. Challenging the predominant view that the *Diario* is "a privileged eyewitness document of the discovery . . . an accurate ethnographic record," Peter Hulme prefers to see it as the "first fable of European beginnings in America" (*Colonial Encounters: Europe and the Native Caribbean, 1492–1797* [London: Methuen, 1986], 17–18). But even in his salutary skepticism regarding the unlikely privilege of a text that is "a transcription of a copy of a lost original," Hulme, like Varela and Fuson, considers the *Diario*'s mediated transmission a contingent rather than essential problem, secondary to what he has identified as the presence of the pristine discourses of "Oriental civilization" and "savagery" in the text attributable to Columbus. Clearly, in my argument, no aspect of the *Diario* is left untouched by the presence of the editorial voice.

11. The entry for 21 November reads:

Para creer qu'el cuadrante andava bueno, le movía ver diz que el norte tan
alto como en Castilla. Y si esto es verdad, mucho allegado y alto andava con
la Florida; pero ¿dónde están luego agora estas islas que entre manos traía?
Ayudava a esto que hazía diz que gran calor, pero claro es que si estuviera
en la costa de la Florida que no oviera calor, sino frío; y es también manifiesto que cuarenta y dos grados en ninguna parte de la tierra se cree hazer
calor si no fuese por alguna causa de *per accidens*, lo que hasta oy no creo yo
que se sabe.

(Varela, 61)

To see the North Star as high as in Castile would persuade him, he says,
that the quadrant was working well. (And if this is true he would have been
near and traveling in the same latitude as Florida. But where are these islands that he had at hand?) It helped him to this conclusion, he says, that it
was very hot. (But it is clear that if he were on the coast of Florida it would
not be hot, but cold; and it is also manifest that in 42 degrees latitude nowhere on earth is it thought to be hot, if it were not for some accidental
cause, which up to now I do not believe is known.)

(Dunn & Kelley, 163–65)

Dunn and Kelley have added the parentheses to their translation in order
to signal Las Casas's interventions, but, as noted earlier, Las Casas silently
and seamlessly embedded his observations into the third-person paraphrase.

12. Mikhail M. Bakhtin, *The Dialogic Imagination*, trans. Caryl Emerson
and Michael Holquist (Austin: University of Texas Press, 1981), 293–94.

13. Julia Kristeva develops her basic theory of intertextuality in *Le texte
du roman* (Paris: Mouton, 1970) and in *Sémiotiké, recherches pour une sémanalyse* (Paris: Seuil, 1969).

14. See, for example, Laurent Jenny, "The Strategy of Form," in *French
Literary Theory Today*, ed. Tzvetan Todorov (Cambridge: Cambridge University Press, 1982), 34–63; Jonathan Culler, "Presupposition and Intertextuality," in his *The Pursuit of Signs* (Ithaca: Cornell University Press, 1981),
100–118; Gérard Genette, *Palimpsestes: La littérature au second degré* (Paris:
Seuil, 1982).

15. Genette, *Palimpsestes*, 286.

16. My discussion of rhetorical paraphrase is based on Michael Roberts,
Biblical Epic and Rhetorical Paraphrase in Late Antiquity (Liverpool: Francis
Cairns, 1985).

17. Quoted by Roberts, *Biblical Epic*, 30.

18. These three discourses are also evident in the letter to Luis de Santángel (15 February 1493), which appears also to be a summary of the journal, although it differs substantially from Las Casas's *Diario* in that it emphasizes the economic aspects of the enterprise and is homogeneously
testimonial in point of view; see Varela, 139–46.

19. I discuss Las Casas's marginalia in the *Diario* in the next essay, "In
the Margins of Columbus."

20. Las Casas's later manipulation of the *Diario* when he assimilated it

into the *Historia* bears out this tendency to subordinate (or suppress) the less savory aspects of Columbus's account and enhance those that place the Indians in a favorable light. David Henige's detailed comparison of the *Diario* and its version in the *Historia* demonstrates that Las Casas showed a liberal hand in further editing and revising his own edition as he incorporated it into the history; see Henige, "To Read Is to Misread, To Write Is to Miswrite: Las Casas as Transcriber," *Hispanic Issues: Amerindian Images* (Minneapolis: University of Minnesota Press, 1992).

21. Columbus refers to a "libro" in the letter/prologue, but it was not what we know today as the *Diario*. Presumably it was to have contained maps and/or drawings; see Varela, 17. If he ever managed to compose it, it has not been found.

22. Columbus wrote of his intention to describe in his journal "todo este viaje muy puntualmente, de día en día, todo lo que yo hiziese y viese y passasse" (Varela, 16–17; this entire voyage very punctually, day by day, everything that I would do and see and experience).

23. On the "academic" prologue, see A. J. Minnis, *Medieval Theory of Authorship: Scholastic Literary Attitudes in the Later Middle Ages* (London: Scolar Press, 1984). On medieval literary pedagogy, see Minnis's volume and Judson Boyce Allen, *The Ethical Poetic of the Later Middle Ages: A Decorum of Convenient Distinction* (Toronto: University of Toronto Press, 1982).

24. On Las Casas's treatment of other aspects of the *Diario* in his transcription of the text in the *Historia*, see Henige, *In Search of Columbus*, 54–64. The question of intention in literary analysis has become problematic in contemporary literary theory. For a sober critical summation, see Annabel Patterson, "Intention," in *Critical Terms for Literary Study*, ed. Frank Lentricchia and Thomas McLaughlin (Chicago: University of Chicago Press, 1990), 135–46. Paul de Man put it this way: "the subject remains endowed with a function that is not grammatical but rhetorical, in that it gives voice, so to speak, to a grammatical syntagm. The term *voice*, even when used in a grammatical terminology . . . is, of course, a metaphor inferring by analogy the intent of the subject from the structure of the predicate" (quoted by Patterson, 145).

25. Alberto Porqueras Mayo, *El prólogo como género literario: Su estudio en el Siglo de Oro español* (Madrid: Consejo Superior de Investigaciones Científicas, 1957).

26. Even the Caribs, later described as fierce, are written off as formidable only in contrast to the absolute timidity of the Taínos. I examine this aspect of the *Diario* more fully in "Voyage to Paradise."

27. See, for example, the polemical treatise Las Casas presented in 1550–51 at the Valladolid debate on the nature of the Indians, *Del único modo de atraer a todos los pueblos a la verdadera religión* (Mexico: Fondo de Cultura Económica, 1942), and the *Historia de las Indias*, where the log becomes an intertext in the common sense of the term. In the prologue to the *Historia* Las Casas affirms his ideological intentions and his goal in writing the book:

quise . . . librar mi nación española del error y engaño gravísimo y perniciosísimo en que vive y siempre hasta hoy ha vivido, estimando destas océanas gentes faltarles el ser de hombre, haciéndolas brutales bestias incapaces de virtud y doctrina.

([Madrid: Biblioteca de Autores Españoles, 1957], 15)

I wanted . . . to deliver my Spanish nation from the grave and pernicious error and self-deception in which it lives and has always lived to date, believing that these oceanic peoples lack humanity, making them out to be brutish beasts incapable of virtue and instruction.

Columbus's log is employed by Las Casas precisely to subvert this pejorative vision of the Indians.

IN THE MARGINS OF COLUMBUS

1. The very proliferation of notes suggests that in Las Casas's mind they played an important rhetorical role in underscoring the portions of the text he felt were especially significant.

2. Anthony Pagden has noted that the *Historia* is heavily text-dependent and argues that Las Casas fills its pages with an overwhelming number of citations in order to display his erudition and thus buttress the authority of his own eyewitness testimony about life in the Indies; see his *"Ius et Factum*: Text and Experience in the Writings of Bartolomé de Las Casas," *Representations* 33 (Winter 1991):147–62. I will argue further that the citations are not only a rhetorical element but the very stuff of Las Casas's historical discourse, which depends on the commentary of the citations and paraphrases to carry out its "reading" of the Discovery.

3. On the deconstructionist notion of the supplement, see Jonathan Culler, *On Deconstruction: Theory and Criticism After Structuralism* (Ithaca: Cornell University Press, 1982), esp. 102–6.

4. On Las Casas as biographer, see Santa Arias, "Retórica e ideología en la *Historia de las Indias* de Bartolomé de Las Casas" (Diss., University of Wisconsin, Madison, 1990). On the interpolated story in the *Historia*, see Antonio Benítez Rojo, "Bartolomé de Las Casas: Entre el infierno y la ficción," in his *La isla que se repite: El Caribe y la perspectiva posmoderna* (Hanover, N.H.: Ediciones del Norte, 1989), 69–104.

5. Pagden, *"Ius et Factum,"* 157.

6. Arias argues that Las Casas identified with Columbus and that traces of that transference can be found throughout the *Historia*; see "Retórica e ideología en la *Historia de las Indias,"* esp. 86–99.

7. Las Casas, "Memorial de los remedios," in *Obras escogidas*, ed. Juan Pérez de Tudela y Bueso (Madrid: Biblioteca de Autores Españoles), 121.

8. I am relying to a great extent on Varela's description of the manuscripts in *Fray Bartolomé de Las Casas: Obras Completas*, vol. 14, p. 12, since I have only been able to consult Sanz's facsimile.

9. I do not include under my definition of "marginal commentary" the corrections to the text itself made by Las Casas. Although they are a useful indicator of how Las Casas massaged the text, they do not constitute a creative contribution.

10. The abbreviation "nõ" was acknowledged by de Lollis only the first four times it appeared.

11. Most of the major translations into other European languages follow this same pattern. On the editing history of the *Diario*, see Samuel Eliot Morison, "Texts and Translations of the Journal of Columbus' First Voyage," *Hispanic American Historical Review* 19 (1939):235–61; Robert H. Fuson, "The *Diario de Colón*: A Legacy of Poor Transcription, Translation, and Interpretation," in *In the Wake of Columbus*, ed. Louis de Vorsey, Jr., and John Parker (Detroit: Wayne State University Press, 1985), 51–75; and David Henige, "Samuel Eliot Morison as Translator and Editor of Columbus's *diario de a bordo*," *Terrae Incognitae* 20 (1988):69–88.

12. Of the most recent and important translations, Cioranescu's French version presents a limited selection of Las Casas's commentary in the notes; his prevailing criterion of selection appears to have been geographical. Gaetano Ferro's Italian translation similarly omits some commentary, at times justifying the omission with pronouncements on the commentary's irrelevance. The question such pronouncements immediately raise is, of course, to whom is the commentary irrelevant? Certainly not to Las Casas.

13. In her edition of Las Casas's *Colección de obras completas* (Madrid: Alianza, 1989), Varela writes: "A primera vista puede que sorprenda la inclusión [del Diario y la Carta] en la *Colección*, inclusión que se justifica por sí misma: Las Casas no fue sólo un copista fiel de la obra colombina, como se verá más adelante, sino también un anotador del texto en cuyos márgenes dejó muchas apostillas valiosísimas" (14:11; At first glance the inclusion of the *Diario* and letter in the *Colección* may be surprising, an inclusion which justifies itself: Las Casas was not only a faithful copyist of Columbus's works, as will be seen shortly, but also an annotator of the text in whose margins he left very valuable annotations). In that case, one is tempted to ask, why weren't the notes alone published in the *Colección*? Varela may feel some personal awkwardness here since in her *Cristóbal Colón: Textos y documentos completos* she (paradoxically, in hindsight) includes both the *Diario* and the "Relación" and characterizes Las Casas precisely as "un copista fiel, incluso cuando no acertaba a dar con el sentido del pasaje" (xxiii; Las Casas was a faithful copyist, even when he did not succeed in making the passage make sense).

14. Compare, for example, the *Diario* entry for 30 October in Fernández de Navarrete's *Colección de los viages . . .* (Buenos Aires: Guaranía, 1945) and in *Colección de documentos y manuscritos compilados por Fernández de Navarrete* (Nendeln, Lichtenstein: Kraus-Thomson, 1971).

15. J. A. Vázquez has done a valuable preliminary study of the nature and content of the commentary itself; see his "Las Casas's Opinions in Co-

lumbus's Diary," *Topic* 21 (Spring 1971):45–56. Note, however, that what I am proposing here is significantly different—that the annotations and the main text be read organically. This, of course, requires that the text be published integrally, precisely as it appears in the manuscript.

16. Rumeu de Armas has argued that Las Casas was working with an already-summarized version of the Columbian text, to which he then added his own commentary and corrections. This, of course, would make the Las Casas text at least twice removed from the original. See Rumeu, "El *Diario de a bordo* de Cristóbal Colón: El problema de la paternidad del extracto," *Revista de Indias* 36 (1976):7–17.

17. An assimilated version of the Columbian texts, apparently derived from a somewhat different source than the one used by Las Casas, appears in Ferdinand Columbus's *Vida del Almirante*, which survived only in an Italian translation; the Spanish original was lost.

18. The generous margins probably served to facilitate annotation as well as to highlight the notes themselves. A possible model or antecedent for Las Casas's treatment of the marginal commentary is the sixteenth-century Spanish practice of annotating official correspondence from the colonies to facilitate reading when the documents circulated through the Council of the Indies. The Council was apparently increasingly concerned precisely with the size of the margins of the documents it received, and legislation was passed at the end of the sixteenth century to ensure they be of generous proportions with respect to the main text; see Antonia M. Heredia, "Las cartas de los virreyes de Nueva España a la corona española en el siglo XVI," *Anuario de Estudios Americanos* 31 (1974):441–596, and "La carta como tipo diplomático indiano," *Anuario de Estudios Americanos* 34 (1977):65–95. Las Casas himself appeared at various times before the Council and was undoubtedly familiar with documents similarly annotated. While the purpose of annotating documents at the Council was typically to summarize or record responses to specific petitions contained in the text, Las Casas adds evaluative and critical annotations to Columbus's texts.

19. Varela transcribes "entenderse" in contrast to Sanz's "estenderse." Comparison with the facsimile text leaves little doubt that Sanz was correct.

20. For a striking contrast to Las Casas's reading, see Peter Martyr d'Anghiera's bucolic reading of Columbus in *De Orbe Novo decades*.

21. Soon after composing this letter Columbus was returned to Spain from Española in shackles by Bobadilla, chief justice and royal commissioner of Ferdinand and Isabella; see Samuel Eliot Morison, *Admiral of the Ocean Sea* (Boston: Little, Brown, 1942), 562–72.

22. Varela includes the fragments of this lost *diario* that were excerpted by Las Casas in her *Textos y documentos completos* (220–42) and considers them part of the "Relación," a text she believes to have been summarized by Las Casas in his edition. Rumeu's recent publication of *El Libro Copiador de Cristóbal Colón*, containing a copy of the "Relación" that is essentially coeval to Las Casas's transcription, supports my conviction that Las Casas

must also have consulted and extracted passages from a separate account of the third navigation in composing the *Historia*.

23. The *encomienda* placed a group of Indians under the control of a Spanish colonist. In exchange for religious instruction and tutoring in Spanish customs and language, the Indians were forced to work the mines and fields. Such was the remuneration Columbus himself claimed he would give to the captives he took during the first voyage.

24. I am working from Las Casas's copy of "Carta a doña Juana de la Torre, ama del príncipe don Juan" as edited by Varela (269–70). The letter is transcribed verbatim, with the marginal notes, in the *Historia de las Indias* (482–87). A translation of the complete version of the letter, based on the *Raccolta* edition, appears in Morison (289–98).

25. I am paraphrasing Anthony Pagden's lucid assessment of Las Casas's contributions to the debate on the nature of the Amerindians; see his *The Fall of Natural Man: The American Indian and the Origins of Comparative Ethnology* (Cambridge: Cambridge University Press, 1982), 119.

26. Antonio Gómez Moriana has done an illuminating comparative analysis of Las Casas's and Ferdinand Columbus's treatment of the same passage from the *Diario* in their respective histories of the Discovery. He argues that Ferdinand does an economic reading of the Columbian text, in contrast to Las Casas's missionary reading—an analysis that supports my argument here that Las Casas's rewriting of the Columbian texts subordinates the commercial dimension of Columbus's discourse in favor of its Christian dimension. See Gómez Moriana, "Narration and Argumentation in the Chronicles of the New World," in *1492–1992: Re/Discovering Colonial Writing*, ed. René Jara and Nicholas Spadaccini (Minneapolis: Prisma Institute, 1989), 97–120.

27. Quoted by Alejandro Cioranescu, "La 'Historia de las Indias' y la prohibición de editarla," *Anuario de Estudios Americanos* 23 (1966):363–76. Cioranescu suggests that Las Casas's intended audience may have been only his fellow Dominicans at the convent in Santo Domingo. Given the scope, tone, and tenor of the text, this possibility seems highly improbable. Since Las Casas entrusted to the Dominicans the preservation of the manuscript and its publication, there is good reason to believe, as Cioranescu also suggests, that he hoped they would come to advocate his positions after his death.

VOYAGE TO PARADISE

1. A notable exception is Mary B. Campbell's chapter on Columbus's "Letter to Sánchez" (i.e., "Letter to Santángel") and "Journal" (i.e., the *Diario*) in *The Witness and the Other World: Exotic European Travel Writing, 400–1600* (Ithaca: Cornell University Press, 1988). Campbell considers these texts to have been informed by the literary genre of the romance.

2. Hayden White, Dominick LaCapra, and Hans Kellner, among others,

have shown how the study of the historical text is enhanced by considering it as a story about the past. See, for example, the works by these three authors listed in the bibliography.

3. Paul Carter, *The Road to Botany Bay: An Exploration of Landscape and History* (Chicago: University of Chicago Press, 1987), 69.

4. A similar notion is proposed by Michel de Certeau, who argues that stories constitute "symbolic languages of space" (*The Practice of Everyday Life*, trans. Steven F. Rendall [Berkeley: University of California Press, 1984]). I prefer Carter's formulation here because of its greater specificity. De Certeau's argument that every story is a travel story—"a spatial practice"—erases what to my mind is a fundamental distinction between stories that are about journeys and those that are not.

5. "Christoferens," from the Latin *fero* (to carry, to speak of, to endure, to spread abroad). Alain Milhou offers a detailed assessment of the ideological context that, he argues, explains the significance of Columbus's assumption of this particular name; see his *Colón y su mentalidad mesiánica en el ambiente franciscanista español* (Valladolid: Seminario Americanista de la Universidad de Valladolid, 1983), esp. 55–90.

6. The classical paradigm is the errant geography of Herodotus, the traveler-geographer of the fifth century B.C., not Erathosthenes of Cyrene, who wrote a geographical treatise in the third century B.C.

7. Michel Butor, "Travel and Writing," *Mosaic* 8 (1974):1–16.

8. Samuel Eliot Morison, quoting Franco Machado, reminds us that in the fifteenth-century Portuguese literature of exploration *descobrir* could mean any of the following: to find a land of whose existence one had previous knowledge, albeit vague or erroneous; to find a place not known to exist (the predominant modern sense); and to explore territory previously found (*Portuguese Voyages to America in the Fifteenth Century* [Cambridge: Harvard University Press, 1940], 143–44). All these connotations, we may note, entail the acquisition of knowledge about a place initially constituted as an enigma. Thus, in the literature of exploration to write about a place is to make known what was essentially unknown by inscribing it into the cultural discourses that render it familiar and thus "thinkable." Naming is above all a way of thinking about a place by setting it in context with and in relation to other names and thereby rendering it, in Paul Carter's words, "a place that could be communicated."

9. The literature on the Discovery is dominated by discussion of what Columbus thought about his findings, whether he realized the land to be a "new world," and what that phrase actually meant in his day. In contrast, I am concerned with the Discovery as it was *written*, and my essay proposes a reading, not the history of an idea. Thus, I will not be claiming that Columbus wrote about a destination known to him (as some have argued) but rather, and this is an essential distinction, that Columbian writing articulates the destination as if it were already known.

10. Mikhail M. Bakhtin, "Forms of Time and of the Chronotope in the

Novel: Notes Toward a Historical Poetics," in *The Dialogic Imagination*, trans. Caryl Emerson and Michael Holquist (Austin: University of Texas Press, 1981), 84–258. Bakhtin holds that the chronotope is responsible for generating meaning, by defining the spatiotemporal characteristics of genre and thereby the conditions for process and event in the text.

11. The phrasing is borrowed from Steven Hutchinson, *Cervantine Journeys* (Madison: University of Wisconsin Press, 1992), 84.

12. A similar notion of time is evident in the nonreligious travel literature of the Spanish Middle Ages, such as Clavijo's *Embajada a Tamorlán* or Tafur's *Andanzas*, as Barbara W. Fick has noted in *El libro de viajes en la España medieval* (Santiago de Chile: Editorial Universitaria, 1976).

13. Pierre d'Ailly's text and Columbus's marginal annotations are available in a bilingual Latin-French edition, *Ymago Mundi*, 3 vols., ed. Edmond Buron (Paris: Maisonneuve Frères, 1930). The copy owned by Columbus is preserved in the Biblioteca Colombina, in Seville.

14. Samuel Y. Edgerton, Jr., "From Matrix to *Mappaemundi* to Christian Empire: The Heritage of Ptolemaic Cartography in the Renaissance," in *Art and Cartography: Six Historical Essays*, ed. David Woodward (Chicago: University of Chicago Press, 1987), 10–50.

15. For a general assessment of the influence of Ptolemy on Columbus, see George E. Nunn, *The Geographical Conceptions of Columbus: A Critical Consideration of Four Problems* (New York: American Geographical Society, 1924), esp. 54–90.

16. David Woodward, "Medieval *Mappaemundi*," in *The History of Cartography*, ed. J. B. Harley and David Woodward (Chicago: University of Chicago Press, 1987), 1:286–370.

17. On the relation between the portolan chart and the *portolano*, see Armando Cortesão, *History of Portuguese Cartography*, vol. 1 (Coimbra: Junta de Investigações do Ultramar, 1969).

18. Tony Campbell, "Portolan Charts from the Late Thirteenth Century to 1500," in *The History of Cartography*, ed. J. B. Harley and David Woodward (Chicago: University of Chicago Press, 1987), 1:371–463. For an excellent summary of the development and significance of portolan cartography, see Yoko K. Fall, "Les cartes a rumbs et leur utilisation au XIV et au XV siècle," *Studia* 47 (1989):23–39.

19. Morison, *Admiral of the Ocean Sea* (Boston: Little, Brown, 1942), 286. A portolan chart at the Bibliothèque Nationale in Paris has been attributed to Columbus, but the attribution is not generally accepted; see Harley and Woodward, *History of Cartography*, 1:452. Various remarks in the *Diario* suggest that Columbus made or directed the making of several "cartas de navegar"; see, for example, the prologue to the *Diario* (Varela, 17), and the *Diario* entries for 25 September and 3 October (Varela, 24, 26). Several contemporaries of Columbus testified that they had seen a Columbian chart of the voyage to Paria on the South American mainland; among these witnesses was the navigator and cartographer Alonso de Hojeda, who captained the

later expedition, in which Vespucci participated, to the same area. See Paolo Revelli, *Cristoforo Colombo e la scuola cartografica genovese* (Genova: Consiglio Nazionale delle Ricerche, 1937), 227.

20. Juan de la Cosa served as pilot on Columbus's first and second voyages. For a reproduction of his map, see J. B. Harley, *Maps and the Columbian Encounter* (Milwaukee: Golda Meir Library of the University of Wisconsin, 1990), 60.

21. Quoted by David Woodward, "Medieval *Mappaemundi*," in *The History of Cartography*, 287.

22. I have borrowed the term "textual cartography" from Tom Conley, "Montaigne and the Indies: Cartographies of the New World in the *Essais*, 1580–88," in *1492–1992: Re/Discovering Colonial Writing* (Minneapolis: Prisma Institute, 1989), 223–62.

23. Evidence of Columbus's involvement in the cartographic trade is abundant. Oviedo, in the *Historia general*, explains that the Admiral had once made his living by drawing navigational charts (bk. 1, chap. 4). Ferdinand, in chap. 7 of the *Vida*, notes that his father had once sent Toscanelli a small sphere to demonstrate his geographical theories. Las Casas also underscores Columbus's cartographic abilities, citing evidence found in the Columbian texts. Revelli refers to the eyewitness testimony of several contemporaries who had seen Columbus's portolan chart of the third voyage; see Revelli, *Cristoforo Colombo*, 227. Hojeda, who apparently used Columbus's directions for his own voyage to the mainland, described the chart as a "carta de marear los rumbos y vientos por donde [Columbus] había llegado a la Paria" (Revelli, 227; chart for navigating the rhumbs and winds by which [Columbus] had arrived at Paria). This chart is probably the same one Columbus promised to send the Crown in the "Relación del tercer viaje" (Varela, 219).

24. Revelli, *Cristoforo Colombo*, 226.

25. See Morison's *Portuguese Voyages* and *Admiral of the Ocean Sea*, chap. 4, and also Avelino Teixeira da Mota, *O essencial sobre Cristovão Colombo e os portugueses* (Lisbon: Imprensa Nacional–Casa de Moeda, 1987).

26. *Alonso de Chaves y el libro IV de su "Espejo de navegantes,"* ed. P. Castañeda, M. Cuesta, and P. Hernández (Madrid: Industrias Gráficas España, 1977).

27. G. Pereira collected these rutters in *Roteiros portuguezes da viagem de Lisboa a India nos séculos XVI e XVII* (Lisbon: Imprensa Nacional, 1898).

28. For a summary of Veen's instructions, see João Rocha Pinto, *A viagem: Memória e espaço* (Lisbon: Livraria Sá Da Costa Editora, 1989), 64–65.

29. *O manuscrito "Valentim Fernandes,"* ed. António Baião (Lisbon: Academia Portuguesa da Historia, 1939). See also Avelino Teixeira da Mota, *Evolução dos roteiros portugueses durante o século XVI* (Coimbra: Revista da Universidade de Coimbra, 1969).

30. Garcie's text was not printed until the early 1500s. David W. Waters describes it as "an outstanding piece of objective, factual, scientific writ-

ing," in *The Rutters of the Sea: The Sailing Directions of Pierre Garcie* (New Haven: Yale University Press, 1967), 9.

31. Campbell notes an interesting contrast between the Columbian journal, which emphasizes the psychological aspects of description, and Marco Polo's account of his travels in the Far East (a text Columbus read and annotated profusely), where description assumes an annunciatory form; see Campbell, *The Witness and the Other World*, 194.

32. Duarte Pacheco Pereira, *Esmeraldo de situ orbis* (Lisbon: Imprensa Nacional, 1892). For Ca' da Mosto's "Navegações," and Usodimare's "Carta," see *As viagens dos Descobrimentos*, ed. José Manuel García (Lisbon: Editorial Presença, n.d.), 73–146. Ca' da Mosto's account was first published in 1507, Usodimare's not until 1802.

33. In his prologue, Pacheco describes his work as a book on "cosmografia e marinharia" but one that also discusses "a natureza da jente desta ethiopia & ho seu modo de viver & asy direi do comercio que nesta terra pode haver" (4; the nature of the people of this Ethiopia [Guinea] & their way of life, & likewise I will tell of the commerce that may be obtained in this country).

34. It is unlikely that these early-sixteenth-century voyage narratives would have been influenced by the *Diario* or its source, which undoubtedly did not circulate for security reasons. The *Diario* and the *Historia de las Indias*, which contained many and lengthy direct quotations from it, were not published until the nineteenth century.

35. For a study of the tendency to temporalize spatial relationships in the development of scientific theories of space, see A. M. Amorim, "Temporalização do espaço versus espacialização do tempo," *Revista da Universidade de Coimbra* 29 (1984):259–70.

36. The temporalization of space was, of course, commonplace in historical writing, but it was clearly a new phenomenon in the nautical travel writings of the late-fifteenth and sixteenth centuries.

37. Alvise Ca' da Mosto, "Navegações," in García, *As viagens dos Descobrimentos*, 73–138.

38. References to the *Diario* in Ferdinand's *Vida del Almirante* also confirm its filiation with the *roteiro*.

39. Campbell, *The Witness and the Other World*, 27. It is just this distinction that compels me to disagree with Rocha Pinto's argument that simply the introduction of a strict chronology in nautical writings of the mid-sixteenth century constitutes a "temporalization of space" absent in earlier texts.

40. Walter J. Ong reminds us that the earliest writing known, the cuneiform script of the Sumerians (c. 3500 B.C.), is predominantly account-keeping. In contrast, the earliest written narratives are biblical texts, which, though also intended as records, are not fashioned as lists but as reconstitutions of coherent sequences of events. Ong argues that narrative's origins are oral, unlike the list, which seems to have originated with writing; in-

deed, script seems to have arisen precisely to make lists possible. His theory is supported by narrative's capacity, whether oral or written, to communicate events as the experience of those events. Whereas the list is a form of preserving information, narration, in establishing coherent relations among events, is a form of recording and of understanding experiences; see his *Orality and Literacy: The Technologizing of the Word* (London: Methuen, 1982), 99.

41. Letter 71 (5 September 1493) in Fernández de Navarrete, 2:131–33.

42. Las Casas worked with a copy of the original text. His source is unclear, but in all likelihood he had access to a copy in the Columbus family archives (Varela, xvi–xvii). The text is plagued with anachronistic interpolations, whether introduced by Las Casas or someone else is impossible to determine in the majority of cases. See two earlier essays in this volume, "This present year of 1492" and "All these are the Admiral's exact words" for a discussion of this problem.

43. The first mention of the existence of an autonomous daily pilot's log in diary form, according to Rocha Pinto (*A viagem*, 127), is the testimony of an anonymous Portuguese pilot (c. 1531–1550) that "Noi pilotti portoghesi abbiamo un *libro ordinario*, dove notiami a giorno per giorno il viaggio que facciamo, e per qual vento, e in quanti gradi di declinazion è il sole" (his emphasis, quoted from Giovanni Battista Ramusio, *Navigazioni e Viaggi*, 6 vols, ed. Marica Milanesi [Torino: Giulio Einaudi Editore, 1978–80]; We Portuguese pilots keep a book in which we write daily about the voyage and the route, the winds we sail by, and the degrees of declination of the sun). Note, however, that the term "libro ordinario" closely resembles Las Casas's terminology, "libro de navegación y descubrimiento," and the Crown's more general "este vuestro libro" in referring to Columbus's much earlier text. Thus the anonymous Portuguese example hardly seems conclusive to establish the characteristics or dating of a new genre. Most likely the old Portuguese term *livro a navegar* referred to a type of text that shared many of the technical characteristics of the later *diario de bordo*. The *Dicionário da linguagem de Marinha antiga e actual* (Lisbon: Centro de Estudos Históricos e Cartografia Antiga, 1990) defines the "livro a navegar" as a book in which the quarter officer registered information relevant to the navigation observed during his four-hour vigil, such as directions, distance traveled, time, and lands sighted.

44. Rocha Pinto concludes that the systematic organization of navigation along chronological lines characteristic of the *diario de bordo* was a mid-sixteenth-century development. Clearly, the evidence of Columbus's *Diario* either refutes this claim or, if Rocha Pinto is correct, must be considered an unprecedented innovation and an anomaly in the context of nautical literature. Perhaps a more plausible explanation for the apparent contradiction is that all the texts prior to the mid-sixteenth century that Rocha Pinto examined which did not keep a strict chronology of the navigation were concerned with the Indian voyages carried out by the Portuguese primarily in coastal waters and often within sight of land. A systematic chronology

in nautical writing is more likely a product of the need to record regular fixes during extended periods of navigation on the high seas. Unlike his Portuguese predecessors, of course, Columbus navigated in midocean, out of sight of land.

45. Revelli (226–27) noted the *Diario*'s uniqueness in this respect, calling it the earliest *diario* known to exist.

46. For example, consider the "erroneous" locations given in the *Diario*, which placed Española and Cuba at 26° N, on a line with Hierro island in the Spanish Canaries, rather than at 20° N, the correct longitude but closer to Portuguese territories. Clearly, as Henige has observed, political expediency, not geographical accuracy, dictated this location; see Henige, *In Search of Columbus*, 115.

47. *Pintar* in this context means "to draw on a map or chart." Similarly, *pintura* was synonymous with "map" or "chart" in the nautical terminology of the Mediterranean basin; see *Dicionário da linguagem de Marinha antiga e actual*.

48. While *roteiros* contained detailed and specific sailing directions, including information on landmarks, depths, shallows, and currents, *livros de marinharia* (books of seafaring) were "heterogeneous compilations resulting from notes accumulated by pilots, to record all information which might be worthwhile in the practice of their professions" and *livros de armação* contained the record of the goods or equipment carried on board; *Portugal-Brazil: The Age of the Atlantic Discoveries*, ed. Max Justo Guedes and Gerald Lombardi (Lisbon: Bertrand Editora, 1990), 227.

49. The unusual hybrid nature of the *Diario* suggests that it may have been an amalgam of various different types of texts originally written on board and later synthesized by Columbus to form the "Libro de su primera navegación y descubrimiento" that Las Casas worked into what we know today as the *Diario*. In this respect the *Diario* is reminiscent of Pacheco Pereira's *Esmeraldo* and Ca' da Mosto's "Navegações," neither of which, however, would have been available to Columbus prior to 1492–93.

50. There is some controversy regarding the authorship of the "Carta a Luis de Santángel" (which also exists in an almost identical version addressed to Rafael [sic, for Gabriel] Sánchez). See "Reading Columbus," earlier in this volume.

51. Prior to Rumeu's publication of the *Libro Copiador* in 1989, the only known eyewitness accounts of the second voyage were those of Michele de Cuneo, an old friend of Columbus's, Guillermo Coma, a gentleman volunteer, and Dr. Diego Alvarez Chanca, the expedition's physician, who sailed with the fleet in 1493. The four *relaciones* from the second voyage are dated January 1494, 20 April 1494, 26 February 1495, and 15 October 1495. From this period there are also three petitions by Columbus, "Memorial a Antonio Torres" (30 January 1494), "Memorial de la Mejorada" (July 1497), and an undated "Memorial a los Reyes sobre la población de las Indias." With the *relaciones*, they comprise the most complete statement available on the early development of a colonial policy for the Indies.

52. For the text of the instructions to Columbus for the second and fourth voyages see Morison, 199–202 and 307–10.

53. *The Letters of Amerigo Vespucci and Other Documents Illustrative of His Career*, trans. Clement R. Markham (London: Hakluyt Society, 1944), 42.

54. The Italian text reads, "questa mia ultima navigatione he dechiarato, conciosa che in quelle parte meridionala el continente io havia retrovato de più frequenti populi et animali havitato de la nostra Europa o vero Asia o vero Affrica, et ancora l'aere più temperato et ameno che in que banda altra regione da nui cognosciute, como de sotto intenderai"; quoted by Edmundo O'Gorman, *The Invention of America* (Bloomington: Indiana University Press, 1961), 166.

55. Several explorations of the mainland found by Columbus in 1498 were conducted prior to Vespucci's letter claiming to have discovered it, including the Ojeda (1499), Yáñez Pinzón (1500), and Cabral (1500) expeditions. The latter resulted in the discovery of Brazil. One of the members of the Cabral crew, Pero Vaz de Caminha, described it to the king of Portugal in a letter dated 1 May 1500.

56. The letter was written circa 18 October 1498. The translation is from O'Gorman, *The Invention of America*, 100.

57. The most elaborate argument for denying Columbus the "discovery" of America is O'Gorman's in *The Invention of America*.

58. Explicit references to the Indies as the site of the Terrestrial Paradise are made in the *Diario* entry for 21 February and in the "Relación del tercer viaje."

59. Cf. Hutchinson, "It goes without saying that places aren't inert physical shells, but localities of experience or of being where interaction not only 'takes place' but also 'makes place'" (*Cervantine Journeys*, 84).

60. In the *Diario* the noun appears once—"quando venía al descubrimiento" (15 January)—but this is in Las Casas's third-person paraphrase, and it is impossible to determine what the original form may have been. Dunn and Kelley have translated it as "when he came (on the voyage of) discovery" (341), but a more idiomatic translation would be "when he came to discover." Note that here *descubrimiento*, despite its nominal form, plays an adverbial and not a substantive function.

61. *The Life of the Admiral Christopher Columbus by His Son Ferdinand*, ed. and trans. Benjamin Keen (Westport, Conn.: Greenwood Press, 1978), 16–17.

62. An English translation of the document appears in Jara and Spadaccini, *1492–1992: Re/Discovering Colonial Writing*, 397.

63. Wilcomb E. Washburn is one of the few historians to acknowledge Columbus's extensive use of metaphor and appreciate its potential significance for the study of the meaning of "discovery." See his "The Meaning of 'Discovery' in the Fifteenth and Sixteenth Centuries," *American Historical Review* 68, no. 1 (October 1962):1–21.

64. Quoted by Campbell, *The Witness and the Other World*, 52, from *The Christian Topography of Cosmas, an Egyptian Monk*, trans. J. W. McCrindle

(London: Hakluyt Society, 1897). For an appraisal of Cosmas's work, see C. Raymond Beazley, *The Dawn of Modern Geography* (New York: Peter Smith, 1949), 1:273–303.

65. An example of Columbus's use of *negocio* in its spiritual sense occurs in the *Diario* entry for 14 February. In the midst of a terrible storm, he consoles himself with the following thought:

> Y como antes oviese puesto fin y endereçado todo su negocio a Dios y le avía oído y dado todo lo que le avía pedido, devía creer que le daría complimento de lo començado y le llevaría en salvamento.
>
> (Varela, 127)

> And (he writes here) that, since earlier he had entrusted his destiny and all of his enterprise to God, Who had heard him and given him all he had asked for, he ought to believe that God would grant him the completion of what he had begun and would take him to safety.
>
> (Dunn & Kelley, 369)

Although the English translation does not reflect it, *salvamento* has the connotation of saving from physical peril as well as salvation in the spiritual sense.

66. According to Claude Carozzi,

> si on lit dans l'ordre chronologique les documents relatifs á l'Au-delà du XI–XIII siècle, on se rend compte que progressivement apparaissent des paysages et des itinéraires concrets et qu'une cosmographie de plus en plus cohérent vient structurer cet ensemble de lieux visités par les voyageurs.
>
> ("La géographie de l'Au-delà et sa signification pendant le haut Moyen Age," *Popoli et Paesi nella Cultura Altomedievale* 2 [1983]:424)

> if one reads the documents concerned with the Other World from the eleventh through the thirteenth century in chronological order, one realizes that concrete lands and itineraries appear ever more frequently, and that an increasingly coherent cosmography structures the places visited by the travelers.

Such a phenomenon appears paradoxical to us because we have lost all sense of the immanence of the sacred so profoundly felt by people in the Middle Ages.

67. See Cesare Segre, "*L'Itinerarium Animae* nel duecento e Dante," *Letture Classensi* 13 (1984):9–32.

68. See Beazley, *Dawn of Modern Geography*, esp. 1:190–96.

69. Kirkpatrick Sale's recent popular assessment is especially shrill in its contention that Columbus was mad: "By the time he was ready to spell it [the discovery of the location of Paradise] out, in his summary letter to the Sovereigns two months later, it fairly exploded, page after page, in a very long and muddled mishmash of theology and astronomy and geography and fantastic lore, rambling, repetitive, illogical, confusing, at times inco-

herent, self-serving, servile and vainglorious all at once—and quite loony"; Sale, *The Conquest of Paradise: Christopher Columbus and the Columbian Legacy* (New York: Knopf, 1990), 175. Only a reader unfamiliar with the medieval world view and its modes of discourse would be so bewildered by Columbus's assumption that Paradise lay in the vicinity of the Indies.

70. On the background of Columbus's spirituality, see Milhou, *Colón y su mentalidad mesiánica;* Pauline Moffitt Watts, "Prophecy and Discovery: On the Spiritual Origins of Christopher Columbus's 'Enterprise of the Indies,'" *American Historical Review* 90, no. 1 (1985):73–102; Delno C. West, "Wallowing in a Theological Stupor or a Steadfast and Consuming Faith: Scholarly Encounters with Columbus's *Libro de las profecías,*" in *Columbus and His World,* ed. Donald T. Gerace (Fort Lauderdale, Fla.: Bahamian Field Station, 1987), 45–56; and Djelal Kadir, *Columbus and the Ends of the Earth: Europe's Prophetic Rhetoric as Conquering Ideology* (Berkeley: University of California Press, 1992).

71. For a discussion of how flawed Columbus's calculations were deemed to be by most of his contemporaries see Morison, *Admiral of the Ocean Sea,* esp. chaps. 6 and 7.

72. The parenthetical "says he" appears in the Spanish but was omitted without explanation by Dunn and Kelley from their translation. I have inserted it to avoid confusion.

73. The people of these lands, Columbus adds, "cavan el oro y lo traen al pescueço, a las orejas y a los braços e a las piernas, y son manillas muy gruessas, y también ha piedras y ha perlas preciosas y infinita espeçería" (Varela, 55; they dig for gold and wear it on their necks, on their ears, on their arms and legs, and the bracelets are very heavy; also there are precious stones and pearls and infinite spices).

74. For Columbus's source on the location of Paradise, see Pierre d'Ailly, *Ymago Mundi* (Louvain, 1480 or 1483) and the numerous annotations in Columbus's hand contained in the margins of his own copy of the text, preserved at the Biblioteca Colombina.

75. For an analysis of the literal inconsistencies of the *Diario,* see David Henige, *In Search of Columbus: The Sources for the First Voyage* (Tucson: University of Arizona Press, 1991). Henige demonstrates, through a rigorous and comprehensive examination of the text, that the *Diario* is riddled with lacunae, anomalies, and obvious computational errors in its recording of navigational data. For example, he notes that the text even fails to mention in which direction Columbus sailed when he departed from San Salvador (Guanahaní), how far or how long he sailed, or the bearings of his course to the next island on the itinerary, Santa María de la Concepción.

76. On the significance of Jerusalem in the Franciscan tradition within which Milhou situates Columbus's ideology, see *Colón y su mentalidad mesiánica,* esp. chaps. 3–4.

77. I disagree with Juan Gil, who argues for a literal interpretation of Columbus's use of the biblical phrase "nuevo cielo y tierra" to support his case that Columbus was Jewish; see Gil's "Nuevo cielo y nueva tierra: Exé-

gesis de una idea colombina," *Homenaje a Pedro Sainz de Rodríguez* (Madrid: Fundación Universitaria Española, 1986), 2:297–309.

78. On the importance of the prophetic discourse of the *Libro de las profecías* to Columbus's articulation of his enterprise, see Milhou, *Colón y su mentalidad mesiánica*, esp. 199–230, as well as Djelal Kadir, "Imperio y providencia en el Nuevo Mundo: Colón y *El libro de las profecías* (1501)," *Revista de Crítica Literaria Latinoamericana* 14, no. 28 (1988):329–35, and especially his recent *Columbus and the Ends of the Earth*.

79. A quotation in the *Libro de las profecías* explains the literal and figurative senses of Jerusalem:

> Quadruplex sensus sacre Scripture aperte insinuatur in hac dictione: Ierusalem. hystorice enim significat civitatem illam terrestrem, ad quam peregrini petunt; allegorice significat Ecclesiam militantem; tropologice significat quamlibet fidelem animam; anagogice significat celestem Ierusalem, sive patriam, vel regnum celorum.
>
> (de Lollis, 2:77)

> The fourfold interpretation of Holy Scripture is clearly implicit in the word Jerusalem. In a historical sense, it is the earthly city to which pilgrims travel. Allegorically, it indicates the Church in the world. Tropologically, Jerusalem is the soul of every believer. Anagogically, the word means the Heavenly Jerusalem, the celestial fatherland and kingdom.
>
> (West & Kling, 101)

80. In the "Relación" he explains:

> no porque yo crea que allí, adonde es el altura del estremo, sea navegable, ni agua, ni que se pueda subir allá; porque creo que allá es el Paraíso Terrenal, adonde no puede llegar nadie salvo por voluntad divina."
>
> (Varela, 216)

> not because I believe that there, at the highest point, it is navigable, nor [that it is] water, nor that it is possible to go up there; because I believe that the Terrestrial Paradise is there, and no one can reach that place except with divine permission.

81. Among the most famous such voyages were those of St. Brendan and Owein. For a study of the genre and its influence, see Segre, "*L'Itinerarium Animae* nel duecento e Dante."

82. *The Travels of Sir John Mandeville* (New York: Dover, 1964), 200–202. The book first appeared in the late fourteenth century.

83. A long fragment of this *diario* corresponding to the period 30 May–31 August 1498 survives in Las Casas's *Historia* (chaps. 127–49 are devoted to the third voyage). Varela (220–42) has edited the fragment as if it had been part of the "Relación del tercer viaje." Yet Las Casas appears to have blended passages from a rutterlike account with passages bearing a strong resemblance to the erudite, treatiselike account of the third voyage found in the "Relación." Compare, for example, the literal treatment given the

topic of Paradise in the entry for 17 August (Varela, 241) and the highly mystical, figurative treatment of the same topic in the "Relación" proper.

84. Leonardo Olschki, *Storia letteraria delle scoperte geografiche* (Florence: Leo S. Olschki, 1973), 1–9.

85. After this essay was completed, a translation of a research proposal by Michel de Certeau, "Travel Narratives of the French in Brazil: Sixteenth to Eighteenth Centuries," appeared in *Representations* 33 (Winter 1991):221–25. Although de Certeau's subject matter is not Columbian, the methodology he outlines for studying these travel narratives as combinations of the "practices of scientific investigation and their figurations in a literary space-time" complements my approach. It is regrettable that de Certeau did not live to bring his intriguing proposal to fruition.

86. Columbus attributes this passage to Seneca's *Medea* in his *Libro de las profecías*.

GENDER AND DISCOVERY

1. Michel de Certeau, *The Writing of History*, trans. Tom Conley (New York: Columbia University Press, 1988), xxv.

2. See, for example, Louis Montrose on this image in Elizabethan writing, "The Work of Gender in the Discourse of Discovery," *Representations* 33 (Winter 1991):1–41; Hugh Honour, *The New Golden Land: European Images of America from the Discoveries to the Present Time* (New York: Pantheon Books, 1975); and Bernadette Bucher, *Icon and Conquest: A Structural Analysis of the Illustrations of de Bry's "Great Voyages,"* trans. Basia Miller Gulati (Chicago: University of Chicago Press, 1981).

3. Djelal Kadir's illuminating analysis of the language of the "Capitulaciones" underscores the proprietary and imperialistic motives the document described and authorized; see *Columbus and the Ends of the Earth: Europe's Prophetic Rhetoric as Conquering Ideology* (Berkeley: University of California Press, 1992), especially 67–76.

4. Rumeu (1126–31) speculates that the vagueness of the references to Columbus's destination in the "Capitulaciones" and other prediscovery documents may have been the product of a conscious and deliberate attempt by Isabella and Ferdinand to thwart the possibility of rival expeditions by other European monarchies.

5. I have used Las Casas's version of the text of the "Capitulaciones" which appears in volume I, chapter 33 of the *Historia de las Indias*. The original document, in Spanish and signed by Isabella and Ferdinand, has disappeared, but four well-authenticated early copies are described by Jane (1:27). For an English translation of the "Capitulaciones," see Jane, 1:26–29.

6. Quoted by J. H. Elliott, *The Old World and the New, 1492–1650* (Cambridge: Cambridge University Press, 1970), 22.

7. Tzvetan Todorov, *La Conquête de l'Amérique: La Question de l'Autre* (Paris: Seuil, 1982), 48–49.

8. The following passage, from Jane's translation of the "Capitulaciones," gives a sense of the flavor of that document:

> Your Highnesses appoint the said Don Christopher their Viceroy and Governor-General in all the said Islands and Mainlands which, as has been said, he may discover or acquire in the said Seas, and that for the Government of each and every one of them he may name three persons for each Office and that Your Highnesses may take and choose the one most suitable to your service, and thus the lands which Our Lord allows him to discover and acquire in the service of Your Highnesses will be better governed. Item, that of all the Merchandise whatsoever, whether Pearls, Precious Stones, Gold, Silver, Spiceries, and other Things and Merchandise of whatever kind, name, or description that may be, which may be bought, bartered, found, acquired, or obtained within the limits of the said Admiralty. . . .
> (Jane, 28)

9. José Antonio Maravall explains that Columbus's act of taking possession of the islands he discovered followed the juridical formula of taking possession established in the Alfonsine texts. These texts, the most complete expression of Europe's juridico-political culture prior to the Discovery, according to Maravall, defined a territory not only as space but as a qualitative entity: To take possession of a territory implied an elaborate process of intepreting the relationship of "belonging to," of establishing a right of possession; see his *Estudios de historia del pensamiento español* (Madrid: Ediciones Cultura Hispánica, 1984), 2:397–99. In essence, this process is what my analysis will elucidate—that is, the terms in which the justification of the relationship of possession and domination mandated in the "Capitulaciones" is articulated in the Columbian texts.

10. Earlier, in the essay "In the Margins of Columbus," I view this phenomenon "from the margins" of the *Diario*, where Las Casas's criticisms of Columbus's cupidity render these passages antagonical components in a rhetoric of contraposition at the service of Las Casas's condemnation.

11. Las Casas, in his edition of the *Diario*, often alternates between the first- and third-person narrative voices in these passages, but this is clearly his editorial manipulation. Columbus's original text was undoubtedly narrated wholly from the first-person point of view.

12. In their translation, Dunn and Kelley (69) render "hombres, todos mançebos" as "people—all young." But when applied to a woman, the adjective *manceba* had a pejorative sense in fifteenth-century Spanish: "Este término se toma siempre en mala parte, por la muger soltera que tiene ayuntamiento con hombre libre" (Covarrubias, *Tesoro de la lengua*, 784; This term is always used pejoratively, for the unmarried woman who engages in carnal copulation with a free man).

13. The earlier portion of the passage in question reads

> Y para ver todo esto me moví esta mañana, porque supiese dar de todo relación a Vuestras Altezas, y también adónde pudiera hazer fortaleza, y vide un pedaço de tierra que se haze como isla, aunque no lo es, en que avía seis casas, el cual se pudiera atajar en dos días por isla, aunque yo no veo ser

neçessario, porque esta gente es muy símpliçe en armas, como verán Vuestras Altezas de siete que yo hize tomar para le llevar y deprender nuestra fabla y bolvellos.

(Varela, 33)

And I bestirred myself this morning to see all of this, so that I could give an account of everything to Your Highnesses, and also to see where a fort could be made. And I saw a piece of land formed like an island, although it was not one, on which there were six houses. This piece of land might in two days be cut off to make an island, although I do not see this to be necessary since these people are very naive about weapons, as Your Highnesses will see from seven that I caused to be taken in order to carry them away to you and to learn our language and to return them.

(Dunn & Kelley, 75)

14. Rare is the occasion when Columbus remarks on an unattractive Indian. When he does so, as on 13 January, he concludes that the man in question must be a cannibal. Physical unattractiveness appears as an exception, significantly linked to a moral aberration: "El cual diz que era muy disforme en el acatadura más que otro que oviese visto: tenía el rostro todo tiznado de carbón. . . . Juzgó el Almirante que devía ser de los caribes que comen los hombres" (Varela, 114; The Admiral says that he was quite ugly in appearance, more so than others that he had seen. He had his face all stained with charcoal. . . . The Admiral judged that he must be from the Caribs who eat men; Dunn & Kelley, 329).

15. In the letter to the Crown dated 4 March 1493 an almost identical passage includes an additional element that the Indians lack, private property:

Todos, ansí mugeres como hombres, andan desnudos como sus madres los parió, aunque algunas mugeres traen alguna cosita de algodón o una foja de yerva con que se cubijan; no tienen fierro ni armas, salvo unas çimas de cañas en que ponen al cavo un palillo delgado agudo; todo lo que labran es con piedras; y no e podido entender que alguno tenga bienes propios.

(Rumeu, 2:437)

All of them, women and men alike, go about naked like their mothers bore them, although some women wear a small piece of cotton or a patch of grass with which they cover themselves. They have neither iron nor weapons, except for canes on the end of which they place a thin sharp stick. Everything they make is done with stones [stone tools]. And I have not learned that any one of them has private property.

As André Saint-Lu has noted, lack of clothing appears repeatedly throughout Columbus's writing as a symbol for barbarism; see his "La perception de la nouveauté chez Christophe Colomb," *Etudes sur l'impact culturel du Nouveau Monde* (Paris: Editions L'Harmattan, 1981), 1:11–24.

16. In a rare moment of generosity (and no doubt self-interest), Columbus qualifies his comparison of the Indians to animals: "que aunquesta gente sean desnudos y paresca al huir que devan ser salvajes y vestias, yo les çertifico [a Vuestras Altezas] que son agudísimos y huelgan de saver

cosas nuevas" (Letter of 26 February 1495; Rumeu, 2:510; although these people may be naked and seem like savages and beasts when they flee, I certify to Your Highnesses that they are very bright and they enjoy learning new things).

17. Stephen Greenblatt, *Marvelous Possessions: The Wonder of the New World* (Oxford: Clarendon Press, 1991), 110.

18. The assertion that the Caribs are not very different from the other Indians, except for their long hair, does not mesh with an observation in the *Diario* that affirmed their considerable difference in appearance (13 January; Varela, 114). The apparent contradiction can perhaps be explained by the context: that here the similarity between the more aggressive Caribs and the peaceable Arawaks is noted to establish Spanish superiority with respect to both groups.

19. Aristotle, *Politics*, bk. 1 ch. 5, 1132, in *Basic Works*, ed. Richard McKeon. Claude Kappler's encyclopedic *Monstres, démons et merveilles a la fin du Moyen Age* (Paris: Payot, 1980) demonstrates how Aristotelian notions of difference helped define the conceptualizations of monstrosity in the Middle Ages. The medieval mind melded the Aristotelian notion with the Augustinian contribution that monstrosity found its justification in the Divine Plan, to marvel at the plurality of the universe and at the same time feel repulsed by difference as a marker of inferiority.

20. My translation, unlike Dunn and Kelley's (193–95), underscores the suggestion implicit in this passage that not carrying weapons (worthy of the name) is a function of the Indians' extreme cowardice.

21. That this process culminates in the "Relación" of the third voyage is at least partially explained by the historical circumstances. By the third voyage the enterprise of the Indies had fallen into such disrepute that in order to achieve the colonization of Española, the Crown was obliged to offer a pardon to any criminals (heretics, sodomites, and counterfeiters excepted) willing to sail with Columbus.

22. On the symbolism of gardens in classical and medieval literature, see A. Bartlett Giamatti, *The Earthly Paradise and the Renaissance Epic* (Princeton: Princeton University Press, 1966).

23. Some scholars maintain that Columbus did not know Polo's account until he received a copy of it in 1497 from the Englishman John Day. The early Columbian texts strongly suggest, however, that the author was familiar with Polo's text, particularly with its geography, during the first and second voyages, as I argue below. The most recent proponent of the theory that Columbus was not aware of Polo's *Travels* until the late 1490s is Juan Gil, in the introductory essay to his edition of *El libro de Marco Polo anotado por Cristóbal Colón. El libro de Marco Polo: versión de Rodrigo de Santiella*. Madrid: Alianza, 1987. (Thanks to F. Provost for pointing out my oversight in the manuscript stage of this book.)

24. The quotations are from *The Travels of Marco Polo* (New York: Dorset Press, 1987), 290 and 296. Columbus refers to Kin-sai in the *Diario* entries for 21 October (Quisay) and 1 November (Quinsay) 1492 and in the Letter

of 26 February 1495 (Quisaye) (Rumeu, 2:492–93 and 510). Polo stated that the Khan resided in Cambalic. The paradisiacal-erotic associations of Kinsai may explain, at least in part, Columbus's geographic confusion in substituting Kin-sai for Cambalic as the expressed destination of the voyage.

25. As Catherine MacKinnon observes, eroticization is a primary mechanism of the subordination of women in patriarchal cultures; see her *Sexual Harassment of Working Women: A Case of Sexual Discrimination* (New Haven: Yale University Press, 1979), 221.

26. Gilberto Araneda Triviños argues that the anti-idyllic, antiparadisiacal vision present in the letter of the fourth voyage destroys and supplants the myth of the Indies-as-Paradise found in the earlier writings; see his "Los relatos colombinos," *Ideologies and Literature* 3, no. 1 (Spring 1988): 81–96. In my reading, however, the idealizing and denigrating components are complementary operations in Columbus's interpretation of difference in a gender-specific mode. Helen Carr observes this same conjunction of the positive and the negative in the feminization of the Amerindian in colonial North American culture:

> So man/woman, husband/wife, seducer/seduced, rapist/victim, can all be transferred to the European/non-European relationship and the European right to mastery made natural. Secondly, by transferring this difference, all the ambivalence towards woman's unknowable otherness can also be projected on to the non-European. So the first effect of transferral is to naturalize the desire for, and legitimize the right to, possession; the second is to provide a language in which to express the fear of the Other's incalculable potential for resisting and for damaging the would-be possessor.
>
> ("Woman/Indian: The 'American' and His Others," in *Europe and Its Others*, ed. Francis Barker et al. [Colchester, Eng.: University of Essex, 1985], 2:49)

27. See Rolena Adorno, "El sujeto colonial y la construcción de la alteridad," *Revista de Crítica Latinoamericana* 14, no. 28 (1988):55–68.

28. Hélène Cixous and Catherine Clément, *The Newly Born Woman*, trans. Betsy Wing (Minneapolis: University of Minnesota Press, 1986), 79.

29. Luce Irigaray, "This Sex Which Is Not One," in *New French Feminisms*, ed. Elaine Marks and Isabelle de Courtivron (New York: Schocken, 1981), 105.

30. Dunn and Kelley, citing Morison, translate "y tres niños" as "and three children." That these three are not included in the count of the young and adult female "heads" suggests "boys" as a more accurate translation. Dunn and Kelley have a tendency to opt for ungendered translations, even when the context clearly calls for distinguishing between masculine and feminine; see note 12 above.

31. The quotations are from Antonello Gerbi, *Nature in the New World: From Christopher Columbus to Gonzalo Fernández de Oviedo*, trans. Jeremy Boyle (Pittsburgh: University of Pittsburgh Press, 1985), 18. Gerbi himself

underscores, if only implicitly and probably unconsciously, the erotic nature of Columbian discourse, for his impressions are recorded in a sentimental mode filled with sexual allusions, which appear to have affected the English translator in his word choice: "But his [Columbus'] glance dwells lovingly on every detail of the islands. . . . His pen, at times so dry and energetic, now becomes a brush whose delicate strokes caress the tiny islands. . . . With a sort of lover's awkwardness he seeks to wax poetic, and produces a flood of warbling nightingales, blossoming springtimes, May meadows, and Andalusian nights" (17).

32. Noé Jitrik discusses the discourse of appropriation in the Columbian texts from a Marxist perspective; see his *Los dos ejes de la cruz* (Puebla, Mexico: Editorial Universidad Autónoma de Puebla, 1983). However, he does not perceive the fundamental role that feminization and eroticization of the sign "Indies" plays in the texts. When the issue of gender is taken into account, what at first appears as an idiosyncratic dichotomy assumes its full sociocultural significance.

APPENDIX

My translation follows Rumeu's transcription as literally as possible, in order to recreate the awkwardness, the clumsiness that characterizes much of the original. Where the literal translation verged on incomprehensibility, I have added a word or phrase in brackets for clarification. Rumeu modernized the punctuation in his transcription, and I have followed his lead.

1. The Spanish, "y no fue contradicho," has the sense of "without resistance or opposition" and implies in this context that there was no verbal or physical opposition to Columbus's taking of possession.

2. I have here translated Rumeu's transcription literally, though it does not make sense. My best guess is that there was either a copying error in the original or a transcription error by Rumeu. It probably should read "e así nombre nuevo" (and [to the others] likewise a new name); cf. an almost identical passage in the letter to Santángel, which reads "e así a cada una nombre nuevo" (Varela, 140).

3. This is probably an allusion to the accounts of Marco Polo and to the papal embassies to the Far East in the thirteenth and fourteenth centuries by Plano Carpini, Rubruck, Monte Corvino, and Pordenone. Pordenone's account was distilled in John Mandeville's *Travels*, a book Columbus knew well.

4. I have translated this passage literally, but I believe it contains several errors that result in ambiguities and apparent contradictions in Columbus's predicament and actions. Compare it to its counterpart in the letter to Santángel:

> y al cabo de muchas leguas, visto que no había innovación y que la costa me levava al setentrión, de adonde mi voluntad era contraria, porque el ivierno era ya encarnado [y] yo tenía propósito de hazer del al austro, y tanbién el

viento me dio adelante, determiné no aguardar otro tiempo, y bolví atrás fasta un señalado puerto.

(Varela, 140)

and after [sailing] many leagues, having seen nothing novel and that the coast was taking me northward, where I did not want to go, because it was already winter [and] my purpose was to make from it to the south, and moreover the wind pushed me forward [to the south], I decided not to wait for a change in weather, and I turned back to a notable port.

5. Columbus sailed with two caravels (*Niña* and *Pinta*) and a larger *nao*, the *Santa María*, which ran aground on a reef on the night of 24–25 December. This portion of the text is underscored in the manuscript.

6. This passage appears to be an allusion to Martín Alonso Pinzón, who throughout the voyage had a tendency to disregard Columbus's orders and strike out on his own.

7. The Spanish, "naos y navíos," refers to two types of vessels larger than the caravels Columbus preferred.

8. This king must be Guacanagarí, who befriended Columbus and came to his aid when the *Santa María* ran aground. La Navidad fort, erected to house the Spaniards who remained on the island, was at least partly constructed with lumber from the *Santa María*. *Agí*, a hot red pepper, was one of the very first Taíno words to be introduced to Europeans.

9. I have translated *cielo* as "heaven" (rather than "sky") because the context would seem to imply that the author believes that the Indians saw the Europeans as beings of divine origins.

10. Rumeu includes whatever fragments of the mutilated passages he could decipher. In most cases, I have translated the fragments. Here, however, the three damaged lines do not provide sufficient context for translation.

11. None of the Spanish connotations of *quadra* make sense in this context. In Italian, the word means "quadrant," which also seems anomalous in this context. So I have based my translation on *quartum*, which is used in an almost identical passage in the Latin version of the letter of 15 February addressed to Sánchez (see Major, 11).

12. Variant spelling of *Española*.

13. The literal meaning of *señorío* (seigniory) is "feudal lordship."

14. A *fusta* is a small vessel of Moorish or Turkish origin; see James J. Pontillo, "Nautical Terms in Sixteenth-Century American Spanish" (Diss., State University of New York at Buffalo, 1975).

15. Pedro de Villacorta, a member of the crew of the first voyage and among Columbus's favorites.

16. Later renamed San Juan de Puerto Rico by Columbus.

17. The *Diario* puts Columbus in the Atlantic just off the coast of Portugal, near Lisbon and the mouth of the Tagus River, on 4 March 1493.

Bibliography

Bibliographical entries for the editions and translations of Columbus's journals, letters, and other documents appear on page xv.

Adorno, Rolena. "El sujeto colonial y la construcción de la alteridad." *Revista de Crítica Literaria Latinoamericana* 14, no. 28 (1988):55–68.

Ailly, Pierre d'. *Ymago Mundi: Texte latin et traduction française des quatre traités cosmographiques de d'Ailly et des notes marginales de Christophe Colomb*. 3 vols. Ed. and trans. Edmond Buron. Paris: Maisonneuve Frères et Editeurs, 1930.

Albuquerque, Luis de. *Dúvidas e certezas na história dos descobrimentos portugueses*. 2 vols. Lisbon: Vega, 1991.

Alegría, Ricardo E. *Las primeras representaciones gráficas del indio americano, 1493–1523*. Barcelona: Instituto de Cultura Puertorriqueña, 1978.

Alexandre, M. "Entre ciel et terre: Les premiers débats sur le site du Paradis (Gen. 2, 8–15 et ses réceptions)." In *Peuples et pays mythiques*, eds. François Jouan et Bernard Deforge, 187–224. Paris: Les Belles Lettres, 1988.

Allen, Justin Boyce. *The Ethical Poetic of the Later Middle Ages: A Decorum of Convenient Distinction*. Toronto: University of Toronto Press, 1982.

Amorim, A. M. "Temporalização do espaço versus espacialização do tempo." *Revista da Universidade de Coimbra* 29 (1984):259–70.

Anghiera, Peter Martyr d'. *Décadas del Nuevo Mundo*. Mexico City: Porrúa, 1964.

———. *De Orbe Novo decades*. Trans. F. A. MacNutt. 2 vols. New York and London, 1912.

Araneda Triviños, Gilberto. "Los relatos colombinos." *Ideologies and Literature* 3, no. 1 (Spring 1988):81–96.

Arias, Santa. "Retórica e ideología en la *Historia de las Indias* de Bartolomé de Las Casas." Diss., University of Wisconsin, Madison, 1990.

Aristotle. *The Basic Works of Aristotle*. Ed. Richard McKeon. New York: Random House, 1941.

Atiya, Aziz Suryal. *The Crusade in the Latin Middle Ages*. London: Methuen, 1938.

Bakhtin, Mikhail M. *The Dialogic Imagination*. Trans. Caryl Emerson and Michael Holquist. Austin: University of Texas Press, 1981.

Bataillon, Marcel. *Etudes sur Bartolomé de Las Casas*. Paris: Centre de Recherches de l'Institut d'Etudes Hispaniques, 1965.

———. "Historiografía oficial de Colón y Pedro Mártir a Oviedo y Gómara." *Imago Mundi* 5 (September 1954):23–39.

Bataillon, Marcel, and André Saint-Lu. *El Padre Las Casas y la defensa de los indios*. Trans. Javier Alfaya and Barbara Mc Shane. Barcelona: Ariel, 1976.

Beazley, C. Raymond. *The Dawn of Modern Geography*. Vol. 1. New York: Peter Smith, 1949.

Bellini, Giuseppe. "'. . . andaban todos desnudos . . .': Alle origini dell' 'incontro' tra l'Europa e l'America." *Columbeis II*, 181–201. Genoa: Università di Genova, 1987.

Benítez Rojo, Antonio. *La isla que se repite: El Caribe y la perspectiva posmoderna*. Hanover, N.H.: Ediciones del Norte, 1989.

Bernáldez, Andrés. *Memorias del reinado de los Reyes Católicos*. Ed. Manuel Gómez Moreno and Juan de M. Carriazo. Madrid: Consejo Superior de Investigaciones Científicas, 1962.

Bertone, Giorgio. "L'occhio, l'ancora, la scrittura: Lo sguardo del l'Almirante." *Columbeis II*, 153–80. Genoa: Università de Genova, 1987.

Bhabha, Homi K. "The Other Question: Difference, Discrimination, and the Discourse of Colonialism," *Literature, Politics, Theory*. Ed. Francis Baker et al., 149–72. London: Methuen, 1986.

Boas, George. *Essays on Primitivism and Related Ideas in the Middle Ages*. Baltimore: Johns Hopkins University Press, 1948.

Bogliolo Bruna, Giulia, and Alberto Lehmann. "Amazzoni o Cannibali, vergini o madri, sante o prostitute: Donne amerindie e alterità nelle 'relazioni' de alcuni viaggiatori francesi (secoli XVI–XVIII)." *Columbeis III*, 215–64. Genoa: Università di Genova, 1988.

Brenkman, John. *Culture and Domination*. Ithaca: Cornell University Press, 1987.

Buarque de Holanda, Sérgio.*Visão do Paraíso: Os motivos edenicos no descobrimento e colonização do Brasil*. Rio de Janeiro: José Olympio Editora, 1959.

Bucher, Bernadette. *Icon and Conquest: A Structural Analysis of de Bry's "Great Voyages."* Trans. Basia Miller Gulati. Chicago: University of Chicago Press, 1981.

Butor, Michel. "Travel and Writing." *Mosaic* 8 (1974):1–16.

Ca' da Mosto, Alvise. "Navegações." In *As viagens dos descobrimentos*, ed. José Manuel Garcia, 73–138. Lisbon: Editorial Presença, 1983.

Campbell, Mary B. *The Witness and the Other World: Exotic European Travel Writing, 400–1600*. Ithaca: Cornell University Press, 1988.

———. "'The Object of One's Gaze': Landscape, Writing, and Early Medieval Pilgrimage." In *Discovering New Worlds: Essays on Medieval Exploration and Imagination*, ed. Scott D. Westrem, 3–15. New York: Garland Publishing, 1991.

Campbell, Tony. "Portolan Charts from the Late Thirteenth Century to 1500." In *The History of Cartography*, ed. J. B. Harley and David Woodward, 1:371–463. Chicago: University of Chicago Press, 1987.

Carbia, Rómulo D. "La historia del descubrimiento y los fraudes del Padre Las Casas." *Nosotros* 72 (1931):139–54.

Carozzi, Claude. "La géographie de l'Au-delà et sa signification pendant le haut Moyen Age." *Popoli e Paesi nella Cultura Altomedievale* 2 (1983):423–81.

Carpentier, Alejo. *El arpa y la sombra.* Mexico City: Siglo XXI, 1980.

Carr, Helen. "Woman/Indian: The 'American' and His Others." In *Europe and Its Others*, ed. Francis Barker, et al., 2:46–60. Colchester, Eng.: University of Essex, 1985.

Cartas de particulares a Colón y relaciones coetáneas. Ed. Juan Gil and Consuelo Varela. Madrid: Alianza, 1984.

Carter, Paul. *The Road to Botany Bay: An Exploration of Landscape and History.* Chicago: University of Chicago Press, 1987.

Certeau, Michel de. *The Practice of Everyday Life.* Trans. Steven F. Rendall. Berkeley: University of California Press, 1984.

———. *The Writing of History.* Trans. Tom Conley. New York: Columbia University Press, 1988.

———. "Travel Narratives of the French in Brazil: Sixteenth to Eighteenth Centuries." *Representations* 33 (Winter 1991):221–25.

Chartier, Roger. "Texts, Printing, Readings." In *The New Cultural History*, ed. Lynn Hunt. Berkeley: University of California Press, 1989.

Chaunu, Pierre. *L'Expansion européenne du XIII au XV siècle.* Paris: Presses Universitaires de France, 1969.

Chaves, Alonso de. *Alonso de Chaves y el libro IV de su "Espejo de Navegantes."* Ed. P. Castañeda, M. Cuesta, and P. Hernández. Madrid: Industrias Gráficas España, 1977.

Cioranescu, Alejandro. *Colón, humanista: Estudios de humanismo atlántico.* Madrid: Editorial Prensa Española, 1967.

———. "La 'Historia de las Indias' y la prohibición de editarla." *Anuario de Estudios Americanos* 23 (1966):363–76.

Cixous, Hélène, and Catherine Clément. *The Newly Born Woman.* Trans. Betsy Wing. Minneapolis: University of Minnesota Press, 1986.

Colón, Fernando [Ferdinand Columbus]. *Vida del Almirante Don Cristóbal Colón.* Mexico City: Fondo de Cultura Económica, 1947.

———. *The Life of the Admiral Christopher Columbus by His Son Ferdinand.* Ed. and trans. Benjamin Keen. Westport, Conn.: Greenwood Press, 1978.

Conley, Tom. "Montaigne and the Indies: Cartographies of the New World in the *Essais*, 1580–88." In *1492–1992: Re/Discovering Colonial Writing*, ed. René Jara and Nicholas Spadaccini, 223–62. Minneapolis: Prisma Institute, 1989. [Reprint of *Hispanic Issues* 4 (1989).]

Conti, Simonetta. *Un secolo di bibliografía colombiana, 1880–1985.* Genoa: Cassa di Risparmio di Genova e Imperia, 1986.

Cortesão, Armando. *History of Portuguese Cartography.* Vol. 1. Coimbra: Junta de Investigações do Ultramar, 1969.

———. *Os descobrimentos portugueses.* Vol. 1. Lisbon: Livros Horizonte, 1975.

Culler, Jonathan. *The Pursuit of Signs*. Ithaca: Cornell University Press, 1981.
———. *On Deconstruction: Theory and Criticism After Structuralism*. Ithaca: Cornell University Press, 1982.

Curtius, Ernst Robert. *European Literature and the Latin Middle Ages*. Princeton: Princeton University Press, 1953.

Dainville, F. de. *La géographie des Humanistes*. Paris: G. Beauchesne et Fils, 1938.

Dalché, Patrick Gautier. "Comment penser l'Océan? Modes de connaissance des *finis orbis terrarum* du nord-ouest (de l'Antiquité au XIII siècle)." In *L'Europe et l'océan au Moyen Age*, 217–33. Nantes: Cid Editions, 1988.

Danzer, Gerald. *Cartographic Images of the World on the Eve of the Discoveries*. Chicago: Newberry Library, 1988.

Degli Innocenti, Mario. "Ancora sulla letteratura dei viaggi oltremondani: La 'Leggenda del Paradiso Terrestre.'" *Italia Medievale e Umanística* 29 (1986):63–88.

Dicionário da linguagem de Marinha antiga e actual. Lisbon: Centro de Estudos Históricos e Cartografia Antiga, 1990.

Diffie, Bailey W., and George D. Winius. *A Fundação do Império Portugues, 1415–1580*. Vol. 1. Trans. João Rosa Ferreira. Lisbon: Vega, n.d.

Dubois, J., et al. *A General Rhetoric*. Trans. Paul B. Burrell and Edgar M. Slotkin. Baltimore: Johns Hopkins University Press, 1981.

Edgerton, Samuel Y. "From Mental Matrix to *Mappaemundi* to Christian Empire: The Heritage of Ptolemaic Cartography in the Renaissance." In *Art and Cartography: Six Historical Essays*, ed. David Woodward, 10–50. Chicago: University of Chicago Press, 1987.

Elliott, J. H. *The Old World and the New, 1492–1650*. Cambridge: Cambridge University Press, 1970.

Fall, Yoko K. "Les cartes a rumbs et leur utilisation au XIV et au XV siècle." *Studia* 47 (1989):23–39.

Fasce, Silvan. "Colombo, il Paradiso Terrestre e Mircea Eliade." *Columbeis* I, 199–205. Genoa: Università di Genova, 1986.

Faulhaber, Charles B. "The Letter-Writer's Rhetoric: The *Summa dictaminis* of Guido Faba." In *Medieval Eloquence: Studies in the Theory and Practice of Medieval Rhetoric*, ed. James J. Murphy, 85–111. Berkeley: University of California Press, 1978.

Fernandes, Valentim. *O manuscrito "Valentim Fernandes."* Ed. Antonio Baião. Lisbon: Academia Portuguesa da Historia, 1939.

Fernández de Navarrete, Martín. *Colección de documentos y manuscritos compilados por Fernández de Navarrete*. Nendeln, Lichtenstein: Kraus-Thomson, 1971.

Fernández de Oviedo y Valdés, Gonzalo. *Historia general y natural de las Indias, islas, y Tierra-Firme del mar océano*. Ed. José Amador de los Ríos. 4 vols. Madrid: Imprenta de la Real Academia de la Historia, 1851–55.

Fick, Barbara W. *El libro de viajes en la España medieval*. Santiago de Chile: Editorial Universitaria, 1976.

Frake, Charles O. "Cognitive Maps of Time and Tide Among Medieval Seafarers." *Man* 20 (1985):254–70.

Friede, Juan, and Benjamin Keen. *Bartolomé de Las Casas in History*. De Kalb: Northern Illinois University Press, 1971.

Frye, Northrop. "The Journey as Metaphor." In *Northrop Frye: Myth and Metaphor: Selected Essays, 1974–1988*, ed. Robert D. Denham, 212–26. Charlottesville: University Press of Virginia, 1990.

Fuson, Robert H. "The *Diario de Colón*: A Legacy of Poor Transcription, Translation, and Interpretation." In *In the Wake of Columbus*, ed. Louis de Vorsey, Jr., and John Parker, 51–75. Detroit: Wayne State University Press, 1985.

Genette, Gérard. *Palimpsestes: La littérature au second degré*. Paris: Seuil, 1982.

Gerbi, Antonello. *Nature in the New World: From Christopher Columbus to Gonzalo Fernández de Oviedo*. Trans. Jeremy Boyle. Pittsburgh: University of Pittsburgh Press, 1985.

Gertz, Sun Hee Kim. "Metarhetorical Texturing in Medieval Prologues." *Deutsche Vierteljahrsschrift für Literaturwissenschaft und Geistesgeschicht* 64 (1990):591–603.

Giamatti, A. Bartlett. *The Earthly Paradise and the Renaissance Epic*. Princeton: Princeton University Press, 1966.

Gil, Juan. "El rol del tercer viaje colombino." In *Temas colombinos*, ed. Juan Gil and Consuelo Varela, 1–28. Seville: Escuela de Estudios Hispanoamericanos de Sevilla, 1986.

———. *Mitos y utopías del descubrimiento: Colón y su tiempo*. Vol. 1. Madrid: Alianza, 1989.

———. "Nuevo cielo y nueva tierra: Exégesis de una idea colombina." *Homenaje a Pedro Sainz Rodríguez*, 2:297–309. Madrid: Fundación Universitaria Española, 1986.

———, ed. *El libro de Marco Polo anotado por Cristóbal Colón. El libro de Marco Polo: Versión de Rodrigo de Santiella*. Madrid: Alianza, 1987.

Giucci, Guillermo. "The Conquest of America: From the Marvelous to the Exotic." Diss., Stanford University, 1987.

Gómez Moriana, Antonio. "Narration and Argumentation in the Chronicles of the New World." In *1492–1992: Re/Discovering Colonial Writing*, ed. René Jara and Nicholas Spadaccini, 97–120. Minneapolis: Prisma Institute, 1989.

González Echevarría, Roberto. *Myth and Archive: A Theory of Latin American Narrative*. Cambridge: Cambridge University Press, 1990.

Gould, Alicia B. *Nueva lista documentada de los tripulantes de Colón en 1492*. Madrid: Real Academia de la Historia, 1984.

Grabois, Aryeh. "Medieval Pilgrims, the Holy Land and Its Image in European Civilisation." In *The Holy Land in History and Thought*, ed. Moshe Sharon, 65–79. Leiden: E. J. Brill, 1988.

Graf, Arturo. *Miti, leggende e superstizione del Medio Evo*. Torino: Ermano Loescher, 1892.

Greenblatt, Stephen. *Marvelous Possessions: The Wonder of the New World*. Oxford: Clarendon Press, 1991.

Hanke, Lewis. *All Mankind Is One: A Study of the Disputation Between Bartolomé de Las Casas and Juan Ginés de Sepúlveda on the Intellectual and Religious Capacity of the American Indians*. De Kalb: Northern Illinois University Press, 1974.

Harbsmeier, Michael. "On Travel Accounts and Cosmological Strategies: Some Models in Comparative Xenology." *Ethnos* 50, nos. 3–4 (1985):273–312.

Harley, J. B. *Maps and the Columbian Encounter*. Milwaukee: Golda Meir Library of the University of Wisconsin, 1990.

Heers, Jacques. *Christophe Colomb*. Paris: Hachette, 1981.

———. "Le projet de Christophe Colomb." *Columbeis I*, 7–26. Genoa: Università di Genova, 1986.

Henige, David. *In Search of Columbus: The Sources for the First Voyage*. Tucson: University of Arizona Press, 1991.

———. "Samuel Eliot Morison as Translator and Editor of Columbus's *diario de a bordo*." *Terrae Incognitae* 20 (1988):69–88.

———. "To Read Is to Misread, To Write Is to Miswrite: Las Casas as Transcriber." *Hispanic Issues: Amerindian Images*. Minneapolis: University of Minnesota Press, 1992.

Henige, David, and Margarita Zamora. "Text, Context, Intertext: Columbus's *diario de a bordo* as Palimpsest." *The Americas* 46, no. 1 (July 1989):17–40.

Heredia, Antonia M. "Las cartas de los virreyes de Nueva España a la corona española en el siglo XVI." *Anuario de Estudios Americanos* 31 (1974):441–596.

———. "La carta como tipo diplomático indiano." *Anuario de Estudios Americanos* 34 (1977):65–95.

Herrnstein Smith, Barbara. *Contingencies of Value: Alternative Perspectives for Critical Theory*. Cambridge: Harvard University Press, 1988.

Hodgen, Margaret T. *Early Anthropology in the Sixteenth and Seventeenth Centuries*. Philadelphia: University of Pennsylvania Press, 1964.

Honour, Hugh. *The New Golden Land: European Images of America from the Discoveries to the Present Time*. New York: Pantheon Books, 1975.

Horozco de Covarrubias, Sebastián. *Tesoro de la lengua castellana o española*. Madrid: Ediciones Turner, 1979.

Howard, Donald R. *Writers and Pilgrims: Medieval Pilgrimage Narratives and Their Posterity*. Berkeley: University of California Press, 1980.

Hulme, Peter. *Colonial Encounters: Europe and the Native Caribbean, 1492–1797*. London: Methuen, 1986.

———. "The Log of Christopher Columbus: A Review Essay." *Culture and History* 6 (1989):25–36.

Humboldt, Alexander Freikerr von. *Cristóbal Colón y el descubrimiento de América*. Trans. Luis Navarro y Calvo. Buenos Aires: Centro Difusor del Libro, 1946.

Hutchinson, Steven. *Cervantine Journeys*. Madison: University of Wisconsin Press, 1992.

Irigaray, Luce. "This Sex Which Is Not One." In *New French Feminisms*, ed. Elaine Marks and Isabelle de Courtivron. New York: Schocken, 1981.

Jaffe, Samuel. "Gottfried von Strassburg and the Rhetoric of History." In *Medieval Eloquence: Studies in the Theory and Practice of Medieval Rhetoric*, ed. James J. Murphy, 288–318. Berkeley: University of California Press, 1978.

Jara, René, and Nicholas Spadaccini, eds. *1492–1992: Re/Discovering Colonial Writing*. Minneapolis: The Prisma Institute, 1989. [Reprint of *Hispanic Issues* 4 (1989).]

Jenny, Laurent. "The Strategy of Form." In *French Literary Theory Today*, ed. Tzvetan Todorov, 34–63. Cambridge: Cambridge University Press, 1982.

Jitrik, Noé. *Los dos ejes de la cruz: La escritura de apropiación en el Diario, el Memorial, las Cartas y el Testamento del enviado real Cristóbal Colón*. Puebla, Mexico: Editorial Universidad Autónoma de Puebla, 1983.

Jos, Emiliano. "La génesis colombiana del descubrimiento." *Revista de Historia de América* 14 (June 1942):1–48.

Kadir, Djelal. "Imperio y Providencia en el Nuevo Mundo: Colón y El Libro de las Profecías (1501)." *Revista de Crítica Literaria Latinoamericana* 14, no. 28 (1988):329–35.

———. *Columbus and the Ends of the Earth: Europe's Prophetic Rhetoric as Conquering Ideology*. Berkeley: University of California Press, 1992.

Kappler, Claude. *Monstres, démons et merveilles a la fin du Moyen Age*. Paris: Payot, 1980.

Keen, Benjamin, ed. and trans. *The Life of the Admiral Christopher Columbus by His Son Ferdinand*. Westport, Conn.: Greenwood Press, 1978.

Kellner, Hans. *Language and Historical Representation: Getting the Story Crooked*. Madison: University of Wisconsin Press, 1989.

Kimble, George H. T. *Geography in the Middle Ages*. New York: Russell and Russell, 1968.

Kristeva, Julia. *Le texte du roman*. Paris: Mouton, 1970.

———. *Sémiotiké, recherches pour une sémanalyse*. Paris: Seuil, 1969.

LaCapra, Dominick. *History and Criticism*. Ithaca: Cornell University Press, 1985.

Ladero Quesada, Miguel Angel. "L'Espagne et l'océan a la fin du Moyen Age." In *L'Europe et l'océan au Moyen Age*, 115–30. Paris: Cid Editions, 1988.

Larner, John. "The Certainty of Columbus: Some Recent Studies." *History* 15 (1988):3–23.

Las Casas, Bartolomé de. *Apologética historia*. Madrid: Biblioteca de Autores Españoles, 1958.

———. *Del único modo de atraer a todos los pueblos a la verdadera religión*. Mexico: Fondo de Cultura Económica, 1942.

———. "Diario del primer y tercer viaje de Cristóbal Colón." In *Bartolomé* de Las Casas: Colección de obras completas, vol. 14, ed. Consuelo Varela. Madrid: Alianza, 1989.

————. Historia de las Indias. 3 vols. Hollywood, Fla.: Ediciones del Continente, 1985.

————. Historia de las Indias. Ed. Juan Pérez de Tudela. 2 vols. Madrid: Biblioteca de Autores Españoles, 1957.

————. Historia de las Indias. Mexico City: Fondo de Cultura Económica, 1951.

Le Goff, Jacques. Medieval Civilization: 400–1500. New York: Basil Blackwell, 1989.

MacKinnon, Catherine A. Sexual Harassment of Working Women: A Case of Sexual Discrimination. New Haven: Yale University Press, 1979.

McSpadden, George E. Don Quijote and the Spanish Prologues: Glimpses of the Genius of Cervantes at Work. 2 vols. Potomac, Md.: José Porrúa Turanzas, 1979.

Madariaga, Salvador de. Christopher Columbus: Being the Life of the Very Magnificent Lord Don Cristóbal Colón. New York: Frederick Ungar Publishing, 1967.

Mahn-Lot, Marianne. Bartolomé de Las Casas et le droit des Indiens. Paris: Payot, 1982.

————. "Iles des bienhereux et Paradis terrestre." Revue Historique 289, no. 1 (1989):47–50.

Mandeville, John. The Travels of Sir John Mandeville. New York: Dover, 1964.

Manzano, Juan Manzano. Colón y su secreto: El predescubrimiento. Madrid: Ediciones Cultura Hispánica, 1982.

Maraval, Pierre. Lieux saints et pèlerinages d'Orient: Histoire et géographie des origines a la conquête arabe. Paris: Editions du Cerf, 1985.

Maravall, José Antonio. Estudios de historia del pensamiento español. Serie segunda: La época del renacimiento. Madrid: Ediciones Cultura Hispánica, 1984.

Martinell Gifre, Emma. Aspectos lingüísticos del descubrimiento y la conquista. Madrid: Consejo Superior de Investigaciones Científicas, 1988.

Martínez Crespo, Alicia. "Los libros de viajes del siglo XV y las primeras crónicas de Indias." In Literatura hispánica en la época de los Reyes Católicos y descubrimiento. Actas del Congreso Internacional Sobre Literatura Hispánica en la Epoca de los Reyes Católicos y el Descubrimiento, ed. Manuel Criado de Val, 423–30. Barcelona: PPU, 1989.

Martini, Dario G. Cristoforo Colombo tra ragione e fantasia. Genoa: Edizioni Culturali Internazionali, 1986

Menéndez Pidal, Ramón. La lengua de Cristóbal Colón. Madrid: Espasa-Calpe, 1978.

————. El padre Las Casas: Su doble personalidad. Madrid, 1963.

Mignolo, Walter. "Colonial Situations, Geographical Discourses and Territorial Representations: Toward a Diatopical Understanding of Colonial Semiosis." Dispositio 14, nos. 36–38 (1989):93–140.

Milani, Virgil I. The Written Language of Christopher Columbus. Buffalo: State University of New York, 1973.

Milhou, Alain. *Colón y su mentalidad mesiánica en el ambiente franciscanista español.* Valladolid: Seminario Americanista de la Universidad de Valladolid, 1983.

Minnis, A. J. *Medieval Theory of Authorship: Scholastic Literary Attitudes in the Later Middle Ages.* London: Scolar Press, 1984.

Montrose, Louis. "The Work of Gender in the Discourse of Discovery." *Representations* 33 (Winter 1991):1–41.

Moreiras, Alberto. "*Theatrum analyticum* y el tercer viaje del Almirante." *Ideas '92* 6 (Spring 1990):43–52.

Morison, Samuel Eliot. *Admiral of the Ocean Sea.* Boston: Little, Brown, 1942.

———. *Christopher Columbus, Mariner.* Boston: Little, Brown, 1955.

———. *Portuguese Voyages to America in the Fifteenth Century.* Cambridge: Harvard University Press, 1940.

———. "Texts and Translations of the Journal of Columbus' First Voyage." *Hispanic American Historical Review* 19 (1939):235–61.

Mund-Dopchie, Monique. "L'extrême-Occident de l'Antiquité classique et la découverte du Nouveau Monde: Une manipulation de textes a des fins idéologiques." *Nouvelle Revue du Seizième Siècle* 8 (1990):27–49.

Murphy, James J. *Rhetoric in the Middle Ages: A History of Rhetorical Theory from Saint Augustine to the Renaissance.* Berkeley: University of California Press, 1974.

Nardi, Bruno. "Osservazioni sul medievale 'accessus ad auctores' in rapporto all'*Epistola a Cangrande.*" In *Saggi e note de critica dantesca,* 268–308. Milan: Riccardo Ricciardi, 1966.

Newton, Arthur Percival. "Travellers' Tales of Wonder and Imagination." In *Travel and Travellers of the Middle Ages,* ed. Arthur Percival Newton. New York: Knopf, 1926.

Nunn, George E. *The Geographical Conceptions of Columbus: A Critical Consideration of Four Problems.* New York: American Geographical Society, 1924.

O'Gorman, Edmundo. *Cuatro historiadores de Indias, siglo XVI.* Mexico City: Sep Setentas, 1972.

———. *The Invention of America: An Inquiry into the Historical Nature of the New World and the Meaning of Its History.* Bloomington: Indiana University Press, 1961.

Olschki, Leonardo. *Storia letteraria delle scoperte geografiche.* Florence: Leo S. Olschki, 1973.

Ong, Walter J. *Orality and Literacy: The Technologizing of the Word.* London: Methuen, 1982.

Organización de los Estados Americanos and Instituto Panamericano de Geografía e Historia. *Precedentes Cartográficos del Descubrimiento de América.* Mexico City: Instituto Panamericano de Geografía e Historia, 1989.

Pacheco Pereira, Duarte. *Esmeraldo de situ orbis.* Lisbon: Imprensa Nacional, 1892.

Pagden, Anthony. "*Ius et Factum*: Text and Experience in the Writings of Bartolomé de Las Casas." *Representations* 33 (Winter 1991):147–62.

———. *The Fall of Natural Man: The American Indian and the Origins of Comparative Ethnology.* Cambridge: Cambridge University Press, 1982.

Pastor, Beatriz. *Discurso narrativo de la conquista de América*. Havana: Casa de las Américas, 1983.

Patch, Howard Rollin. *The Other World According to Descriptions in Medieval Literature*. Cambridge: Harvard University Press, 1950.

Pereira, G. *Roteiros portuguezes da viagem de Lisboa a India nos seculos XVI e XVII*. Lisbon: Imprensa Nacional, 1898.

Pérez de Tudela, Juan. *Mirabilis in altis: Estudio crítico sobre el orígen y significado del proyecto descubridor de Cristóbal Colón*. Madrid: Consejo Superior de Investigaciones Científicas, 1983.

Pérez Fernández, O. P., Isacio. *Cronología documentada de los viajes, estancias y actuaciones de Fray Bartolomé de Las Casas*. Bayamón, P.R.: Centro de Estudios de los Dominicos del Caribe, 1984.

————. *Inventario documentado de los escritos de Fray Bartolomé de Las Casas*. Bayamón, P.R.: Centro de Estudios de los Dominicos del Caribe, 1981.

Phelan, John Leddy. *The Millennial Kingdom of the Franciscans in the New World*. Berkeley: University of California Press, 1956.

Phillips, J. R. S. *The Medieval Expansion of Europe*. Oxford: Oxford University Press, 1988.

Polo, Marco. *The Travels of Marco Polo*. New York: Dorset Press, 1987.

Pontillo, James J. "Nautical Terms in Sixteenth-Century American Spanish." Diss., State University of New York at Buffalo, 1975.

Porqueras Mayo, Alberto. *El prólogo como género literario: Su estudio en el Siglo de Oro español*. Madrid: Consejo Superior de Investigaciones Científicas, 1957.

Portugal-Brazil: The Age of the Atlantic Discoveries. Ed. Max Justo Guedes and Gerald Lombardi. Lisbon: Bertrand Editora, 1990.

Prescott, William H. *History of the Reign of Ferdinand and Isabella, the Catholic*. 3 vols. Philadelphia: J. B. Lippincott, 1882.

Provost, Foster. *Columbus: An Annotated Guide to the Scholarship on His Life and Writings, 1750–1988*. Detroit: Omnigraphics, Inc., for The John Carter Brown Library, Brown University, 1991.

Pupo-Walker, Enrique. *La vocación literaria del pensamiento histórico en América. Desarrollo de la prosa de ficción: Siglos XVI, XVII, XVIII y XIX*. Madrid: Gredos, 1982.

Quartino, Luigina. "Colombo e i mostri." *Columbeis III*, 165–73. Genoa: Università di Genova, 1988.

Rabassa, José. "Columbus and the New Scriptural Economy of the Renaissance." *Dispositio* 14, nos. 36–38 (1989):271–302.

Ramos Pérez, Demetrio. *Las variaciones ideológicas en torno al descubrimiento de América: Pedro Mártir de Anglería y su mentalidad*. Valladolid: Seminario Americanista de la Universidad de Valladolid, 1981–82.

————. *La primera noticia de América*. Valladolid: Seminario Americanista de la Universidad de Valladolid, 1986.

Real Academia de la Historia. *Bibliografía Colombina: Enumeración de libros y documentos concernientes a Cristóbal Colón y sus viajes*. Madrid: Establecimiento Tipográfico de Fortanet, 1892.

Revelli, Paolo. *Cristoforo Colombo e la scuola cartografica genovese.* Genova: Consiglio Nazionale delle Ricerche, 1937.

Richard, Jean. "Voyages réels et voyages imaginaires, instruments de la connaissance géographique au Moyen Age." In *Culture et travail intellectuel dans l'Occident médiéval,* ed. Geneviève Hasenohr and Jean Longère, 211–20. Paris: Editions du Centre National de la Recherche Scientifique, 1981.

Roberts, Michael. *Biblical Epic and Rhetorical Paraphrase in Late Antiquity.* Liverpool: Francis Cairns, 1985.

Rocha Pinto, João. *A viagem: Memória e espaço. A literatura portuguesa de viagens. Os primitivos relatos de viagem ao Indico, 1497–1550.* Lisbon: Livraria Sá Da Costa Editora, 1989.

Rojas, Fernando de. *Celestina.* Ed. Dorothy Sherman Severin. Trans. James Mabbe. Warminster: Aris and Phillips, 1987.

Roux, Jean-Paul. *Les explorateurs au Moyen Age.* Paris: Fayard, 1985.

Ruano, Eloy Benito. *La leyenda de San Borondón, octava isla canaria.* Valladolid: Seminario Americanista de la Universidad de Valladolid, 1978.

Rumeu de Armas, Antonio. "El *Diario de a bordo* de Cristóbal Colón: El problema de la paternidad del extracto." *Revista de Indias* 36 (1976):7–17.

———. *Nueva luz sobre las Capitulaciones de Santa Fe de 1492 concertadas entre los Reyes Católicos y Cristóbal Colón.* Madrid: Consejo Superior de Investigaciones Científicas, 1985.

Saint-Lu, André. "La perception de la nouveauté chez Christophe Colomb." In *Etudes sur l'impact culturel du Nouveau Monde,* 1:11–24. Paris: Editions L'Harmattan, 1981.

Sale, Kirkpatrick. *The Conquest of Paradise: Christopher Columbus and the Columbian Legacy.* New York: Knopf, 1990.

———. "What Columbus Died Believing: "The *True* Geographic Concepts of the Great Discoverer." *Terrae Incognitae* 21 (1989):9–16.

Sanford, Charles L. *The Quest for Paradise: Europe and the American Moral Imagination.* Urbana: University of Illinois Press, 1961.

Sanz, Carlos. *El nombre América: Libros y mapas que lo impusieron.* Madrid: Librería General, 1959.

Sariola, Sakari. *Power and Resistance: The Colonial Heritage in Latin America.* Ithaca: Cornell University Press, 1972.

Scholes, Robert. *Protocols of Reading.* New Haven: Yale University Press, 1989.

Segre, Cesare. "*L'Itinerarium Animae* nel duecento e Dante." *Letture Classensi* 13 (1984):9–32.

Struever, Nancy. *The Language of History in the Renaissance.* Princeton: Princeton University Press, 1970.

Sumption, Jonathan. *Pilgrimage: An Image of Medieval Religion.* London: Faber and Faber, 1975.

Taviani, P. E., C. Varela, J. Gil, and M. Conti, eds. *Relazione e lettere sul secundo, terzo, e quarto viaggio* (Nuova Raccolta Colombiana). 2 vols. Rome: Istituto Poligrafico e Zecca dello Stato, 1992.

Teixeira da Mota, Avelino. *Evolução dos roteiros portugueses durante o século XVI.* Coimbra: Revista da Universidade de Coimbra, 1969.

————. *O essencial sobre Cristovão Colombo e os portugueses.* Lisbon: Imprensa Nacional–Casa da Moeda, 1987.

Todorov, Tzvetan. *La Conquête de l'Amérique: La Question de l'Autre.* Paris: Seuil, 1982.

Usodimare, Antonioto. "Carta." In *As viagens dos descobrimentos,* ed. José Manuel Garcia, 139–46. Lisbon: Editorial Presença, 1983.

Vázquez, J. A. "Las Casas's Opinions in Columbus's Diary." *Topic* 21 (Spring 1971):45–56.

Vespucci, Amerigo. *The Letters of Amerigo Vespucci and Other Documents Illustrative of His Career.* Trans. Clement R. Markham. London: Hakluyt Society, 1944.

Vignaud, Henri. *Histoire critique de la grande entreprise de Christophe Colomb.* 2 vols. Paris: H. Welter, 1911.

————. *Le vrai Christophe Colomb et la légende.* Paris: Picard, 1921.

Vigneras, Louis-André. *La búsqueda del paraíso y las legendarias islas del Atlántico.* Valladolid: Seminario Americanista de la Universidad de Valladolid, 1976.

Washburn, Wilcomb E. "The Meaning of 'Discovery' in the Fifteenth and Sixteenth Centuries." *American Historical Review* 68, no. 1 (October 1962):1–21.

Waters, David W. *The Rutters of the Sea: The Sailing Directions of Pierre Garcie.* New Haven: Yale University Press, 1967.

Watts, Pauline Moffitt. "Prophecy and Discovery: On the Spiritual Origins of Columbus's 'Enterprise of the Indies.'" *American Historical Review* 90, no. 1 (1985):73–102.

West, Delno C. "Wallowing in a Theological Stupor or a Steadfast and Consuming Faith: Scholarly Encounters with Columbus' *Libro de las Profecías.*" In *Columbus and His World,* ed. Donald T. Gerace, 45–56. Fort Lauderdale, Fla.: Bahamian Field Station, 1987.

White, Hayden. *The Content of the Form: Narrative Discourse and Historical Representation.* Baltimore: Johns Hopkins University Press, 1987.

————. *Tropics of Discourse: Essays in Cultural Criticism.* Baltimore: Johns Hopkins University Press, 1978.

Woodward, David. "Medieval *Mappaemundi.*" In *The History of Cartography,* ed. J. B. Harley and David Woodward, 1:286–370. Chicago: University of Chicago Press, 1987.

————. "Reality, Symbolism, Time, and Space in Medieval World Maps." *Annals of the Association of American Geographers* 75, no. 4 (1985):510–21.

Zamora, Margarita. "El prólogo al *Diario* de Cristóbal Colón." *Insula: Revista de Letras y Ciencias Humanas* no. 522 (June 1990):16–17.

Zavala, Silvio A. *Las instituciones jurídicas en la conquista de América.* Mexico City: Editorial Porrúa, 1971.

Index

Compositor:	Wilsted & Taylor
Text:	10/13 Palatino
Display:	Palatino
Printer:	Thomson-Shore, Inc.
Binder:	Thomson-Shore, Inc.